GW00341105

WEBSITE NEWS UPDATED WEEKLY
WWW.INDEXONCENSORSHIP.ORG • CONTACT@INDEXONCENSORSHIP.ORG
TEL: 020 7278 2313 • FAX: 020 7278 1878

Editor-in-chief Ursula Owen • **Editor** Judith Vidal-Hall • **Web Managing Editor** Rohan Jayasekera
Eastern Europe Editor Irena Maryniak • **Editorial Production Manager** Natasha Schmidt • **Publisher**
Henderson Mullin • **Development Manager** Hugo Grieve • **Membership and Promotions** Tony Callaghan
Project Manager Ruairi Patterson • **Director of Administration** Kim Lassemillanté • **Volunteer Assistants**
James Badcock, Ben Carrdus, Gulliver Cragg, Avery Davis-Roberts, Ioli Delivani, Hanna Gezelius, Monica
Gonzalez Correa, Frances Harvey, Andrew Kendle, Agustina Lattanzi, Najlae Naaoumi, Gill Newsham, Ben
Owen, Jason Pollard, Shifa Rahman, Neil Sammonds, Andrew Smith, Mike Yeoman
Cover design Sheridan Wall • **Design and production** Jane Havell Associates • **Printed by** Thanet Press, UK

CONTENTS

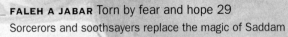

INDEX ON CENSORSHIP

for free expression

Third Annual
Freedom of Expression
Awards

7pm 26 March 2003

**Royal College of Physicians
11 St Andrews Place, Regent's Park, London NW1 4LE**

hosted by

JEREMY PAXMAN

entertainment by a special guest comedian

**awards presented by
Michael Grade, David Hare,
Geoffrey Hosking and Sheena McDonald**

Tickets are available for a minimum donation of £150 per person. For tickets or further enquiries, including information on booking corporate tables and how to sponsor an award, please contact Ruairi on 020 7278 2313 or email ruairi@indexoncensorship.org

The *Index on Censorship* Freedom of Expression Awards dinner was inaugurated in 2001 to honour those who risk their lives defending this important right. Previous awards have been hugely successful in attracting attention to the work done by the nominees for prizes. The awards dinner is an enjoyable gala evening, with stars from the media, entertainment and business worlds in attendance.

All proceeds go to fund *Index*'s work.

To nominate recipients ⇨ www.indexoncensorship.org

*Background: Anna Politkovskaia receives her award for the
Most Courageous Defence of Free Expression 2002 from Geoffrey Hosking*

STATES OF FEAR

URSULA OWEN

It was a speech designed to arouse Americans at home: it ended up sowing fear and hatred abroad. In his State of the Union address, President Bush's now famous assertion that Iran, Iraq and North Korea constituted an 'axis of evil' that threatened world peace, suggested, without any evidence, some sort of alliance such as the 'axis powers' of World War II (Germany, Italy and Japan). His statement put the three countries 'on notice' and helped put the US on a higher level of war preparation.

A year on, *Index* examines the state of these three nations, and speculates particularly on the bizarre – and counter-productive – inclusion of Iran (Aryeh Neier, p22). Though we have heard much about their governments and leaders, little is heard from the citizens of these countries. *Index* reports from *inside* 'the axis of evil' (p20), finding out who these people are, how they live, what their newspapers are saying (p58), what they feel about their governments and their futures.

As we know, Iraqi citizens live in a state of fear, trapped between a hugely repressive regime and devastating sanctions: Faleh Jabar tells us how they are dealing with this (p29). Meanwhile, as the world waits to see what will happen next, the US administration is trying to insulate us, through that subtlest form of censorship, euphemism, from what war does to human beings. 'Serious consequences', 'collateral damage', 'regime change', ' taking out', 'cleansing' – this is warspeak, shrouding war's bitter reality.

And the face of war has changed. Violence has become more fragmented – 152 small wars you may have missed have been fought since World War II. They have often involved massive displacements of people. Conflicts are seen as more threatening to the world's security, and military intervention is used to defend human rights. *Index* looks at some of the controversial debates, many of them going on behind closed doors, about the way that humanitarian aid is delivered, and its consequences. While Caroline Moorehead (p148), in her disturbing and instructive article on life in post-war Afghanistan, tells us that 'humanitarian intervention has become more uncertain, more precarious and more political', David Rieff (p196) warns that humanitarian aid workers, by moving from the principle of neutrality to advocacy for intervention in civil wars and ethnic cleansing, are losing sight of their purpose. ❏

ANTI-SEMITISM AND THE ARABS

From Mai Ghoussoub (Lebanese/British), sculptor and writer, and Moshe Machover (Israeli/British), professor emeritus at King's College London

Let us for a moment give Harold Evans the benefit of the doubt and grant that his article is a genuine search for truth and peace ('The voice of hate', *Index* 4/2002). Far be it from us to defend or condone the criminal acts committed by the so-called 'martyrs', who in dying take with them children, men and women in a bus, restaurant or nightclub. Nor do we wish to deny that there is a growing discourse in the Arab and Muslim world that draws on the cesspit of European anti-Semitism. In recent decades, many Arabs have been searching for reasons for the total inhumanity of the Israeli occupation wherever they can find them.

The propaganda of the Israeli state and its Zionist allies deliberately conflates the terms 'Jew' and 'Israeli'. Ironically, it is finally succeeding – in the Arab world. If the friends of Israel consistently confuse opposition to Israel with anti-Semitism, little wonder that some of the victims of Israeli oppression and those who identify with them also end up in the same confusion.

Like the Zionist establishment, Evans refuses, despite his protestations to the contrary, to make any distinction between Jewish and Israeli; but he screams with horror when some powerless people don't make this distinction and rushes to call them 'anti-Semites', equating them with the powerful Jew-haters of the 1930s. Evans is writing for a Western audience; his readers naturally think of anti-Semitism in the traditional European context, in which it was directed against a persecuted minority. In the present Arab context – while still a deplorable phenomenon – it has quite a different meaning.

[Throughout his article] Evans twists the facts to prove that the victims of today are the Israeli occupiers, not the occupied Palestinians. If Evans were really seeking a just, peaceful solution for that blood-soaked area in the Middle East, he should have tried to acknowledge the suffering of *all* the people involved. Evans is rightly horrified by the murder of Jewish-Israeli children; less so, it would seem, by that of Palestinian children, which he hardly mentions. And he compels us to play his own game for we must remind him that many more Palestinian children have lost their lives in this conflict. We abhor the need to give numbers and statistics – the idea is somehow demeaning: for every single child who has died in this conflict deserved to have a life and a future and his or her death is a tragedy that destroyed not only their young lives but those of their parents and loved ones.

But here are a few dry statistics from *Jewish Peace News*:

- Number of days since the beginning of the current Intifada to 30 October 2002: 763
- Average number of trees uprooted in the occupied territories per day: 896
- Average number of homes demolished by the Israeli army in the occupied territories per day: 15
- Total number of homes demolished: 12,099
- Area of land confiscated in the West Bank and East Jerusalem by the Israeli authorities since the beginning of the Intifada: 63.05 square miles (Manhattan, New York, is 22.7 square miles)
- Average number of Palestinians injured by Israeli forces and settlers per day: 27
- Average number of Israelis injured by Palestinians (including soldiers and settlers) per day: 6
- Number of Palestinian teachers detained by the Israeli army: 75
- Percentage of Palestinian children between six months and five years who suffer from chronic malnutrition: 45 per cent
- Number of journalists injured by the Israeli army: 254
  These numbers do not include the dead.

Again, we are forced by Evans' enumeration of the wrongdoing of 'the Arabs' to list tragedies and suffering and to compare them. But when he writes: 'The brilliance of the whole campaign of anti-Semitism is its stupefying perversity: the Arab and Muslim media and mosque depict Israelis as Nazis . . . media and mosque peddle the same Judophobia that paved the way to Auschwitz,' is not Evans deploying against 'Arabs' and 'Muslims' the same stereotyped plot terminology and conspiracy theories that anti-Semites have used against the Jews? Evans has an inflated idea of the Arab media and their organisation. The reality is almost the reverse: there is hardly any organised social or political strategy in the Arab world.

Peace is really in trouble. To secure it, the anti-Jewish upsurge in the Arab world must be fought. But it does not need voices like that of Evans: they do more harm than good.

Victims' reactions are rarely saintly. The crimes of the victims may often look as ugly as those of their victimisers, but seekers of peace and justice do not use the victim's wrongdoing to whitewash the victimiser. ❏

For the complete version of this letter ⇨ www.indexonline.org

REPORTING THE EARTH

ANDREW WASLEY

ENVIRONMENTAL REPORTING HAS
BECOME ONE OF JOURNALISM'S
MOST DANGEROUS BEATS

'About 20 people attacked me with spears, machetes and about three bottles of hydrochloric acid,' says Arbi Kusno. 'They started striking at me straight-away with their blades. Luckily, I was not hit on my front, only on my back. When I fell they didn't stop or say anything, they just went for it.

'My back was wounded with 17 gashes, each gash being 20 centimetres long and four deep. My hand was severed, one ear was wounded and there was only 1cm left of the other. My only thought was to surrender to the Almighty and nothing else.'

Arbi Kusno, an Indonesian journalist, writes for *Lintas Khatulistiwa* newspaper and several news magazines. He was attacked and very nearly killed by thugs believed to be working for timber barons as he returned home from an assignment probing rampant illegal logging in the Pangkalan Bun region of Indonesia.

'Twenty-seven bags of blood were used on me,' says Kusno. 'My own blood was exhausted. I was almost taken to the morgue; I was actually on my way there because they thought I had died. But I was still conscious, though I couldn't speak. I wiggled my foot, which was seen by a nurse who exclaimed, "He's still alive, he's still alive!"' Kusno currently cannot eat or dress unaided, is still awaiting a full police investigation into the attack and needs to raise funds to enable him to make a trip overseas for specialist treatment.

His testimony – some of which was included in a recent documentary, *Rotten Trade*, broadcast on BBC World – is particularly disturbing, but not unusual for reporters investigating the corrupt and violent world of illegal logging in Indonesia.

'Journalists looking at this illegal trade are almost as likely to face real danger as the activists working alongside them,' says Faith Doherty,

Indonesia 1999: illegal logging. Credit: A Ruwindrijarto / Telepak

senior campaigner with the Environmental Investigation Agency, herself kidnapped and brutally beaten alongside a colleague while documenting logging in an Indonesian national park. 'The people involved in the trade are violent criminals; foreign correspondents, and particularly local journalists and their "fixers", are all under threat, especially those that go the extra mile to expose information about environmental abuse.'

Kusno's experiences echo those of colleagues in the Philippines who, while reporting on illegal logging a decade ago, first highlighted the dangers facing media personnel examining such issues. Marites Vitug received death threats and then outrageous criminal libel actions as a result of her reports, which linked a regional congressman and a local timber tycoon to destructive logging practices.

'Reporting on the environment in the Philippines is about power,' she says. 'A handful of families control the country's forests, coastal resources and land; and they are wealthy, well connected and entrenched. That is why environmental reporting is not safe.'

In the years following Vitug's harassment, Philippine reporters looking at mining, illegal logging and the trade in endangered species have suffered increasing intimidation, threats and violence. One of them, Nesino P Toling, was shot dead while working at his desk. Many journalists were forced to leave the country, give up the trade or find ever more creative and elaborate ways to conduct their investigations.

It is situations such as this that led one commentator to claim recently that 'reporting the earth is fast becoming one of journalism's most dangerous beats'. Indeed, as issues concerning the health of the planet appear to creep up the news agenda – partly, say analysts, in response to a perceived ecological crisis and partly because of events such as the Earth Summit in Johannesburg – press freedom organisations have warned of the increasing dangers facing journalists reporting on environmental affairs.

'Reporters attempting to cover difficult environmental issues do experience problems, particularly in politically unstable parts of the world,' says Aidan White of the International Federation of Journalists. The IFJ and the International Federation of Environment Journalists have documented cases of environmental journalists running into trouble in Eastern Europe, Russia, China, West Africa, South America and parts of Asia.

Most recently, a reporter from the Brazilian television network Record covering a Greenpeace action in the Amazon had to be rescued after coming under threat from members of the logging community. A peaceful

10   INDEX ON CENSORSHIP 1 2003

blockade of a major timber smuggling river route turned violent after logging barges attempted to ram protesters; in the ensuing confusion, several activists were hurt and the reporter, along with campaigners, was forced to seek sanctuary at the local airport.

In Russia, the case of Grigorii Pasko brought the hazards of environmental reporting to international attention. Pasko, a military journalist with the newspaper of the Russian Pacific fleet, *Battle Watch*, was first jailed in 1999 for 'misusing his office as a military journalist' after passing video footage to a Japanese TV company that showed nuclear waste being dumped at sea. Following international outrage he was freed, only to face a second trial late last year that resulted in a four-year jail sentence (*Index* 2/02).

Equally disturbing, but less well known, is the case of Igor Kravchuk, a reporter with the Russian daily *Vesti*. Kravchuk revealed that impoverished sailors from Russia's northern Pacific port were stripping submarines of communications equipment and radioactive components to sell to organised crime. Following his reports, Kravchuk claims that his telephone was bugged by Russian security services, his professionalism was questioned and that while covering the trial of two sailors accused of selling equipment he was threatened with jail.

Analysts claim that such cases have killed off some investigative environmental reporting in the former USSR. 'The Pasko case was a particularly resounding blow for environmental journalism,' says Anatoly Lebedev, who compiles a yearly anthology of environmental reporting in the Far East. 'Journalists are shunning tough environment stories for easier topics and there are regions where such issues are not being covered at all.'

But, despite the dangers, journalists in some parts of the world continue to file stories. The IFEJ points towards the case of Xhemal Mato, an Albanian TV journalist who, despite threats of arson and kidnapping by organised criminals, continued to report on the threats to endangered wildlife in Albanian national parks.

In Algeria, Mohamed Rebah continued to document chronic environmental problems in a country where reporters have been killed by government and Islamists for refusing to stay silent. In Ghana, Ben Ephson, an environment correspondent for *Business in Ghana* magazine, was arrested and jailed for six months as a result of stories he filed. IFEJ also highlights the case of Barbara D'Achille, who, while investigating development issues in Peru for *El Comercio* newspaper, was shot and killed by a little-known guerrilla movement.

In India, Tehelka.com, an internet news site that has built its reputation through investigative reporting of ecological, governmental and corruption issues, faces a financially precarious future as a direct result of sustained harassment from the authorities (*Index* 4/2002). Tarun Tejpal, Tehelka's founder, says his offices have been repeatedly raided by tax, customs, police and various anti-corruption agencies since the sting two years ago, and that because of a high-profile 'vendetta' mounted by the authorities, funding for the project has all but dried up.

Vir Sanghvi, editor of the *Hindustan Times*, one of India's big circulation dailies, says the effect of the 'Tehelka scam' has been to prevent other journalists from pursuing corruption. 'The messenger gets shot and the accused is the one who pulls the trigger.'

In the West, environmental reporters have also been subjected to harassment and intimidation, particularly those covering ecological protests or involved in exposing corporate activities. 'There is a documented history of intimidation against those who speak out on the environment, and journalists are one category of people in the firing line,' says Andy Rowell, one of the UK's leading environment journalists and author of *Green Backlash*.

Rowell says the major obstacle in the way of getting genuine, accurate, environmental journalism into the public arena is the corporate nature of much of the mainstream media. 'You only have to look at the way much of the mainstream press covered the Genoa [anti-G8] protests last year to realise there are political agendas at play.'

Such a view is backed up by the IFJ: 'We've seen instances where corporate ownership of the media has affected the nature of coverage of environmental issues,' says White. He cites the case of one European media conglomerate that also owns and manages water supply facilities: the company was fined millions of dollars in 1999 for violating ecological regulations, but its media largely failed to report on what was effectively a major environmental scandal.

The case echoes that of the ITN/Shell affair, in which the UK TV news provider was accused of allowing corporate interests to prevent the broadcast of a news feature exploring oil-related environmental pollution and human rights atrocities in Nigeria. An ITN offshoot, Corporate Television Networks, had made promotional films for Shell.

In the US, questions have been raised on whether NBC's TV coverage of environmental pollution of the Hudson River in New York might be affected by the fact that its corporate flagship, the General Electric Corporation, had originally caused the pollution. Reporters also highlighted what they describe as a worrying trend by the big news corporations to cut back on ecological reporting; they cited AOL Time Warner's recent decision to cut environmental coverage on CNN, one of its subsidiaries.

In the UK, the Medialens organisation is more direct: 'Why expect the corporate media to report accurately on the machinations of corporate business?' it asks. The organisation, which has compiled numerous dossiers on UK press coverage of major ecological concerns, claims there is a disturbing trend among reputable news providers of failing to report accurately on difficult issues such as climate change because of an inherent partnership with big business and economy.

When Exxon oil chief Lee Raymond – dubbed by Greenpeace the Darth Vader of global warming – was entertained by the UK government only months before the collapse of the Larsen B ice shelf as a result of global warming, Medialens controversially brought reporters to book for failing to flag the operational history of Raymond's company and its contribution to global warming.

While civil society initiatives, research, advocacy and publicity campaigns assist organisations such as the IFJ in raising awareness of the dangers facing environmental reporters out in the field, tackling the root causes is seen as more problematic. 'We need governments and international bodies to make human rights and press freedom issues an immediate priority,' says White. 'At the moment, there appears to be a lack of will to do so.' He claims that many action plans drawn up at events such as the Earth Summit will fail because of a lack of free media in many of the countries with the most acute environmental problems.

In such an apparently negative climate, reporting the Earth looks set to continue being an increasingly dangerous beat: 'At the end of the day, we are dealing with contentious issues,' says Rowell. 'Much of the time, corporations and others are not prepared to have their dirty linen aired in public.' ❏

Andrew Wasley *is a journalist specialising in media and human rights*

SMALL ISLAND, BIG PROBLEM

TABITHA MORGAN

RESTRICTIONS ON THE MEDIA IN
NORTHERN CYPRUS ARE INCREASING
AS THE SOUTHERN PART OF THE
ISLAND MOVES CLOSER TO MEMBERSHIP
OF THE EUROPEAN UNION

It now seems fairly certain that the Republic of Cyprus will be admitted to the European Union at the Copenhagen Summit in mid-December. In practice, this refers only to the southern part of the divided island and is likely to mean further isolation for the Turkish-speaking Cypriots in the north – unless, that is, there is some resolution of the 28-year-old partition of the island, a stronger possibility under the new government in Ankara than at any time previously.

Growing dissatisfaction with the policies of 78-year-old Turkish Cypriot leader Rauf Denktash, whom the UN blames for blocking attempts to find a political solution, has resulted in more overt criticism than at any time in his long, highly autocratic, one-man rule. This has been met with an unprecedented media crackdown. Over the years, Denktash, whose political career began in the early 1950s when Cyprus was still under British rule, has persuaded the Turkish Cypriot community that he alone is their best defence against the Greeks. His photograph, along with that of Mustafa Kemal Ataturk, founder of the Turkish Republic, gazes down benignly from the walls of government buildings and shops throughout the territory north of the UN-manned Green Line that divides the island.

In 1983, Denktash unilaterally declared independence from the south, announcing the establishment of the Turkish Republic of Northern Cyprus (TRNC), even today recognised only by Turkey. Greek and Turkish Cypriots had largely lived apart since 1963, with sporadic outbursts of violence between the two communities. Joint government fell apart after the island's complex constitution, bequeathed by the British and designed to protect the interests of the Turkish Cypriot minority, proved unworkable. In 1974, after the colonels in Athens attempted to stage a right-wing coup on the island, Turkey invaded on the grounds that it was intervening to protect Turkish Cypriots from further inter-communal violence.

Nicosia, Northern Cyprus 1997:
Rauf Denktash prepares to snap
his critics. Credit: STR /AFP

For most of his time in office, few have felt the need to challenge either Denktash's style or his policies, which were broadly seen as being in the best interests of the continuing survival of the Turkish Cypriot community. Today, however, many believe Denktash has become little more than a mouthpiece for Ankara.

Not that you would necessarily discover this from reading the abundant Turkish Cypriot press. The population of less than 200,000 can choose from no fewer than ten daily papers, giving the tiny breakaway statelet one of the highest concentrations of newspapers per capita anywhere in the world. Ironically, given many people's views on the role of Turkey on the island, it is the mainland Turkish papers that sell best. Conservative dailies *Sabah* and *Hurriyet* have a daily circulation of 13,000 between them, while sales of the most popular Turkish Cypriot paper, *Kibris*, never exceed 10,000 a day. Turkish Cypriot journalist Hasan Kahvecioglu says Northern Cyprus is the victim of 'a daily cultural bombardment from the mainland'.

For Kahvecioglu, and increasing numbers who share his views, it is time for Turkey to step back from Northern Cyprus and allow Turkish Cypriots to take control of their own affairs. History, culture and religious traditions set Turkish-speaking Cypriots apart from mainland Turks; the former resent the presence of more than 60,000 Turks, known as 'settlers', who have moved – or been moved – to Northern Cyprus since 1974. 'We have more in common with Greek Cypriots than with these people from Anatolia,' said a young Turkish Cypriot lawyer.

However, economic dependence makes it unlikely that the ties to Turkey will weaken. An international embargo on trade with the breakaway north means its economy is kept going solely by annual injections of cash from Turkey. Without any possibility of international commerce, growing numbers of the younger generation argue that local initiative and private enterprise in their part of the island are being stifled. Many of the most enterprising have left. According to Muharrem Faiz of Comar, a Turkish Cypriot market research company, the majority of his contemporaries are critical of their government's relationship with Turkey. 'Turks always say Cypriots are lazy,' he says. 'In fact, this is just old-fashioned colonialist rhetoric designed to legitimise a policy that is creating a culture of dependency.'

Despite the close relationship between Northern Cyprus and its powerful neighbour, major differences exist between the two in the way the media operates. 'Turkey's media is about profit,' says Kahvecioglu. 'Our media is about making political capital.' Newspapers in the TRNC, like those in the south, are overtly financed and supported by political parties and, broadly speaking, fall into pro- or anti-government camps. Economies of scale make a viable commercial press impossible.

The leading pro-government paper in the north, *Kibris*, is owned by businessman Asil Nadir, who also owned the Industrial Bank of Cyprus, one of several banks in Northern Cyprus that collapsed two years ago, leaving thousands of Turkish Cypriots unable to recover their savings. According to one diplomat in Nicosia, the authorities have made little effort to compel Nadir to refund the money because 'he uses his paper like a weapon, holding it to the heads of the Turkish Cypriot administration.'

The biggest opposition newspaper, *Afrika*, claims to be the only truly independent paper in Northern Cyprus and consequently enjoys a far less secure existence. Founded under the name *Avrupa* in 1997, the paper was accused by the authorities of seeking to undermine Turkey's security forces which have been deployed in the north of the island since 1974. After the management was unable to pay a US$200,000 fine, its computers and equipment were confiscated and its offices fire-bombed (*Index* 2/2002). It has, nevertheless, continued to be a source of annoyance to the Turkish Cypriot authorities; Sener Levent, the paper's founding editor, recently spent six weeks in prison after being found guilty (under an old British law) of defaming Denktash and undermining his office.

It remains to be seen whether EU harmonisation laws rushed through the Turkish parliament last August will have any impact on journalists working in Northern Cyprus. Under the new laws, journalists found guilty of libel no longer risk a custodial sentence, only a fine. Levent, meanwhile, is awaiting the outcome of no less than 75 legal cases brought against him by the authorities. He and several other journalists were due to appear in court at the end of November, charged with trespassing as they reported on a rally in support of a suspended schoolteacher last December.

The teacher, Nilgun Orhan, was suspended from her job after writing an article in *Avrupa* criticising the presence of Turkish troops on Cyprus. It began: 'I am writing to you from a divided and invaded island . . .' Orhan has since been charged with 'creating hatred and mistrust of the state and undermining its power'.

As far as Kahvecioglu is concerned, the main problem facing journalists in Northern Cyprus is self-censorship. Discussion of the Cyprus problem, known as 'the national issue', is taboo. 'It is like the Quran,' he says, 'a sacred belief you cannot question, that is untouchable.' He adds: 'Anyone who criticises Denktash's policies is instantly branded a traitor.' As a result, Cyprus's relationship with Turkey, the continued presence of more than 30,000 Turkish troops on the island and increased contact with Greek Cypriots are simply not addressed in the media.

A quick glance at a single day's papers from both sides of the divided island confirms that far fewer column inches in the north are devoted to solving the Cyprus problem than in the south. In part this may reflect Turkish Cypriots' feelings of alienation from any decision-making process on Cyprus's future. 'We do not have a National Council to discuss these subjects, as they do in the south,' said a Turkish Cypriot doctor in Nicosia who asked not to be named. 'Everyone knows that if Denktash is too sick to continue with the settlement talks, then Turkey will simply find a replacement. We have no say in the matter.'

The present talks between Denktash and his Greek Cypriot counterpart Glafcos Clerides have been going on for nearly a year. It is not the first time they have crossed swords; both are veterans on the Cypriot political scene. Now, as then, they have got nowhere and it is unlikely there will be any agreement before the EU is forced to make its decision in December. Progress has not been helped by six months' near political paralysis in Turkey, or by Denktash's poor health. 'Without firm direction from Turkey,' said one Western diplomat, 'there can be no movement on Cyprus.' The newly elected government in Ankara has announced its commitment to joining the European Union but given the magnitude of the problems inside Turkey it seems unlikely that Cyprus will be at the top of its agenda. It has, however, appealed to the EU to delay its decision on the accession of Cyprus in the interests of achieving a resolution of the problem – and Europe appears to be listening. Denktash, who underwent major heart surgery in October, is unlikely to return to the negotiating table until well after the Copenhagen deadline.

This leaves Brussels with the dilemma of whether or not to admit only the southern half of the island into Europe. If it refuses, Greece has threatened to use its veto to block any further European expansion; if it goes ahead as planned, it runs the risk of an irretrievably partitioned island. The previous Turkish government had threatened to annex the north, seal the border with the south and force those who want to visit the north to enter via Turkey.

Paradoxically, this may make it easier for overseas journalists to work in Northern Cyprus. An accredited foreign correspondent working in Turkey, or visiting Northern Cyprus from Turkey, is allowed unfettered access throughout the territory. But if the same correspondent chooses to enter the north overland from the south, he or she will be assigned a minder from the government press and information office detailed to restrict access to the population. Correspondents who fall foul of this restriction are speedily returned to the south and further visits banned.

'Living here is like living in a box,' complains Turkish Cypriot journalist Sevgul Uludag, 'it's hard to explain the level of psychological pressure we are under.' An accumulation of economic hardship, frustration with the lack of progress towards a settlement and restrictions on free speech have led thousands of Turkish Cypriots to conclude that life has to be better elsewhere. As a result they are leaving in record numbers, prompting Turkey's then deputy prime minister, Mesut Yilmaz, to comment that if the Cyprus problem was not resolved, there would be no Turkish Cypriots left on the island in ten years' time.

Meanwhile, some of those who stay defy official restrictions on communications with their neighbours on the other side of the Green Line.
Turkish- and Greek-speaking peace groups keep in touch by email and
meet periodically in Pyla, the only village on the island still inhabited by
both communities. 'It's not easy for us to keep up contact; whenever we
cross over the border, guards take a note of our names and when we get
home we are questioned about why we went,' said a Turkish Cypriot
member of a bi-communal women's group. 'But we are determined to keep
on meeting for as long as we can.'

So far there is little sign that the bi-communal contacts are having any
impact on the Turkish Cypriot administration. Resat Caglar, former
director general of the ministry of foreign affairs and defence in the
northern part of Nicosia, described those in the peace movement as 'naive,
useless do-gooders, distracting attention from the main issue'. And the
longer that 'issue' remains unresolved, the tougher the restrictions on their
freedom of movement and expression are likely to be. ❏

Tabitha Morgan *is a freelance journalist based in Nicosia*

INSIDE THE 'AXIS OF EVIL' . . .

. . . THE PEOPLE AWAIT WHAT THEY CALL THE
'INEVITABLE WAR'. SOME WELCOME LIBERATION FROM
TYRANNICAL REGIMES; FOR MOST, PARTICULARLY
IN IRAQ, LIFE IS ABOUT DAY-TO-DAY SURVIVAL. IN
IRAN THEY ARE ON THE STREETS DEFENDING THEIR
FRAGILE DEMOCRACY; AND IN NORTH KOREA THE
PEOPLE ARE DYING, ONCE MORE, OF HUNGER

250 dinar Iraqi note: banking on Saddam.
Credit: Camera Press / Manfredo Pinzaniti / Grazia Neri

BUSH'S BIG BLUNDER

ARYEH NEIER

SO WHAT EXACTLY MAKES IRAN PART OF THE FAMOUS 'AXIS'?

One of the difficulties with talk about the Axis of Evil is that it suggests that those who make up this axis are linked to each other. On such grounds it seems appropriate to label Hitler's Germany, Mussolini's Italy and Hirohito's Japan as 'the Axis powers'. They were allies. But except for the fact that President George W Bush and his administration see them as enemies of the United States, how are Iran, Iraq and North Korea connected?

As is well known, there is no love lost between Iran and Iraq. They fought a catastrophic eight-year-long war against each other in the 1980s that ended only at a point when both sides were substantially worn out. Since then, relations between them have barely improved. Iranians properly regard Saddam Hussein's regime as the oppressor of their fellow Shia and as the desecrator of some of the holiest places of their faith. Anti-Americanism is a significant factor in both countries – though its extent and depth in the population at large are impossible to estimate – but perhaps no more so than in many countries the US considers its allies. It appears that many Iranians are also antagonistic to a threatened US pre-emptive war against Iraq. Here too, however, there is nothing that seems especially distinctive.

As for North Korea, no one has even suggested a link to Iraq and Iran. To the extent the regime in Pyongyang has friends, they seem to be Russia and China. If we are to talk about an axis involving North Korea, they seem the logical candidates for inclusion. Yet, particularly after 11 September, the Bush administration considers them strategic partners.

Among the three governments designated as the Axis of Evil, the selection of Iran seems most bizarre. Both Iraq and North Korea are totalitarian states. No one may breathe a word of dissent without facing the most severe reprisal. Saddam Hussein's claim that he was re-elected with nothing short of 100 per cent of the vote is indicative. In contrast, political debate in Iran is lively; despite persecution, writers, journalists, academics, lawyers, liberal members of the clergy and many others continue to speak out; elected officials exercise limited authority, but they are chosen democratically; and public opinion constrains the actions of the religious leaders who wield police, judicial and military power.

Kish Island, Iran 2002: new spaces of freedom.
Credit: 135 photos / Omid Salehi

Iraq under Saddam has been an international aggressor, starting wars against Iran and Kuwait. North Korea has maintained a nuclear weapons programme after giving assurances that it was being dismantled. Yet to the extent that is known, Iran has pursued neither course. Hence, if it is not part of an axis, what makes it more evil than a great many other governments around the world?

Of course, there are accusations, perhaps well founded, that Iranian security forces have supported Hezbollah in Lebanon and have covertly shipped arms to the Palestinian Authority. Perhaps this is the reason for its inclusion. If so, it would be useful for the Bush administration to say so. Also, it raises many questions. Among them, of course: what other Middle Eastern governments are engaged in similar activities? And how do Iran's actions differ from those of other governments including, of course, the US when it supported – far more directly than Iran – such forces as UNITA in Angola and the Contras in Nicaragua.

Among the pernicious consequences of labelling Iran as part of the Axis of Evil are that it arouses nationalist – and anti-American – passions that exacerbate the difficulties confronting democratic forces in Iran; and it embitters relations between Iran and the US, making it all but impossible for Americans and, to an extent, other Westerners to assist in bringing about a political opening. Intellectual contacts between Iranians and outsiders are urgently needed. Without them, what may well be the most important struggle anywhere between democrats and religious bigots will be very much harder. In labelling Iran as part of the Axis of Evil, President Bush strengthens the hand of just the forces in Iran he probably sees as the enemy and undermines those bravely trying to transform their government. ❑

Aryeh Neier is president of the Open Society Institute, New York

MEDIA MONGERING

WILLIAM M ARKIN

US Army psyops regimental crest

It was California's Hiram Johnson who said, in a speech on the Senate floor in 1917, that 'the first casualty, when war comes, is truth.' What would he make of the Bush administration? In a policy shift that reaches across all the armed services, Secretary of Defense Donald H Rumsfeld and his senior aides are revising missions and creating new agencies to make 'information warfare' a central element of any US war. Some hope it will eventually rank with bombs and artillery shells as an instrument of destruction.

Rumsfeld's vision of information warfare is disturbing in that it has a way of folding together two kinds of wartime activity involving communications that have traditionally been separated by a firewall of principle.

The first is purely military. It includes attacks on the radar, communications and other 'information systems' an enemy depends on to guide its war-making capabilities. This category also includes traditional psychological warfare, such as dropping leaflets or broadcasting propaganda to enemy troops.

The second is not directly military. It is the dissemination of public information that the American people need in order to understand what is happening in a war, and to decide what they think about it. This information is supposed to be true.

Increasingly, the administration's new policy – along with the steps senior commanders are taking to implement it – blurs or even erases the boundaries between factual information and news on the one hand, and public relations, propaganda and psychological warfare on the other. And, while the policy ostensibly targets foreign enemies, its most likely victim will be the American electorate.

One of Rumsfeld's first steps into this minefield occurred last year with the creation of the Pentagon's Office of Strategic Influence. Part of its stated mission was to generate disinformation and propaganda that would help the United States counter Islamic extremists and pursue the war on terrorism. The office's nominal target was the foreign media, especially in the Middle East and Asia. As critics soon pointed out, however, there was no way – in an age of instant global communications – that Washington could propagandise abroad without that same propaganda spreading to the home front. Faced with a public outcry, Rumsfeld declared it had all been a big misunderstanding. The Pentagon would never lie to Americans. The Office of Strategic Influence was shut down. But the impulse to control public information and bend it to the service of government objectives did not go away.

In autumn 2002, Rumsfeld created a new position of deputy undersecretary for 'special plans', a euphemism for deception operations. The special plans policy czar will sit atop a huge new infrastructure being created in the name of information warfare. On 1 October, in a little-noticed but major reorganisation, US Strategic Command took over all responsibilities for attacks on global information. The Omaha-based successor to the Strategic Air Command had up to this point focused solely on nuclear weapons. Similarly, the country's most venerable and historic bombing command, the 8th Air Force, which carried the air war to Germany in World War II, has been directed to transfer its bomber and fighter aircraft to other commands so that it can focus exclusively on worldwide information attacks.

The Navy, meanwhile, has consolidated its efforts in a newly formed Naval Network Warfare Command. And the Joint Strategic Capabilities Plan (JSCP), prepared by the Joint Chiefs of Staff, now declares information to be just as important in war as diplomatic, military or economic factors. The strategic capabilities plan is the central war-fighting directive for the US military. It establishes what are called 'Informational Flexible Deterrent Options' for global wars, such as the war on terrorism, and separate plans written for individual theatres of war, such as Iraq.

To a large extent, these documents and the organisational shifts behind them are focused on such missions as jamming or deceiving enemy radar systems and disrupting command and control networks. Such activities only carry forward efforts that have been part of US military tactics for decades or longer. But a summary of the strategic capabilities plan and a raft of other Pentagon and armed forces documents made available to the *Los Angeles Times* make it clear that the new approach now includes other elements as well: the management of public information, efforts to control news media sources and the manipulation of public opinion.

The plan summary, for instance, talks of 'strategic' deception and 'influence operations' as basic tools in future wars. According to another Defense Department directive on information warfare policy, military leaders should use information 'operations' to 'heighten public awareness; promote national and coalition policies, aims, and objectives . . . [and] counter adversary propaganda and disinformation in the news.'

Both the Air Force and the Navy now list deception as one of five missions for information warfare, along with electronic attack, electronic protection, psychological attacks and public affairs. A September draft of a new Air Force policy describes information warfare's goals as 'destruction, degradation, denial, disruption, deceit, and exploitation'. These goals are referred to collectively as 'D5E'. In order to do a better job of deception, the joint chiefs have issued a 'Joint Policy for Military Deception' that directs the individual services to work on the task in peacetime as well as wartime. Specifically, it orders the Air Force to develop better doctrine and techniques for incorporating deception into war plans.

The Air Force, in response, now defines military deception as action that 'misleads adversaries, causing them to act in accordance with' US objectives. And, like the other services, it is increasingly folding its 'public affairs' apparatus – that is, the open world of media relations – into the information warfare team. 'Gaining and maintaining the information initiative in a conflict can be a powerful weapon to defeat propaganda,' the Air Force said in its January doctrine.

That echoes a statement by Navy Rear Admiral John Cryer III, who worked on information warfare in the Combined Air Operations Center in Saudi Arabia during the Afghan war: 'It was our belief . . . we were losing the information war early when we watched al-Jazeera,' Cryer said at a conference in October – ie the US perspective was inadequately represented on the Arab equivalent of CNN. 'We came around, but it took a lot longer than it should have.'

Of course, there is nothing wrong with making sure the US point of view gets represented in the news media, abroad and at home. Done properly, that is a prescription for more openness and less unnecessary secrecy. The problem is that Rumsfeld's vision of information warfare seems to push beyond the notion that US ideas and information should compete with the enemy's on a level playing field. And Rumsfeld's vision, with its melding of public information and deception, is taking root in the armed services.

The new Air Force doctrine, for example, declares that the news media can be used not only to convey 'the leadership's concern with [an] issue', but also to avoid 'the media going to other sources [such as an adversary or critic of US policy] for information'. In other words, information warfare now includes controlling as far as possible what the US public sees and reads.

The disinformation campaign being constructed goes against even the military's own stated mission. Truthfulness, the Air Force says, is a key to defeating adversaries. Accordingly, the service branch adds, 'US and friendly forces must strive to become the favoured source of information.'

The potential for mischief is magnified by the fact that so much of what the US military does these days falls into the category of covert operations. Americans are now operating out of secret bases in places like Uzbekistan and the Kurdish enclave in northern Iraq; Special Forces units are said to be inside western Iraq as well. In the meantime, the armed forces are making use of facilities in the Arab states along the Persian Gulf.

In all these cases and more, the US and other Western news media depend on the military for information. Since reporters cannot travel into parts of Iraq and other places in the region without military escort, what they report is generally what they've been told. And when the information that military officers provide to the public is part of a process that generates propaganda and places a high value on deceit, deception and denial, then truth is indeed likely to be high on the casualty list.

That is bad news for the US public. In the end, it may be even worse news for the Bush administration – and for a US military that has spent more than 25 years climbing out of the credibility trap called Vietnam. ❏

William M Arkin is a columnist and writer on military affairs and a former US Army intelligence analyst. This item was originally published by the Los Angeles Times

TORN BY FEAR AND HOPE
FALEH A JABAR

IRAQIS WELCOME LIBERATION FROM
THE EXCESSES OF THEIR REGIME,
BUT ARE MORE CONCERNED WITH
THE EXIGENCIES OF SURVIVAL

For the world, the fate of the Iraqi dictator-patriarch may seem all but sealed. United States rhetoric and diplomacy are both geared to a military campaign with or without the UN, whereas no trace of peaceful effort exists. For Iraqis, who are natural-born sceptics, this could be another ploy in which reality and rhetoric are so interwoven that it is impossible to sort the hope from fear.

Most observers in Iraq are firmly of the opinion that the USA and Iraq are irretrievably locked on a collision course, the purpose of which is not so much disarmament as the elimination of Saddam Hussein. While the silent majority in Iraq welcome such a surgical excision, they fear the rhetoric disguises other ends.

For three decades, the one-party rule of the Baath has dominated their lives. Two generations have known no other president than Saddam, no political party other than the Baath, and no ideology save its nationalist-socialist creed, strongly influenced by Nazism. In their imagination and memory, Saddam represents the sole source of all good and all evil: the prosperity and social welfare of the good days in the 1970s; war, sanctions, poverty and isolation in the 1990s. He has been with them from time immemorial and is bent on staying from here to eternity. And beyond, as the selection of his younger son as his heir implies. Newspapers carry his image on their front pages daily; television screens broadcast footage of him for at least six hours a day. Praise songs are recited in his honour. As one Iraqi poet put it: 'Saddam has been planted under our skin. He is on the radio, in the press, on the walls, with you at home. There is no escape from him.'

Iraqis are told his piercing eyes can penetrate the private thoughts of others, and uncover would-be traitors before they can turn into conspirators. There are myths that claim he is protected by supernatural powers. Has he not survived scores of attempts on his life and nipped countless military coups in the bud? Did not the US and its allies fail to eliminate him in the 1991 war? And they ask themselves the question: 'Are we weak because he is omnipotent, or is he is omnipotent only because we are so feeble?' Above all, they are convinced the tyrant will not leave the stage unless a super-power intervenes. In that lies their only hope.

Yet even this is mitigated by an ancient Babylonian superstition that warns them to fear hope. Inhabitants of the flourishing Mesopotamian civil-isation in the fertile crescent invented a bizarre custom in which days were set aside for the ritual practice of grief in anticipation of calamities that might call it forth. Their collective weeping and wailing was assisted by texts recalling past sorrows, all the better to prepare them for future disaster.

So when their dictator survived the various uprisings across Iraq that followed the Gulf War, the nation concluded grimly that the US had, after all, been conspiring to keep him in power. A host of 'theories' were invented to explain this paradox: he was to be the 'scarecrow' of the Gulf, frightening its rulers into buying even more US arms. A more outlandish theory claimed – with 'proof' – that Saddam had all along been conspiring with both Israel and the US to wipe out the entire Iraqi population, using his deputy Tariq Aziz as the secret go-between.

The new US resolve to remove Saddam Hussein did not overly impress Iraqis at home. But when the ruling elite and their crony business class began to hoard gold (a bad omen) and betray real signs of concern, Iraqis at large began to realise that the republic of fear might, at last, have taken on an egalitarian hue. It was easy to differentiate the smell of fright from the scent of panic. With the escalation of war rhetoric, they cautiously began to move from the agony of doubt to the hope, however modest their expecta-tions, that the single-party, single-tribe system was in real trouble and that they might well be free at last.

But no sooner have they reached this point than doubt sets in once more: is this a Kissinger–like plot to sell fear as a commodity in pursuit of US interests – and is Saddam ready to go along with this, provided he stays in power? They recall how they were let down by the US in 1991; and there are fears that the removal campaign, however welcome, might degen-erate into chaos. Forced into a corner, Saddam might do a Samson and bring the house down with him by unleashing his chemical and biological weapons. Even if his fingers get burnt before they have a chance to press the button, his replacement might turn out to be yet another general with the same authoritarian Arab nationalist ideology, sectarian outlook and tribal

leanings. Washington, many Iraqis assume, would welcome a military coup. The cycle of tyranny will never end.

Debate in Iraq has centred on the reasons for the change in US strategy from containment to 'regime change'. The favoured theory is the ideological shift within the Republican Party from multilateralism to unilateralism: from faith in global harmony as represented by the single market to a world split by the 'clash of civilisations', a trend favoured by the events of 9/11. Given the failure of US attempts to contain Iraq via sanctions, no-fly zones and the food-for-oil programme compared with the quick triumph of the campaign in Afghanistan, the surgical strike in pursuit of regime change was clearly the way to go. Wiser counsels in the State Department lost out.

But euphoria at the overthrow of the Taliban may be misplaced: their regime was already tottering when the US launched its campaign. In addition, the campaign had massive international support, the unanimous backing of the UN, the full cooperation of Afghanistan's neighbours, a ready-made armed opposition within the country and a wealth of intelligence. Saudi money, Pakistani military intelligence and manpower, and generous bribes to tribal confederations did the rest. Iraq is a totally different proposition.

Oversimplified notions, mainly embraced by US defence 'experts', present Iraq as a state without a nation, divided between Kurds, Shia and Sunni, and ruled with brute force by a small Sunni family.

Saddam Hussein came into existence in a small village organised around the tribe. An orphan, he was brought up by his maternal uncle – a disgrace by tribal norms, which favour paternal descent. His was a poor family of a poor house of poor lineage in a poor clan. But his uncle's house and clan were influential. In his adolescence, Saddam embraced a form of Arabist ideology, influenced by Nazi ideas, favoured by his uncle. As a young man, he developed terrorist skills and took part in the attempt on the life of the Iraqi prime minister, General Abdul-Karim Qassim, in 1959. Stage three saw him master the stock-in-trade of an underground activist; and, finally, he acquired command of a mass political party.

Once in power, Saddam began to tailor the Iraqi state and society in his own image – though the process reversed his own life experience. He instituted the rule of a single party based on mass membership; created a formidable clandestine network of secret police and intelligence; positioned his own tribal connections in strategic positions in the military, the bureaucracy and the party; and, finally, ensured that his own 'house' emerged as the strongest family in the strongest lineage of the strongest clan in the strongest party. The 1970s oil boom enabled him to bribe vast swathes of society into allegiance or acquiescence.

This peculiar mix of party, tribe and oil, bribery and ruthless policing is what makes Iraq's political system seemingly invincible: it has survived two wars and a host of would-be coups, uprisings and invasion. But this very mix is itself its Achilles heel.

Why would a massive, silent majority long for a successful invasion of their country? The answer lies in the enormous gulf that now exists between official state nationalism and popular patriotism. The identity of interest that existed between the two in the 1970s, when over 1.8 million joined the Baath Party and Iraqis at many levels enjoyed the benefits of the enhanced oil revenues, is long gone. Though it survived the loss and privations imposed by the Iran–Iraq war, it was no match for the austerity of the 1990s. No longer was the party the only route to social, political and economic preferment; gone were the handsome salaries in government departments, big contracts and lucrative import-export licences. Taxes, which had contributed less than 0.5 per cent of state revenue, went up, free medical care and education disappeared in the wake of a devastating war that saw a US$60 billion surplus reduced to a US$50 billion deficit. Loyalty was consumed by galloping inflation; bribery disappeared along with social services. Returning from the front, the war generation watched war profiteers and the fat cats of the inner party flaunting a lifestyle no longer available to them, the backbone of the party. This was the beginning of the fatal divide.

In return for its largesse, the state had exacted total allegiance. No political or ideological dissent was tolerated. The majority acquiesced; those who challenged the regime lost their lives, among them thousands of leftists, liberals, Islamists, Kurdish nationalists, even members of the Baath Party itself. Organised social and political opposition was almost wiped out. Mass deportation and resettlement left deep scars among Kurds and Shia. Now it had to deal with restlessness within party ranks and within the 1 million-strong army, but without the means.

The invasion of Kuwait in August 1990 was an attempt to refill the state's depleted coffers by seizing its neighbour's treasure. Defeat dealt the final blow to national unity; fear of the regime was no longer the motivating force in society. The bite of economic sanctions reduced the once thriving salaried middle classes to paupers. Incomes went down from the level of

Saudi Arabia (cUS$4,000 per annum) to less than that of Bangladesh (cUS$300). The cost of getting to work was more than the monthly salaries of civil servants and teachers; inflation wiped out their savings; along with other social services, health and education now had to be paid for.

People started to sell whatever they could lay their hands on: a special market was opened to trade in things like window frames and doors as people dismantled their homes. Women turned increasingly to prostitution, turning whole neighbourhoods into red-light districts; violent crime soared; gangs of school drop-outs roamed the streets stealing and begging. Taxes increased dramatically. Food-for-oil programmes make little difference; monthly salaries cover basic needs for one week, free provisions another two. Once renowned for labour shortages, the market is glutted with the unemployed.

But if the middle and lower classes are selling, who is buying? The old fat cats and the nouveau riche seized the moment. Together with the political elite and the intelligence community, they live for the moment, seeking out fortune-tellers, buying amulets, talismans and charms to ward off evil. Sorcerers and magicians of all kinds have emerged in this promising new market. Food has become a means of control: ration vouchers in the gift of the government are weapons of mass mobilisation that ensure dissent is kept at bay.

With the decline and corruption of the police and law courts, protection of life and property has become the responsibility of reconstructed tribes and clans that have been officially empowered to administer justice, collect taxes and police urban communities. Non-tribal urban society is the majority.

While the elite classes seek spiritual solace in magic, poor folk resort to mosques and religious institutions for less spiritual ends. The secret of the spread of popular religion lies in the distribution of everything from food to medicine by the religious charities. And the more the state withdraws from the provision of social services, the more the religious networks expand. The Saudis attempted to exploit the vacuum left by the failure of the state to promote their particular Wahabi brand of Islam, an orthodox, Hanbalite version of rigid, medieval Islam, and stem what is seen as Shia expansion. The security services turned a blind eye to the flow of Saudi money and literature through the porous borders; the sectarian divide is encouraged in a society already deeply fragmented along ethnic and tribal lines. Matters of war and peace will undoubtedly be decided in Washington, but the outcome of any military confrontation will depend on Saddam's riposte. For him, it is a war of personal survival.

As the government is forced to acknowledge the divorce between itself and the people, it must also recognise that this increases the chances of outright rebellion. Attempts to infect Iraqis with anti-US and anti-Western Arab and Islamic nationalisms have failed; the anti-US platform in the Middle East has already been occupied by Islamic and nationalist opposition movements.

The regime also has to face up to the fact that the Iraqi army is no match for US or coalition forces. The Iraqi army is one-third its pre-1990 manpower and has half the hardware. War fatigue and poor motivation is evidenced by growing rates of desertion, despite the savage punishments – severing of ears – meted out to those who are caught.

The first, and possibly most effective, tool the regime proposes to use to counter the cracks in its war machine is to emphasise the threat of war to its ruling elites. 'No power is as costly as no power,' goes the official slogan in currency in Baghdad.

Far from being a small group at the top of the regime, Iraq's elites constitute a relatively large tribal core allied to even larger tribal groupings that permeate the army, bureaucracy, security organs, party, business and tribal circles. United by blood, ideological bonds, economic interests and common liability, the different groups that constitute this clan class sense they are wanted dead rather than alive; memory of the savage reprisals that followed the failure of the 1991 anti-government uprisings is still fresh. In the face of the threat of collective elimination, there is a reasonable chance this group may offer a cohesive force to keep up the fighting spirit. Ironically, this sense of wholesale risk has been reinforced by the blunt politics of the US campaign.

In a somewhat desperate effort to build new bridges between party and people, the government is deploying its own brand of Sunni sectarianism. The daily *Babel*, mouthpiece of the president's elder son Udai, has taken to printing anti-Shia articles. At the same time, however, the government has solicited and received supportive fatwas from Shia clerics.

The media in Baghdad are already speaking of a new Vietnam, of street battles and house-to-house combat – a strategy designed to inflict maximum damage with minimal resources and to increase civilian casualties, in the hope that a prolonged and costly war could open up the way for a negotiated compromise. On the theory that such tactics demand media coverage –

unlike the tight control of the media exercised by the military throughout Desert Storm – the government has installed ten media stations in various underground locations.

And should his own disappearance threaten the demise of the state, Saddam has set up a dual control system: Saddam and son, one president, one on the benches. General Kamal Mustafa, the commander of the Republican Guard, could be further insurance.

If the US–UK military campaign goes ahead, it may well plunge Iraq into chaos or prolonged civil war that could consume the very institutional and social forces that are crucial to any post-Saddam reform such as the establishment of the rule of law, power-sharing and nation-building. ❑

Faleh A Jabar is a research fellow at Birkbeck College, University of London. His most recent publications are Ayatollahs, Sufis and Ideologues: State, Religion and Social Movements in Iraq *and* Tribes and Power in the Middle East *(both Saqi Books, London 2002).* The Shi'ite Movement in Iraq *is due in 2003 (Saqi Books)*

Both paintings are by the London-based Iraqi artist **Faisal Laibi Sahi**

THE RETURNEE

MAHDI ISSA AL-SAQR

He sat there staring at the emptiness in front of him. Her sudden absence had confounded him. Out of the loudspeaker the voice of the *muqri* reciting the Quran invaded the surrounding space and buzzed in his ears. It subdued the polite, intermittent whispers of the funeral guests assembled in his front yard. His eyes picked up and dropped the men's polished shoes as they changed positions on the grass under the lawn chairs. A day such as this was coming, of course. He knew that. She would go before him, or he would, but he didn't know the separation would take such a toll on him.

'What tortures me is the idea that once we leave this world, we never return.'

These were her words as they were having tea one day. He told her that no human being or object ever leaves this world as long as the world continues going around, and that living things simply keep returning, only changing their outward appearance.

She felt a little better then.

'So, I'll be back once I'm dead?'

She waited impatiently for his reply.

'You'll be back like the rest of us. Perhaps as a tree blessing the ground with a dense shade, or a bird filling the sky with happiness.'

She looked content and said she'd return in the form of a sparrow that endlessly circles the house and lives in the trees of its garden.

'No, no. Let me think. I don't want things to stand between you and me. I'll come back as a cat and go places with you. Scratch my body against your legs as you read or sit absent-minded.' He laughed and said she'd outlive him.

'Father!' His oldest son, seated next to him, touched his arm and brought him out of his reverie. He stood up and pressed the outstretched hand of one of the mourners. He said a few words and then sat down. Numerous faces had passed in front of him today. Too many to look into carefully. Some were with him at the cemetery. Darkness had fallen then, and a boy brought a lantern that shed some light on the silent faces. They were standing around the graveside as the gravedigger worked hard at deepening the dark hole in the ground. One of the faces hanging over the grave separated itself from the others and, a little later, the sound of water trickling to the ground in the dark behind him shocked his ears. A jarring sound in the midst of silent sleepers. He didn't turn his head, and a minute later the face returned to join the other grim faces. As they piled the wet dirt over the shrouded body, city lights gleamed in the distance. One after another, the headlights of cars pierced the darkness on the road going downtown, like torches carried by ghosts into the throbbing city.

This is how a companion who filled his life with mirth turned into a mere memory. For others, her departure was but a social occasion. They'd lingered a while but eventually left the funeral gathering, each heading off in their own direction. He wished they had never come because this endless movement was wearing him down. His legs ached but he had

Credit: Faisal Laibi Sahi

to observe the conventions, otherwise they would say he had showed no respect for her memory. These rituals, they say, keep the bereaved preoccupied and shield them from the pain of loss. But nothing so far was lessening the pain of her loss. An abyss had yawned open in his soul and brought him endless desolation. They had lived together long enough to know what the other thought without uttering so much as a word. Words stopped being a necessity.

Their eyes alone were enough.

'Take heart. We are all on this road.' He stood up and shook the hand the man extended. No one would argue with this simple fact, but fragile human emotions rarely take notice of hard facts. He heard some of the low, cautious conversations among those around him. Some talked of the latest news and others finalised business deals. Bitterness crept into him. How tired and forlorn he felt. His son noticed that and stopped reminding him to stand up to receive callers or bid them farewell. He apologised for him, mentioning his weak heart. That was true enough because his was a weak heart.

He kept staring in front of him refusing to accept her absence. Then he saw her coming. He hadn't seen her in the neighbourhood before – a small white cat strolling quietly over the green grass, between chairs and men's legs. His face lit up as she approached, and his heart came to life when she stopped under his chair. She sat on the grass, and a little later she scratched herself against his leg. He smiled, and bent to pick her up. Unfazed by the looks in the mourners' eyes or the concern in his son's, he left the funeral assembly. His back was turned to them all as he walked towards the house, his arms around the cat. ❑

Mahdi Issa al-Saqr *was born and still lives in Basra, southern Iraq. From* Shita' bila Matar (Winter without Rain), *Damascus 2001*

Translated by Shakir Mustafa and reprinted from Banipal No. 14, Summer 2002

YUSIF'S TALES

MOHAMMAD KHODAYYIR

When we reconstructed the city after the war, we set aside a plot of land
one by two kilometres overlooking the river. On that we built the printing
house. We raised its twelve stone tiers so that visitors would see it polished
and glittering in sunlight next to the massive marble city towers. Work
on building the house went on day and night for years, and now it pleases
dozens of skilled workers to sit on the broad steps around the building
to bask in the early morning sun and reminisce about those joyful days.
Labourers and craftsmen then disperse on the wide city boulevards leading
to their workplaces as soon as the central city clock chimes fifty.

Our city authorities have attracted from neighbouring towns and cities
scores of blacksmiths, smelters, masons, carpenters, engineers, and bestowed
on them enough honours to raise their status among the public. But
printers, transcribers of manuscripts and writers received even greater
honours. Theirs is the highest building in the city, and their chief is none
other than the famed master we know as Yusif the Printer.

On this sunny spring morning I was walking briskly to the printing
house, climbing up the many stone stairways, manoeuvring my way
through those relaxing on them. One impulse so possessed me that I was
oblivious to several colleagues who were also heading for the southern
gate. Yusif the Printer has promised to share with me a secret he has kept
locked in one of the house's chambers.

My eyes hovered over the impressive mural on the arch of the gate,
coloured in firm chalky strokes, to seek one more time a tiny detail
showing an Arab transcriber bending over an open manuscript. At exactly
this time of day when I report to work I look up to see the ink in his
inkwell sparkling in the sunlight. Other details of the mural conspire with
sunlight at different moments throughout the day. The transcriber detail
diminishes as I go through the reception and service offices, then into the
overwhelming openness of the inner hall. The hall is a thousand square
metres, pierced through the centre by a massive lift shaft whose metal
pillars are visible behind thick glass panels. The printing presses occupy
the entire lower floor.

I cross the hall to the lift, my rubber shoes gliding over its solid glass floor. The coloured plastic chairs all over the hall are vacant at this time of day, and look brilliant under lights from hidden spots in the ceiling. The printing machinery is visible through the glass floor, with fork-lift trucks and carts rolling through the aisles, and separate areas for paper storage, binding and the mechanical repair workshop. The printing presses and the heads of the workers are bathed in that murky basement light familiar in the press area and which the eyes of our veteran printer have known since they first made contact with a printing machine. Below, massive wheels, oiled and gleaming, are spinning huge reels of paper and printing cylinders; paper cutters are delivering the first runs to agile hands. Phosphorescent light from computer screens and monitors showers over faces, machines and outstretched arms. From above, I could hear nothing – the glass ceiling cut out the clatter of wheels and the flutter of paper, not to mention the sucking of inks or the dancing of characters and forms on screens and sheets of paper.

Four lifts run up and down inside the central shaft, but only one has access to the printing floor. The giant glass lift ascends through the lower and middle tiers set aside for proofreaders, calligraphers, cover designers, illustrators, the photo lab and the offices of the administrative staff, then through the eighth floor where the restaurant and clinic are. The lift slows down as it reaches the top four tiers housing writers, transcribers, editors, translators and readers. From it you can see the occupants of these floors in their glass cubicles or in the corridors, even glimpse faces you might not have a chance to see elsewhere. The faces of the city's gifted few who willingly shun publicity: learned scholars like M J Jalal and K Khalifa; the storytellers K M Hasan and M al-Saqr; the poets A Hussein, M al-Azraq, S al-Akhder and S al-Chalabi; and elite journalists and publishers.

The occupants of these top tiers change, which explains why no visitor or worker has ever had a chance to see the city's intelligentsia all together at any given time. Occasionally, their ranks include guests who collect manuscripts and rare books and who wander agog among the cubicles. But, as a rule, all writers, editors or manuscript copiers from this city and neighbouring cities stay at the printing house long enough to finish their work, then leave so that others may take their places. Only Yusif the Printer has been a fixture here, and he might be making the rounds right now on the printing floor, or relishing seclusion in one of the cubicles.

I am a fellow at the house while I work on my novel *Khamarawayh's Last Portrait*, although I knew Yusif before the war when he owned a small press in the city's old business district. Besides the local newspaper he edited, he used to print his own fiction and his friends' non-fiction there. When the city came under intense bombardment in the last year of the war, the press was closed even though at the time it was producing Yusif's autobiography. Our meeting at the house after the war was brief and memorable. He looked old, a profusion of white hair hugging both sides of his red, slender neck. He supported himself on a smooth cane and had a flower in his lapel. It was at that meeting he promised to reveal to me what he had kept a secret at the house.

I got off the lift on the tenth tier where I work among the affiliated writers. In one cubicle, I saw Abdulwahab al-Khasibi, proofreading his only collection of short stories, and from another I heard a diligent translator's renderings of Tagore's reflections. Then I walked past the cubicle occupied by Balquis, the young poet. She's barely fifteen years old, becalmed and not of this world, like a dreamy bird I once saw in a pomegranate tree. She surprised me when she looked up. All I could think of then was Tagore's line: 'The bird wishes it were a cloud, and the clouds wish they were birds.'

Credit: Faisal Laibi Sahi

On the eleventh tier, the transcribers' floor, I see the tired face of an old friend, Oobaid al-Hamdani, and I wonder if he's copying the manuscript on medicinal herbs he found in a discarded box in a subterranean vault. Oobaid once told me about the Muslim medieval storyteller al-Hariri who penned seven hundred copies of his own *Maqamat*. On this tier of the house, only an ancient silence marks the transcribers' cubicles, and the invisible creeping of mice hankering after volumes of paper fragrant with ambergris.

I walked for hours looking for Yusif the Printer. As I reached the twelfth tier, I passed the quarters of the writers who had acquired permanent status. They are the one exception in the house. And why was it that these permanent residents would not complete their work, even if the house were to become a *madrasa* of sorts or a workshop for writing or printing? I was considering a number of possible answers when I caught sight of the veteran printer.

He was in the printing-floor lift ready to descend.

'I've been waiting here for you for hours,' he says. 'The first step dooms those who follow. As soon as you step into a corridor, you end up coming back to it, and when you move up to the next floor, you achieve no actual upward movement.'

This is humour befitting an old man familiar with ascending and descending. His sparkling eyes make me think of a giant press where thousands of machines run day and night to put out a single book composed of endless volumes. I give Yusif a wan smile. After all, it is he alone who knows the rules and secrets of the printing house.

Then he says: 'I read your novel. I think you'll rewrite it. You had Khamarawayh commit suicide the moment he entered chapter K instead of allowing him to materialise anew under a different name.'

His words surprise me.

'When you're unaware of the value of letters,' Yusif adds, 'you sever the chains of words beyond the repair that imagination or grammar can provide.'

I replied: 'I'll write the novel again. That will please me, of course, since it'll help me prolong my stay at the house for one more year. I'll also have more chances to get to know the recluses of the upper floors.'

'You'll stay,' he says gleefully. 'Your affiliation will be extended.'

I had to ask him about the permanent writers on the twelfth tier.

'They're as permanent as ghosts, not individuals with names and accolades. Their works are part of this recurrent phantasmagoria. As soon as they finish a page, a certain part of their being vanishes. If they complete a book they'll disappear entirely. But you see them every morning rewriting one page after another just to relish their presence at the house. What intoxicates them is the vineyard of inks, these ghosts of writers composing transparent pages. If you want, you can join them and never leave the house.'

I was fumbling for an appropriate reply when he remarked: 'We won't succeed in completing a book if we don't really defend our characters. The name Khamarawayh, for instance, is hermeneutic since it reveals a part of the character's truth. A character could escape death by hiding his or her name behind that of another, and not letting that name get swallowed up in the magician's melting pot. Her name alone betrays her transparent symbolism and the shackles from which she'll never be liberated. Give your character more than one name and more than one mien and your book will escape the rottenness of an ending. We fail because our books start to decay before they're finished. We impose on them our imperfection – we die and let the book die with us. What a dismal outcome for an honest and painful ordeal.'

'Yes,' I said, overwhelmed. 'We let our characters live for us.'

'When you approach the truth of genuine creation . . .'

I had the feeling that Yusif suddenly stopped talking and pressed a button on the elevator keypad. The elevator went down through a series of levels and stopped at an unmarked one, the basement, possibly, or an entirely different one. One thing I heard clearly was a suppressed roar. We left the elevator and came to a suite with black walls. Yusif brought out a small key and opened the door. When he turned the lights on I found myself in front of a small printing press, an ancient manual one, and cases of lead letters stacked all around it. The room was airtight, sound- and light-proof, and connected to a smaller side room with a table laden with zinc printing blocks.

'This is my secret, my friend,' Yusif said. 'The treasure of the house.' He was looking at me searching for signs of wonder, joy or interest, then said: 'Here I can work the way I like. I salvaged this machine from the devastation of war. It was in a room in my house. The one I trust most.'

The silent machine generated around itself an aroma of ink, acids, oils, rubber, leather and paper – the remains of several printings of the rare books this press puts out. A structure crouching like a lubricated mythical animal. The mysterious energy the machine emits captivates my spirit and shakes my limbs and sends my heart racing, as if I were feeling with the ends of my fingers the ancient leaves of a volume bound with deer hide. *Kalila wa Dimnah*, or the *One Thousand and One Nights*, Ibn Sina's *Qanun*. Yusif's voice comes to me again, 'On this press the Ottomans printed the first issue of *Anafeer* newspaper and the occupying British authorities used it to print out colonial communiqués. Perhaps it even fell into the Iraqi rebels' hands afterwards. When I bought it in 1940 from a merchant, some of its parts were missing or damaged. A blacksmith I knew made replacement parts and a famed foundry cast new sets of characters. Today, it will print my tales.'

He then pulls out of an open drawer a newly printed sheet and gently places it on the machine. I bring the page close to the bulb over the press. 'If you want to print a genuinely great book,' I hear Yusif say, 'one for yourself and for the ages, you have to set its characters with your own hands patiently, confidently. You will only need a few copies. Ten would immortalise you for a thousand years.'

The page feels as if it were printed on a rough stone tablet. The nicely lined text is surrounded by wide blank margins stained with faint streaks and spots of ink and fingerprints. The page has a full tale printed on it and ends with a dark star rather than a period.

Yusif is still flashing a euphoric smile. 'One story fills out and never gets beyond a page,' he says.

I think about what he has said, and soon realise the discipline and skill involved in his work. You can read Yusif's tales where you choose without ever having to turn the page. The title of the story I'm reading is 'The Mirror of Turdin', and here is its plot:

A giant mirror the astronomer Suleiman al-Saymeri made from a rare polished metal and placed on a green hill outside the city of Turdin was to reflect the three stages of the city. Its past image in the morning, its present at midday, and at sunset the sun would display changing reflections of the city's future. The city's old image gradually appears as the sun ascends, revealing first the Ziggurat, then the irrigation canals of the Hanging Gardens, the Procession Field and the Virgin's Altar. As soon as the details come into full view, the display starts slowly to vanish. At noon, the show lasts but a few minutes, long enough for the inhabitants to recognise their city. But the display at sunset is rare and unpredictable. Twenty years ago it appeared for just seconds before a lucky shepherd and his flock. The future city flashed and dazzled human and animal eyes in an instant that would remain folded in pastoral time. The description of that future place, which the city dwellers wrested from the shepherd, was even more bewildering than the reluctance of the image to appear at all.

He spoke of that city as a colossal and glittering golden hand lining up houses in the shape of a cone. Then another golden hand, more brilliant and much faster than the first, would undo the work before the eye had had a chance to behold it. Since then, people go out to the fields surrounding the mirror hours before sunset and wait for the emergence of a city to come.

In the nights to come, the patient printer will put on his overalls, smeared with patches of ink and oil, and select letters from the cases. He'll bend over the single-page forme to set the reversed characters of the tale with his blackened thumb, then align the rows within its wooden frame. And while we relish the leisure of our nights, he'll secure the type forme to the bed of the press, feed in the ink and lay on a blank sheet of paper. He'll turn the spiral handle gently down in the faint, saffron light of the bulb over the machine.

Years later, my hands will hold one of the ten copies of the magnificent book of tales, illustrated with scenes etched by a house artist. I'll read it on the stone steps outside the building in the deliciously warm sun of the early morning. ❏

Mohammad Khodayyir *was born and still lives in Basra in southern Iraq.*
From Ru'ya Kharif (Autumnal Vision) *published 1995*

Translated by Shakir Mustafa and reprinted from Banipal No. 14, Summer 2002

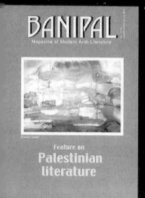

PARTY TIME

NAGMEH SOHRABI

IRAN HAS COME A LONG WAY SINCE
THE HEADY AND DANGEROUS DAYS
OF ITS ISLAMIC REVOLUTION

It's January 2001, 2 am and I'm in a cab returning from a party. The party was an intimate gathering of Iranian artists – film-makers, painters, photographers – and journalists, both Iranian and non-Iranian. Like any other party anywhere else in the world, there was alcohol (albeit of the moonshine kind, made by Armenians and delivered clandestinely straight to the doorsteps of their trustworthy customers) and much dancing. There was nothing, nothing to point out that I was in the Islamic Republic of Iran. Nothing, of course, until my friend and I left the house, wrapped in winter coats and scarves on our head, got into a cab and headed home.

Tehran is by most accounts a generic metropolis, an ugly Third-World city. It is noisy and polluted and, despite the snow-capped mountains standing graciously and disapprovingly over its random sprawl of concrete buildings and, more recently, tower blocks built over fruit orchards, it has little beauty to offer the untrained eye.

Maybe it's the contrast to that chaos that gives Tehran nights such beauty and serenity. Maybe it's the knowledge that in several hours this urban monster will awake with a growl and the streets will once again be filled with old gas-guzzling Paykans – the Iranian cars based on the now extinct British Hillman Hunter – that evoke in the late-night passenger an intense sense of belonging. In my case maybe it was just blissful ignorance that made the ride home so calm and peaceful.

Peaceful, that is, until a white Paykan out of nowhere pulled in front of our cab and forced the driver to brake. Two uniformed men quickly get out of the car and walk towards us. The skinnier one walks to my side of the door, opens it and sticks his head in.

My heart doesn't race faster, it stops. And I am transported back to the early days of the revolution. It is 1981 and I'm a nine-year-old girl. The revolution that ousted the Shah is two years old and what started out as a popular anti-monarchy, anti-imperialist movement is quickly turning into a repressive Islamic state. Night after night 'anti-revolutionary' elements – the same people who only two years back were celebrating the end of the monarchy – are paraded on the television screen and forced to confess. Rumours are flying everywhere: of unveiled women attacked on the streets, of revolutionary police appearing on people's doorsteps, of widespread arrests and executions of various opposition groups. And there are also the checkpoints and roadblocks manned by young bearded boys who stop every car, checking for anything from members of guerrilla groups to the smell of alcohol on people's breath. Sitting in the back of my parents' car, I'd shiver as my father slowed down, then stopped and pulled down the window. The young, often expressionless face would peer through our car, look around, step back and wave us through, and we would continue home in silence.

It is 2001 and I am shivering in the back of a car no longer in the safety of either childhood or my parents' protection.

The uniformed man takes a look at us, opens the passenger-side door and gets in. 'Go back to where you picked up these women. We need to identify that place,' he commands the driver. The driver makes a feeble attempt at protest, turns the car around and heads back to the party.

This is my first encounter ever with the dreaded *komiteh*, the revolutionary militia that throughout the 1980s patrolled the streets and sometimes the homes of many Iranians, regulating and punishing immoral behaviour. With the opposition wiped out and many members of guerrilla groups executed between 1979 and 1982, the Iranian state in the 1980s focused its attention on the ongoing war with Iraq and on increasing its control of the public sphere. I grew up with stories of various parties broken up and the participants jailed, of unmarried couples picked up in the streets and lashed, of women with incomplete Islamic covering rounded up in buses or beaten on the spot. These were stories that filled my childhood and young adolescence and they flooded back as our cab headed towards our point of departure.

But this is not the Iran of the 1980s. Since the surprise election of Mohammad Khatami in 1997, Iran and its image abroad – the 'axis of evil' label notwithstanding – have been changing. Much has been written since then about Iran. With its doors opening and the president's call for a dialogue of civilisations, reporters and scholars who throughout the '80s had little or no direct access to Iran have been travelling back and forth, writing articles, books, making films and providing sound bites. In 1997, most of these latecomers to the Iranian scene treated Khatami and the group of reformists surrounding him as the heroes of the people. The press during

Tehran 2002: partying in the capital.
Credit: 135 photos / Omid Salehi

Tehran 2002: mural commemorating the Iran–Iraq War.
Credit: 135 photos / Omid Salehi

this period exploded on the scene. What came to be known as the reformist camp, advocating democracy and mass participation in the political scene and a lessening of repressive social measures, gained a majority in the parliament. Since 1999, with the increased closure of reformist papers and, specifically, the bloody crackdown on the student protests that year, the same international media that hailed the heroism of Khatami and the reform movement has been talking increasingly of their failure, in particular of the general disappointment with the progress of reform in Iran.

What these reports miss and can never convey is the extent to which Iran *has* changed from the 1980s. Yes, more and more reformists are jailed and some even sentenced to death. Yes, various reformist bills are blocked by the unelected Guardian Council. Yes, increasingly Khatami seems incapable of any type of progress or change. And yes, since 2000 more than 50 publications have been closed down. But none of this was even conceivable in the 1980s when the country was enveloped not just in the pressures of war (bombings, a widespread draft and food rations) but in an atmosphere of fear. The Islamic state ruled the public and the private was in fearful retreat from it.

All this has, I believe, changed irrevocably in the past five years. The closure of more than 50 publications means permission for more than that number to be published. The jailing of various dissidents means the existence of multiple public voices on the political scene. And, even more important, fear seems to have lost its grip, most specifically on the children of the Islamic Revolution itself: the generation under 25 years of age.

For me, the older generation that still remembers another time, that fear still exists but no longer binds. And so I turn to our new passenger, the uniformed man sitting in our car and ask for his identification card.

'I don't need to show you anything,' he replies. 'What is a woman doing in the streets at 2 am?'

'I'm going home,' I reply, my heart pounding in my chest. 'What are you doing in the streets?'

'Plus,' my friend retorts, 'if we've done something wrong, we demand to be taken to the police station, not back to where we came from.'

The man ignores us.

We reach the house and, emboldened by our exchange, I order the man

Vakil Bazaar, Shiraz 2002.
Credit: 135 photos / Omid Salehi

to stay where he is while I go to get the owner of the house. I could hear music coming through the door and people's laughter. I knock loudly, knowing the sound of a knock at this time of the night triggers alarm and, when my friend appears, I explain the situation to him quickly and in English.

His composure surprises me. He shuts the door behind him and approaches the two men, the second having followed us here in his own car. He says something and they disappear in the shadows of the walls surrounding the house. I had been ordered back into the car where I sat nervously, imagining the possible outcomes. It occurred to me as I had been leaving my uncle's house that evening that he had told me not to stay out late: 'You've lived in the US, your parents are there, you have no idea what it's like. If you get arrested and they put you in prison, I have to spend a whole week trying to get you out.' I shook the thought out of my head and just stared at my sweaty palms.

My friend emerges out of the shadows without a glance in our direction and goes in. Five minutes later he rejoins the two men. A minute or so of waiting and all three emerge, shaking hands and smiling. 'You can take them home now,' my friend says to our driver before waving goodbye to us. The two men without a word get into their car and drive away. We sit there in silence and astonishment.

The solution, as it turns out, had been money. I was later informed that if I'd known better, I should've immediately offered around 10,000 tomans (cUS$12) and saved ourselves all the hassle. Because of our naivety, our host had had to pay around US$50. 'Just keep an extra 10–20 dollars in your bag from now on for times like this,' he advised me.

As with the nature of fear, things have also changed socially and politically in the Islamic Republic of Iran. Young bearded militias still set up roadblocks from time to time in the streets of Tehran, stopping cars of young girls and boys. But intimidator and intimidated have both changed. The intimidators of the '80s have become the reformists of the '90s, turning the struggle inwards and attempting to dismantle the roadblocks of the Islamic Republic. In their place is a newer generation, haunted by the fear of losing the only system they have known, driven by the memory of what they see as a Golden Era during which the lines between the powerful and the powerless, the state and the people, the keepers of morality and its abiders were clearly drawn. The intimidated of the '80s was a nation, fresh from an anti-imperialist revolution that had in the course of several years become an Islamic Republic, a nation thrown immediately into a defensive war that quickly became a bloody war of attrition. And in their place is a generation with little memory of the monarchy or of the revolution that brought it down. It is a generation that has come of age in an era of satellite dishes, email, the internet and chat rooms. It is a generation that is oddly both materialistic and idealistic. Dreaming of better economic conditions (achieved either inside Iran or sometimes preferably outside it), it clings to ideals of non-violence and tolerance almost instinctively.

And most important, the fear that acted as the social gel of the '80s no longer binds this generation. Since 1997, the economic situation inherited from the previous era of war and reconstruction has only worsened. Inflation is high and corruption is rampant at all levels. The hardliners, initially cornered and threatened with the loss of absolute power, have struck back relentlessly, countering the reformists' threat of a referendum with arrests, death sentences and fear of bloodshed. And hope, a feeling that permeated Iranian society from 1997 to 2000 has, in most quarters, given way to anger, or worse, disillusion. As one prominent film-maker told me: 'I hate the reformists for making me hope and then taking it away from me.' Yet an entire generation has come into its own awareness during a presidency that unlike all others has refused, absolutely refused, to resort to violence to further its own agenda.

Fear still exists in Iran but no longer as a fog seeping through crowded streets and under people's doors. It's a cloud hanging over their heads and, while everyone knows it's there and everyone fears the gathering storm, they also know that the fog has lifted. ❏

Nagmeh Sohrabi *is a PhD student at Harvard University, USA*

NOT IN OUR NAME EITHER
NILOU MOBASSER

THE BATTLE FOR THE HEARTS AND
MINDS OF THE IRANIAN PEOPLE IS
FOUGHT OUT THROUGH THE VIGOROUS
AND VARIED DAILY PRESS

Three opinion polls conducted in Tehran in the summer of 2002 came up
with remarkably similar results: on average, 74.7 per cent of the capital's
residents favoured talks between Tehran and Washington if Iran's interests
dictated it, although 70.4 of them also said that they mistrusted the US
administration. Despite the fact that the country's leader, Ayatollah Ali
Khamenei, has expressly forbidden ties or talks with the USA and devotes
his harshest words in every speech to 'the Great Satan' and its home-grown
'lackeys', in September the Iranian news agency (IRNA) bravely carried a
report on the averaged-out results of the three polls. So it came as no
surprise when the judge who has banned more than 80 reformist publications since President Mohammad Khatami's election victory in 1997 hauled
the directors of IRNA and one of the three polling centres (the one closest
to the reformists) to court to answer for their sins, at the same time ordering
the closure of the centre in question.

On 7 October, a 'Letter to the Iranian nation from the employees of
polling centres' appeared in a reformist paper's satirical column. It said:

> O noble and brave nation of Iran! As you know, the presentation of
> your views has led to a polling centre being closed and sealed. We,
> the employees of the country's other polling centres, would hereby
> like to request that if, in certain instances, there happens to be a need
> for you, the noble nation, to express your views, please express them
> in a way that will not lead to the closure of other centres and job
> losses for your compatriots.

In view of this charming request and in view of the fact that several
directors of polling institutes subsequently disappeared without trace into
Iran's prisons, it behoves us to be cautious about assuming that Iranian
newspapers reflect the views of 'the noble nation'. Nevertheless, they
continue to be interesting enough to merit a brief perusal, regardless of our
misgivings about whose views they do or do not reflect.

In recent years, Iranian papers have been much preoccupied with domestic affairs, but in the autumn of 2002 the Iraqi crisis received considerable attention on the foreign news pages. On the vexed question of whether the Great Satan or Saddam Hussein is the worse evil, the conservative papers seemed to be fairly clear where they stood: although both the USA and Saddam were to be despised, Saddam Hussein had, even at the height of his belligerence, been little more than 'a pawn'. As he came under increasing pressure from his 'erstwhile master', the conservative newspapers advised the Iraqi ruler to make a clean breast of it:

Perhaps, as a result of ambition, pride and megalomania, Saddam, the US-nurtured pawn, has today turned against the US and Zionism, to the point where he has forced them to eliminate him; assuming this to be the case, it is up to Saddam to prove his enmity towards America and the Zionist regime by disowning his past and revealing how the US encouraged him to attack Iran and Kuwait; to lift the

Former US embassy, Tehran, 4 November 2002: 23rd anniversary of the seizure of US embassy. Credit: 135 photos / Omid Salehi

veil from the behind-the-scenes tale of the chemical bombardment of Halabja and to beg forgiveness from the Almighty, so that the people of the world, especially Muslims, can become more aware of the conspiracy of global arrogance led by the US and the inhuman Zionist regime, and accept his repentance.

The conservative papers also tried to exploit the Iraqi crisis for domestic purposes and to shame the reformists, who were saying that Iran should not side with a doomed dictator and should take a more pragmatic approach to its relationship with the USA. In the words of one conservative commentator:

> Saddam is a criminal. Everyone knows this. But do the so-called reformists not know that the US and its allies were Saddam's accomplices in all the crimes he committed throughout the imposed [Iran–Iraq] war? And that, had it not been for US support and provocation, there would never have been any war? Is it truly not a betrayal of public opinion to tell half the story and to leave the most important part covered and hidden? . . . Is it a service to ward the people off Saddam and drive them into America's arms? . . . The question is not whether America is bad or Saddam is bad. They are both bad. The question is whether Saddam is worse and more dangerous or America. And the one who chooses Saddam as the reply has brazenly betrayed wisdom and lied in a dastardly way to his own people.

Although the reformists recommended pragmatism and opposed the repetition of rigid, ideological formulas that left Iran little room for manoeuvre in the international arena, they were well aware of the implications of a US strike on Iraq, given the fact that Iran's name also figured in Bush's 'axis of evil'. They stressed repeatedly that any US military intervention in Iraq would set a dangerous precedent.

But the most notable recurring theme in the reformist commentaries on the Iraqi crisis was the suggestion that it was the dearth of democracy in Middle East countries that left them vulnerable in the face of the increasingly aggressive US policies. As the managing director of several now-banned reformist dailies, Hamidreza Jala'ipur, put it:

> In the insecure post-11 September world, the only strength of Third World countries lies in the application of the workings of democracy

and it is only governments of this kind that will enjoy strength in today's insecure world.

In the same vein, a commentary on 29 October said:

America is now ready to attack Iraq with the intention of changing its political regime. Although this contravenes the UN Charter, international law and the Iraqi people's right to self-determination, unfortunately, the Baath regime and Saddam's criminal behaviour over the past three decades have created a situation in which, instead of thinking about resisting when attacked, the Iraqi people have in a way become indifferent to the attack and are more concerned about saving themselves than the ruling political system! The bitter fate of criminals like the Taliban and Saddam Hussein at least carries this fundamental message to the statesmen of small, independent countries: only democracy and respect for the people's public and private rights can save a country at critical moments.

And, when US officials began saying that they were considering installing an American military governor in Baghdad after disposing of Saddam Hussein, yet another reformist daily said:

Why should a people who are only suited to being ruled not allow the US to designate a military governor for them just like Britain used to do 100 years ago? If there happens to be a bunch of people in Iraq who say a US commander is better than Saddam the bloodthirsty dictator, what non-nationalistic answer is there to give them? The occasional reports about US programmes to dismember Saudi Arabia, even if they are not very serious, are extremely alarming. Anyone who is not worried about the region's future is deceiving themselves and disregarding the ABC of politics. Nothing but reliance on the people and soliciting their true participation will halt the West's military onslaught.

Finally, the reformists, who like to draw a distinction between the US government and the American people, noted the anti-war protests in the US and echoed the protesters' sentiments:

Unfortunately, narrow-minded people inside Iran have tried to reduce the international sense of fellow feeling with the reformist movement to a conspiratorial alliance with 'global arrogance' and

rank this great social capital among the reformist movement's 'weak points', unaware that it is precisely this enthusiasm and fellow feeling that was directed towards our people in the halcyon days of the reform movement that can prove useful in difficult, critical times . . . In America, they are saying: 'The US president says, You are either with us or against us. This is our reply: We will resist your determination to speak in the name of all the American people. We will not forgo our right to pose questions. We will not sacrifice our conscience for the sake of your hollow promises about our security. We are saying, Not in our name.'

Why should the relatives of our martyrs and the chemical warfare victims in our land not be able to challenge Bush and Donald Rumsfeld's legitimacy and competence? In what sense is Rumsfeld, who shook hands with Saddam in front of TV cameras in 1983 and opened the way for the Iraqi dictator to resort to chemical weapons, qualified to say that he is mounting a military expedition to the Middle East to 'combat weapons of mass destruction and chemical weapons'? Are the victims of the imposed war not more qualified than anyone else, while commiserating with the families of the victims of 11 September and falling into step with the peace lovers in America and Europe, to say to Bush and Rumsfeld, Not in our name? ❏

Nilou Mobasser is an Iranian translator living in the UK

Abyane village, Iran 2002. Credit: 135 photos / Omid Salehi

BORDERLAND: IRANIAN KURDISTAN

Iran's Kurds are counting the days to the US attack on Iraq. They have even given the soubriquet *haji* – a term of respect usually given to one who has made the pilgrimage to Mecca – to George W. Iraqi Kurdistan, in particular the areas under the control of Masood Barzani, represents the land of their dreams: after the collapse of the Baath regime in Baghdad and, with US help, they imagine their secession from Iran and union with Barzani.

In the minds of most Iranians, Kurdistan is their 'Wild West': a strange and dangerous frontier region, hotbed of resistance to the Islamic Revolution during the Iran–Iraq war of 1980–88. Today, on the contrary, such is the level of security, the streets of a town such as Sardasht are far safer than the streets of Tehran. In the capital, a woman who goes out alone after 10pm takes her safety in her own hands; in Sardasht, a mere 20 minutes from the Iraqi border and once a front-line town, anyone may walk the streets at night in safety.

The concentration of state security forces in border towns such as Piranshahr, Sardasht, Oshnaviyeh and Baneh is far beyond anything to which Iranian citizens have become accustomed elsewhere. Daily intrusion in their lives is commonplace; here, security is at saturation point.

Economically, most of the towns in Kurdistan are at rock bottom. Fifteen years after the war and with anti-revolutionary elements cleared from the area, there have still been no investment or development funds from the centre. Unemployment is high. The situation is particularly bad in border towns. For the young men who do not leave for menial work in the big cities or eke out a meagre living in the small border markets, smuggling has become the only option. There are few alternatives, even for graduates, almost all of whom fail to clear the selection process for jobs in government service. Being a Kurd remains a barrier to advancement in the state system; even locally, civil servants are outsiders.

There was a time when agriculture flourished in the border areas. The pollution from chemical bombardments during the Iran–Iraq war and government neglect have largely put an end to this. Many have sold their land and put their all into smuggling.

A mule costs 600,000 tomans [c700 tomans: US$1] – roughly 90 per cent of the money they will have made from their land. They cross the rough, mountainous terrain into Iraq to bring back audio equipment, crystal

ware, tea and, in some areas, a good deal of alcohol. They act as agents for the big boys and are paid 7,000 tomans per load on delivery of the goods to their destinations. Others, known as 'luggers', make the journey on foot and haul the stuff on their backs.

More than half the routes used by the smugglers are still thick with landmines left over from the war. Young men minus a limb are a common sight. Despite having taken the precaution of bribing the law enforcement officers, men are killed daily by trigger-happy Iranian police and border guards. One of the young smugglers says: 'The law enforcement stations along the border earn a minimum of 1 million tomans per night in bribes, but then spray the routes they know we use with a hail of bullets.'

According to another young smuggler, the topsy-turvy system of fines for smuggling is no disincentive. 'If someone is arrested with smuggled tea they have to pay a fine equivalent to four times the value of the load, as well as being sentenced to two years in jail. But if a person smuggling alcohol is arrested, the fine is only 600,000 tomans.' As a result, alcohol, banned in Iran, is coming in by the gallon. ❑

A special correspondent

Translated by Nilou Mobasser
All photographs by **Omid Salehi**, *Iranian photographer and founder of*
135 photos, Tehran

ON THE MAP AT LAST

MICHEL VERRIER

THE KURDS OF IRAQ, IRAN AND
TURKEY AWAIT THE US ATTACK
ON IRAQ WITH A MIXTURE OF
HOPE AND TREPIDATION

Near the Iranian border, the Turkish city of Van descends gently towards an inland sea of 37,000 sq km. Since the Turkish army and Kurdistan Workers' Party (PKK) guerrillas stopped fighting, there has been great relief in the region. But there is still a massive military presence. 'The only reason the army's here is because we're Kurds and they think that's a bad thing,' says Hamdi Demir, once local vice-chairman of Hadep, the pro-Kurdish party the authorities want to ban. He is now a candidate for its successor, Dehap.

From tiny villages to large towns, every rooftop has a satellite dish. Kurdish families in eastern Turkey watch Medya TV, which Ankara describes as 'close to the PKK'. Militarily, Ankara may have won. After guerrilla leader Abdullah Ocalan was arrested in 1999 and called for a cease-fire, his men, who had been fighting in the mountains since the early 1980s, withdrew to northern Iraq. But Turkey lost the media war and stopped trying to confiscate satellite dishes. The army controls the roads but not the airwaves.

In a room decorated with carpets and portraits of famous Kurds, a dozen students of both sexes drink tea and discuss their campaign to save the Kurdish language. Since last winter they have been active in 53 universities. Huseyin, 20, explains that they want the right to learn Kurdish as a second language, like English, Spanish, Farsi or Arabic: 'We don't want it to replace Turkish as the language of education. The government says we do, to discredit us. We collected 2,000 signatures in Van. We wanted to send them to the president of the university. But he made everyone go and sign in person.'

Two months later the authorities claimed the campaign had been orchestrated by the PKK. Several organisers were imprisoned and expelled from the university. After a hunger strike in May, some were tried and sentenced in August by the security court in Istanbul. Also in August, parliament adopted a number of measures to bring Turkey's laws and constitution into line with the Copenhagen criteria, the standards that have to be met by countries wanting to join the European Union. They include the right to study minority languages. But teaching of what the law calls 'languages and accents spoken by Turkish citizens' (Kurdish is a taboo word) must remain private and 'lessons must not contravene the principles, constitution or laws of the Turkish Republic or threaten the integrity of the country'. Enough to make the new laws meaningless.

The students talk about the PKK's change of strategy. Most have followed it on Medya TV. The guerrilla war has been abandoned for a democratic strategy in the four countries where Kurds live: Turkey, Iraq, Syria and Iran. They like the newly formed Kadek (Kurdistan Congress for Freedom and Democracy). 'You've got to move with the times,' said Cemal, who was reading a book Ocalan wrote while in prison.

The state of emergency in force in the Kurdish region for decades was lifted in June 2002, three years after the end of guerrilla activities, though it remains in force in Diyarbakir and Sirvan provinces. But it made little difference. On 30 July, political organisations, associations and NGOs issued a statement in Bingol saying that 'although the state of emergency was lifted three years ago, repression against democratic institutions and organisations continues'.

Unemployment in Van is 80 per cent. There are camps of villagers driven from the countryside. Of 520 villages destroyed because they were accused of supporting the guerrillas, only 90 have been returned to their inhabitants. Ankara wants to rehouse the rest of the people in new buildings built to replace villages. But they are often a long way from the land people used to cultivate. Agriculture and livestock form the basis of the region's economy; if the people cannot go back to that, they refuse to move.

Militias of 'village guards', recruited from pro-government Kurdish tribes, are still active in the villages. Their job was to drive out the guerrillas; some of them have taken over land belonging to displaced families.

Twenty years of war and decades of military rule and special status have encouraged clan warfare and mafia activity. The military are hostile to any assumption of power by the Kurds in their own region, let alone their involvement in central government in Ankara and the institutions of the Turkish Republic. Military intervention by the USA against Iraq could strengthen the army's position. Ankara fears the break-up of Iraq and the proclamation of an independent Kurdish state on its borders, and has set four conditions for any involvement in the inevitable US intervention:

cancellation of US$4bn military debt; credits to offset the economic effects of a new intervention; a guarantee of Iraq's territorial integrity; and no Kurdish state. Even Kurdish control of the Kurds' historic capital of Kirkuk and of the region's oil wealth is unacceptable.

The Iraqi Kurds' uprising at the end of the Gulf War in 1991 had serious repercussions in the region around Van; millions took refuge in the mountains. Turkey's Kurds are closely watching the posturing in Washington and Baghdad. 'If the only aim of US intervention is to depose Saddam and put another dictator in his place, it will do no good,' Demir says. 'But if it's to bring democracy to Iraq, we've nothing to fear. The Iraqi Kurds won't take to the mountains and try to flee here.'

The Kurds often live their history by proxy, across the borders that divide them. Families and tribes have relatives on either side. Demir has two brothers and a sister in Iran. Such situations are common. 'Life's easier for them there,' Demir says. 'Economically and culturally. They can express themselves freely as Kurds. They even have elected representatives to parliament in Tehran.' The sign for Kurdistan on the Tehran ring road may seem harmless. But such things are unthinkable in Ankara, where even the word 'Kurdistan' can get you into trouble.

Iran has more than 10 million Kurds in a population of 70 million. They already enjoy many of the basic rights Turkey's Kurds were denied until this summer. At the end of May last year, the Kurdish Cultural Centre in Tehran organised the first professional conference on the teaching of the Kurdish language. One of President Mohammad Khatami's close associates was present and called on delegates to write a Kurdish textbook.

'Our struggle goes back a long way,' the centre's director, Bahran Valadbaigi, explains. 'In 1945, Iran's Kurds founded the republic of Mahabad; it was put down by the central government a year later. We took part in the 1978 revolution against the Shah, but we didn't get the rights we should have.' At the time, fighters of Abdul Rahman Ghassemlou's Democratic Party of Iranian Kurdistan freed their region again but were then attacked and defeated militarily by the Pasdarans, the Iranian revolutionary guards formed by Ayatollah Khomeini.

But, as in Turkey, a significant part of the Iranian Kurdish movement decided to give up the armed struggle for good. 'It's a generational issue,' Valadbaigi explains. 'Our new strategy takes account of how the world has changed: the fall of the Berlin Wall, the break-up of power blocs, glob-

Suleimania, Iraq 2002: the US dollar and fast-food clones rule in Kurdish-controlled northern Iraq. Credit: AFP Photo / Behrouz Mehri

alisation, the internet. It's based on culture, films, language, research and democracy.'

'The war goes on, but we've replaced the Kalashnikov by the pen,' is how Bakhtiar, a young Kurd from Sanandaj, puts it. Twenty-two Kurdish deputies represent their people in the Tehran parliament. Elected on an independent ticket, they are not free to form a pro-Kurdish party. 'But we want to take part in the exercise of central power,' Valadbaigi stressed. 'We won't be sidelined any more.'

To the Kurds of Iran, the experience of their neighbours in Iraq is like a rerun of the Mahabad Republic; there the Kurds are masters of their own region. US intervention to topple Saddam Hussein would be a precautionary measure, according to Valadbaigi. The Baghdad regime 'decimated our brothers, stopping at nothing, not even chemical weapons,' he says. 'There's no reason to believe he won't try the same thing again.'

Sanandaj, 250km from Tehran, is the capital of the region of Iran officially called Kurdistan. 'It's not our world, but we've had to adapt,' Kayvan, a senior figure in the Kurdish community, tells me outside an imposing Pasdaran building. His wife, who reluctantly wears a black chador, agrees. 'The Czechs and Slovaks separated on friendly terms without fighting. Why aren't we allowed to do the same?' (See Photostory, p44.)

When the PKK leader was arrested, the strength of the demonstrations in Sanandaj took the authorities by surprise. 'Thirty people were killed here,' a Kurd said. 'The demonstration turned violent when young people started chanting slogans in support of Ocalan, then called for freedom for the Kurds of Iran and attacked the Islamic Republic.' 'Before the US bombs Baghdad,' one of his companions adds, 'they should first come here and drop a few on our regime.'

Close to the Iraqi border, the Kermanshah–Baghdad road is lined with the wrecks of tanks and armoured cars left from the Iran–Iraq war of 1980–88. Armed soldiers stand guard behind barbed wire and sandbags. The border crossing at Quasri-e-Shirin is open only two days a week.

The green-and-pink flag of Jalal Talabani's Patriotic Union of Kurdistan (PUK) can be seen everywhere in this part of northern Iraq. Massoud Barzani's Democratic Party of Kurdistan (KDP) controls the adjoining Kurdish region bordering Turkey and Syria. Calm has replaced years of conflict between the two factions in which 3,000 were killed. According to Barham Saleh, prime minister of the regional government, the key to the dispute is the taxes the KDP collects on the Iraqi–Turkish border and distributes in the region it controls. London and Washington have been trying to reconcile the two parties since 1998 and the process is coming to an end. In August, delegations from both sides met in Koisinjaq to get the Unified Kurdish National Assembly, first elected in 1992, working again.

Then, in September, Barzani met Talabani in Salahaddin on the latter's return from Washington, London and Ankara. He had met members of the Iraqi opposition: Kurds, Shi'ites and Iraqi army officers who had fled their country over the last decade. The two men agreed to convene the Kurdish parliament in Irbil in October and unify their parties' positions on the future of Iraq, federalism, democracy and their country's relations with their neighbours.

Saleh believes the situation in Iraqi Kurdistan will remain precarious as long as Saddam rules in Baghdad. 'He must be replaced by a democratic government that is recognised by the Iraqis and includes the Kurds. The present Iraqi state is completely bankrupt. The Arabs know it and are now considering ruling with the Kurds.'

Saleh, who survived an assassination attempt in March last year, thinks that those who consider Kurdish involvement in any US intervention against Saddam is too risky are being shortsighted. He would not go along with 'just any adventure'. But, unlike the Northern Alliance in Afghanistan before the fall of the Taliban regime, Kurdish organisations already control about one-third of the country. 'We had 804 schools in 1991; now we've got more than 2,700. In ten years we have built twice as many as in the 70 years before. We've four times as many doctors. The standard of living here is much higher than in areas controlled by Baghdad.' And 'nobody lives in fear of being woken up by the secret police in the middle of the night'.

Suleimaniyeh, where Saleh lives, has a thriving bazaar. Money there is worth ten times the official dollar exchange rate in Baghdad. There is a central bank, but no access to the international banking system. There is freedom of information and many newspapers, mostly linked to a political party. Many parties also have their own radio and TV stations. It would be premature to speak of an independent press, but people can watch the stations of their choice and are free to surf the internet. KDP publications are available in Suleimaniyeh, though Barzani's and Talabani's parties have not been officially represented in each other's areas since the war between the two groups.

The broad avenue leading to the city centre has hotels, restaurants and shops where alcohol is freely on sale. While some women wear the black chador, many are in Western dress. Covering up for women is neither banned, as in Turkey, nor compulsory, as in Iran. 'Individual liberties are essential,' Saleh says. 'They are enshrined in the law. No official ideology should dictate to anyone how they must live their lives.' Polygamy is banned, as are honour killings of women who refuse an arranged marriage: 'The penalties are very severe.' On this issue, the same policy is enforced in the area controlled by the KDP.

Like the non-Muslim Yazidi Kurds, Turkomen, Assyrians and Chaldean Christians enjoy rights as ethnic or religious minorities, a prerequisite of any democratic development. But in the Halabja region, close to the Iranian border, Ansar al-Islam groups have settled in several villages. If Kurdish

Suleimania, Iraq 2002: park in Kurdish-controlled northern Iraq, off limits to Baghdad since the Gulf War. Credit: AFP Photo / Behrouz Mehri

regional authorities are to be believed, they have links to al-Qaida. This is a serious political threat to the regional government. Freedom of thought, secularism, the availability of alcohol and the lack of constraints on dress invite criticism from the fundamentalists, especially among the poor, who are unable to adopt the Western lifestyle favoured by the leadership.

But on the university campus, where there are 6,000 male and female students, the Islamists appear to have no influence. The sciences are taught in English, and literature, history and geography in Arabic. Since the Kurds took control of the region in 1991, Kurdish has become the language of instruction in primary and secondary schools. The president of Suleiman-iyeh University, Kamal H Khoshnaw, explains that the university institute of 'Kurdology' is working on a unified Kurdish language. (Kurdish has two dialects: Kurmanji, spoken by Kurds in Turkey, Syria and northern Iraqi Kurdistan; and Sorani, used in Iran and eastern Iraqi Kurdistan.) 'They're thinking of adopting the Latin alphabet that the Kurds in Turkey already use and abandoning the Arabic script currently used in Iraq and Iran.'

Talabani says: 'During the war years, since we took to the mountains in 1975, we used to tell ourselves next year we'll be in Kirkuk. We were wrong. But this time I believe it – next year we'll be in Baghdad.' Talabani believes Saddam's time is coming to an end; however, if the US has decided to overthrow the Baghdad regime, it has not yet decided when or how. 'We can't say whether we'll support their intervention until these two questions are answered. Saddam is completely cut off from the Iraqi population; he's incapable of showing the slightest sign of opening. The internet and satellite dishes are banned in Baghdad. The president's word is law, even if the constitution says otherwise. It's a complete reign of terror. If you don't agree, you're hanged.' Between 3 million and 4 million Iraqis – professionals, soldiers and intellectuals – have fled their country to escape the dictatorship.

The PUK leader says Iraq will have a future only as a secular, democratic and federal republic. 'We'd like this new state to be established peacefully, by dialogue, like the transition that took place in Eastern Europe.' But the Baghdad parliament has just confirmed Saddam Hussein in office as president for seven more years, and in the ensuing 'election' he secured 100 per cent of the vote. Talabani wants to give the regime a last chance and has appealed to the president 'to end the one-party system, form a government representative of all the Iraqi people and open the way to free elections'. If that offer is rejected, 'US intervention will be inevitable'.

That could start with air strikes concentrated on the pillars of the regime, the barracks of Saddam's personal troops, the republican guard. 'They will probably hold out for two weeks, three at the most,' says Saadi Pira, the PUK's head of international relations. The Iraqi regular army would not defend the regime in the face of a Washington offensive, the Kurds believe. There would be more desertions and regimental insurrections than at the end of the Gulf War.

It would then be up to Iraqis, Kurds and Arabs to topple the regime; the Iraqi opposition claims it can count on at least 200,000 armed men. It wants to avoid a massive landing of foreign troops. After taking control of the capital and major cities, 'the situation would be rather like post-war Germany,' Pira reckons. 'We'll have to start from the principle that most members of the Baath Party had no other way out. We'll have to integrate them into the new dispensation we'll put in place.'

'If Saddam's regime is defeated, there'll be freedom and democracy,' Talabani assures me. 'Everyone will vote and then we'll decide. We've good relations with all political parties. It's the Baghdad government that divides people and sets them against each other.'

The PUK leader has no fear of a fundamentalist enclave in southern Iraq. 'Mohammad Bakir al-Hakim, head of the supreme council of the Islamic Revolution, won't be sending his people to Kurdistan to close shops that sell alcohol.' Al-Hakim wants a parliamentary regime and the Shia are far from being universally fundamentalist. The Nationalists and the Communist Party were once very powerful among the Shia. 'Of course, the Kurds still dream of a unified Kurdistan,' he concludes, 'but that isn't realistic. It would mean changing Iraq, Turkey and Iran at the same time. We dream of a democratic Iraq. Let's make that dream come true first.'

That would put pressure on Iraq's neighbours. If the Kurds shared power in Baghdad, it would strengthen Kurdish demands in Iran and Turkey. Ankara fears the effects of an autonomous region being established as part of a federal Iraqi state and is demanding a say in the shaping of a new Iraq, particularly around Kirkuk, on the pretext that it must protect the Turkoman minority who live around there. The US will have to avoid creating a second Cyprus in the region, they say in Suleimaniyeh. Iran will not be sorry to see the end of the Baghdad regime, which the US secretly backed in the Iran–Iraq war. While the Iranian leadership is concerned that it may be the next US target, it is fostering close ties with Kurds and Shia who will have an influence in the new government in Baghdad. Al-Hakim is well known in Tehran, having lived there since the early 1980s.

Replacing Saddam Hussein's regime by a government allied to the US would complete the political reshaping of the region that began with the war in Afghanistan. The US would take control of Iraq's oil resources, making it less reliant on Saudi Arabia. That Washington's strategic interests coincide with the Iraqi Kurds' quest for democracy gives the latter grounds for hope that this time they will not be abandoned. ❏

Michel Verrier is a journalist based in Berlin

Translated by Malcolm Greenwood and reproduced from the English-language edition of Le Monde diplomatique, *October 2002* © *Le Monde diplomatique*

ISRAEL: A WEAPONS FILE

In September 1986, Mordechai Vanunu, a technician at Israel's Dimona nuclear site, revealed to the *Sunday Times* that the nuclear military programme based there had produced 'over 200' nuclear warheads. Days later he was tricked into flying to Rome where he was abducted by Mossad agents and secretly transported to Israel. In November, he was tried in camera and sentenced to 18 years' imprisonment, 14 of which were spent in solitary confinement. In 1999, in response to a petition from *Yediot Ahronot* newspaper, the government released about 40 per cent of the trial documents.

The *Bulletin of the Atomic Scientists* estimates that Israel has the world's fifth largest stockpile of nuclear warheads (more than Britain, which it believes has 185). In February 2000, Knesset member Issam Mahoul said Israel had '200 to 300' nuclear weapons; in August of that year, the Federation of American Scientists said that Israel could have produced 'at least 100 nuclear weapons, but probably not significantly more than 200'; the Stockholm International Peace Research Institute estimates 200. Other sources, including *Jane's Intelligence Review,* estimate between 400 and 500 thermonuclear and nuclear weapons.

What Dimona is to Israel's nuclear programme, the Israeli Institute for Biological Research (IIBR) at Nes Ziona is to its chemical and biological warfare (CBW) programme. The high-security facility is absent from aerial survey photographs and maps, on which it has been replaced by orange groves. Except for token visits to Dimona by a Norwegian team in 1961 and a US team in 1969, there has been no international scrutiny. Even the Knesset is denied access.

However, the 1993 report by the Office of Technology Assessment for the US Congress states that Israel has 'undeclared offensive chemical warfare capabilities' and is 'generally reported as having an undeclared offensive biological warfare programme'. Anthony Cordesman of the Centre for Strategic and International Studies states that Israel has conducted extensive research into gas warfare and is ready to produce biological weapons.

According to an exhaustive study by Karel Knip, a Dutch journalist, the IIBR's work has included the synthesis of nerve gases such as tabun, sarin and VX. The October 1992 crash an of El Al cargo plane in Amsterdam that caused at least 47 deaths and caused hundreds of immediate and subsequent mysterious illnesses led to the disclosure in 1998 that flight LY1862 was carrying chemicals including 50 gallons of dimethyl methylphosphonate (DMMP) – enough to produce 594 pounds of sarin. The DMMP was supplied by Solkatronic Chemicals Inc of Morrisville, Pennsylvania, and was destined for the IIBR.

Avner Cohen has catalogued reported uses of biological weapons by Jewish forces during the 1948 war in Palestine. The Israeli historian Uri Milstein alleged that 'in many conquered Arab villages, the water supply was poisoned to prevent the inhabitants from coming back.' Milstein states that one of the largest of such covert operations caused the typhoid outbreak in Acre in May 1948. The Palestinian Arab Higher Committee reported in July 1948 that there was some evidence that Jewish forces were responsible for a cholera outbreak in Egypt in November 1947 and in Syrian villages near the Palestinian–Syrian border in February 1948. In May 1948, the Egyptian ministry of defence stated that four 'zionists' had been captured while trying to contaminate artesian wells in Gaza with 'a liquid which was discovered to contain germs of dysentery and typhoid'.

In 1954, it was widely reported that defence minister Pinchas Lavon had proposed using BW for special operations. Cohen says: 'Israel has presumably employed biological or toxin weapons for special operations.'

In 1955, Prime Minister Ben Gurion ordered the weaponisation and stockpiling of chemical weapons in case of a war with Egypt. Former Mossad agent Victor Ostrovsky claims that lethal tests have been performed on Arab prisoners at the IIBR.

There are allegations that Israel has used CBW on numerous occasions:
• chemical defoliants by the army against Palestinian lands, including Ain el-Beida in 1968, Araqba in 1972 and Mejdel Beni Fadil in 1978;
• armed nuclear missiles in the 1967 and 1973 Arab–Israeli wars;
• chemical weapons in the 1982 war on Lebanon, including hydrogen cyanide, nerve gas and phosphorus shells;
• in the 1980s lethal gases against Palestinian civilians and Palestinian, Lebanese and Israeli Jewish prisoners.

Discussing delivery systems, the *Bulletin of Atomic Scientists* states that Israel's F–16 squadrons based at Nevatim and Ramon are the most likely carriers of nuclear warheads and that a small group of pilots has been trained for nuclear strikes. According to the *Sunday Times*, F–16s crews are also 'trained to fit an active chemical or biological weapon within minutes of receiving the command to attack'. Israel's F–4s, F–15s and Jaguars are also nuclear-capable.

Israel's Jericho I (with a range of 660km) and Jericho II (1,500km) missiles are nuclear-capable. The Shavit satellite launch vehicle is convertible into an intercontinental ballistic missile with a range of 7,800km. Israel also has three Dolphin-class submarines, the Dolphin, the Leviathan and the Tekuma, which are reportedly modified to carry nuclear-tipped cruise missiles. It is widely believed to possess a tactical nuclear capability, including small nuclear landmines, and strategic nuclear warheads that it can fire from cannons.

The UN Security Council regularly calls on Israel 'urgently to place its nuclear facilities under the safeguards of the International Atomic Energy Agency.' Israel has signed but not ratified the Chemical Weapons Convention, but is one of only four countries in the world – with Cuba, India and Pakistan – not to have signed the Nuclear Non-Proliferation Treaty. ❑

Neil Sammonds monitors the Middle East for Index

FOOD FOR WEAPONS: A ROUGH TRADE
ROBIN TUDGE

ECONOMIC INCOMPETENCE, INTERNATIONAL
ISOLATION AND CLIMATIC EXTREMES HAVE
REDUCED NORTH KOREA TO ENDEMIC
FAMINE — BUT DONE NOTHING TO CHECK
ITS NUCLEAR AMBITION

Eating in a Pyongyang restaurant, it's difficult to believe that for the third time in seven years, North Korea is starving to death. More than 3 million people, over ten per cent of the population, are estimated to have died since North Korea's famine cycle began in the mid-1990s. Millions more continue to suffer chronic malnutrition as belated efforts are made to pull the country's economy back from the brink. But for a casual visitor to the country's capital, Pyongyang, the courses keep coming. The food is plain, the choice limited; and sometimes the meals are pre-ordered by your guides so you get what you're given. But to all appearances, there's plenty. Appearance is the word, and the few big cities that foreigners can visit always have food to show. In North Korea you see what you're given, you eat what you're given. But for most of its people, that's long been too little.

For over 50 years, North Korea's rigid adherence to its particular form of socialist self-reliance and its fiercely anti-Western stance have isolated the country internationally, in particular from its former coloniser Japan, the US 'imperialists' who dominate South Korea – the Republic of Korea – and the US 'lackey shop' that is the United Nations. Seven years ago, the government took the unprecedented step of requesting help from outside. It invited international NGOs and donors into the country to observe and assist in staving off a calamitous famine as shortfalls in agricultural output reached millions of tonnes. Millions of tonnes in food and fuels were donated and millions of dollars invested. Since then, and most notably over the past year, the Democratic People's Republic of Korea (DPRK) has, uncharacteristically, made serious efforts on the diplomatic front. And with some success. But, once again, the DPRK is facing famine.

On 30 September 2002, the World Food Programme in Beijing announced that a slump in donations would force it to halt cereal distribution to 3 million hungry women, children and elderly people; a further 1.5

million were deprived of rations midwinter as the WFP cereal shortfall reached 100,000 tonnes. 'Such across-the-board cutbacks would cause acute suffering on a massive scale,' said Rick Corsino, WFP country director for the DPRK. 'As we head into the harsh North Korean winter, those affected will find it very difficult to cope. The tragedy is that the people most at risk stand to bear the entire burden. They are already on the edge.' The barely adequate daily allowance of 200 grams to hundreds of thousands of school-children, the aged and infirm was reduced; in October, cereal distributions to over 460,000 kindergarten children and some 250,000 pregnant and nursing women, who had been receiving 350 and 650 grams a day respectively, was cut by one-quarter; the following month, 925,000 nursery children suffered similar cuts in their 160-grams-a-day entitlement.

These terrifying figures are only estimates of the suffering of the next few months. They mirror those gathered since 1995. UNICEF says mortality rates in the 1990s for children under five rose from 27 per 1,000 to 48 per 1,000, while over 45 per cent of under-fives are still suffering chronic malnutrition and stunted growth. A further 4 million school-aged children are also severely underfed, impairing physical and mental development. (*Index* 1/1998).

Agricultural crises are not unknown to the Korean peninsula, but the odds were stacked against the DPRK following the partition of Korea in 1945. Partition left the South with most of the country's quality arable land. Regardless of tremendous increases in output since the Korean War (1950–53), food has been rationed in the North for decades. By the 1970s, the DPRK was more or less self-sufficient in food, but by the early 1980s food shortages were being reported in the northern provinces as the economy slowed. In the 1990s, the situation deteriorated further as Chinese and Soviet subsidies ended. Fertiliser and pesticide disappeared from the market; the output of tractors and pumps fell; spare parts became almost unobtainable. Broken machines couldn't be fixed; harvests were neither sown nor reaped. Diplomatic isolation, US sanctions – imposed in retaliation for North Korea's self-confessed nuclear ambition – and a bad foreign debt record precluded foreign investment or capital flows.

From 1991, the DPRK could no longer rely on cheap oil bartered from the Soviet Union. As the latter's economy staggered towards free markets and the USSR disintegrated, Russia demanded cash; as did China, in the throes of a similar transition. With no foreign exchange reserves, the DPRK ran out of fuel. Nor could it import new machines, parts, fertilisers or food.

Two-thirds of the DPRK's electricity is generated by hydroelectric power, but from 1995, drought and flood alternated with increasing ferocity, severely damaging the infrastructure. Electricity supplies were intermittent, power cuts shut down refrigerators for vaccines, filter pumps that ensured clean water supplies failed; irrigation systems collapsed, farms were wiped out. According to the ministry of foreign affairs, 1995's flood damage amounted to US$15 billion. The government has never released figures for those who died in the flood.

In late 1995, the UN Food and Agriculture Organisation and WFP found that the nation's 220kg average annual food ration had fallen to around 170 kg, below subsistence needs. The WFP estimated that North Korea needed some 4.7 million tonnes of food to meet the nation's minimum needs, but was 1.2 million tonnes short, US$250 million's worth of rice at market prices. Deficits have fluctuated around this figure ever since.

In 2001, the worst spring drought in 80 years followed the coldest winter in 50 years. Spring's wheat, barley and potato harvests failed; drought scuttled autumn's rice and maize crops. The country's increasingly unstable climate is part of a climatic shift reaching as far as Mongolia and northern China. The Gobi Desert is expanding east as drought becomes increasingly frequent and severe.

Government secrecy has made dealing with N Korea's famine difficult; access to many provinces is still restricted: UNICEF is denied access to 161 counties in six provinces and all residential children's institutions nation-wide. Those deprived of WFP assistance are dependent on the government-run Public Distribution System, traditionally the main channel for food to most of the country's 23 million people. The PDS provides on average 300 grams a day to those on its books – less than half the internationally recommended minimum intake. This year the WFP has had contributions from ten donors, including 250,000 tonnes from the US and 100,000 tonnes from South Korea, but new commitments in Afghanistan and southern Africa have strained its resources beyond the norm; there are unlikely to be additional supplies for the DPRK. Meanwhile, factory workers, soldiers, women and children, who had been drafted to the fields to supply the shortfall in mechanical power, failed to halt the continuing decline in food supplies. Like food, energy also continues to be in crucially short supply.

On the diplomatic front, the closing months of 2002 saw a flurry of activity. Full diplomatic relations have been established with most members of the

*Seoul, S Korea, 15 November 2002:
'Oppose Nuclear Programme' reads
the poster depicting N Korean
leader Kim Jong-Il.
Credit: AP Photo / Yun Jai-hyoung*

European Union, Canada, Australia and New Zealand since 1998. And though it is not averse to keeping its little brother in line (in September last year it was quick to scupper a proposed scheme to turn Sinuijiu – opposite China's Dandong – into a free trade zone) China has resumed food and fuel supplies to the DPRK.

And there has been progress with old enemies too. Though some commentators claim popular support for South Korea's policy of détente – President Kim Dae-Jung's 'Sunshine Policy' – is on the wane in both halves of the peninsula, there has been progress on this front, albeit largely of a symbolic nature. Such as increased meetings between divided families – a situation that affects around one in seven Koreans – and the first North–South football match in front of a 60,000-strong crowd when the teams played under a 'One Korea' flag and a traditional Korean folksong replaced both sides' national anthems. It was a 0–0 draw. Three weeks later, a team of DPRK athletes attended the Asian Games held in Pusan in South Korea.

More tangible moves towards reunification are the construction of road and rail links across the heavily fortified demilitarised zone started in September last year. Both projects have required the partial de-mining of the zone.

In the same month, the Japanese government announced its decision to extend economic assistance to the DPRK and Junichiro Koizumi made the first ever visit by a ruling Japanese prime minister to Pyongyang. Negotiations between the two countries to re-establish diplomatic ties, which have been going on for over a decade, finally broached critical issues when Kim

Jong-Il admitted during the summit meeting that 13 Japanese nationals had been kidnapped in the 1970s and '80s and that five were still alive. They were allowed a brief visit to Japan.

Normalising relations with Japan would release billions of dollars of investment from that country but the DPRK is insisting on reparations for Japan's colonisation of Korea between 1910 and 1945. Japan in turn is making any aid conditional on it not being diverted for military purposes. The US and South Korea have expressed concern over the North's possible misuse of Japanese funds.

But any progress thus far may have been jeopardised by North Korea's admission in late October that it is still in pursuit of a nuclear bomb, a violation of the 1994 Agreed Framework between the US and the DPRK. Under the terms of the agreement, North Korea was to freeze its nuclear weapons programme in exchange for an annual 500,000 metric tonnes of fuel, roughly the amount that had been supplied by the USSR, and two light-water reactors to be built by a US-led consortium. Despite opposition from members of the senate who saw the time as ripe to bring down the communist regime, Bill Clinton pushed the agreement through, delivered the fuel and kept the regime afloat. Much to the relief of the ROK, Japan and China who feared a refugee exodus of huge proportions should the DPRK collapse. The long-delayed ground-laying ceremony for the reactors was in August last year; completion was promised for 2003 but has been delayed by the Bush administration, which has chosen, instead, to include the country in its axis of evil. The Republic of Korea has expressed as diplomatically as possible its irritation at the renewed heightening of tensions on the peninsula this has caused, but at least one US senator is on record as saying that North Korea's nuclear ambition and missile capability pose a greater threat to the US than those of Iraq. The US is also irritated by the DPRK's sale of missile technology to 'unfriendly' countries such as Iraq and Yemen.

In 1998, the North Koreans demonstrated their satellite launch capability by firing a long-range missile across Japan. Like its October 2002 announcement, part of an attention-seeking strategy to work its way out of its present food crisis. National Security Adviser Condoleeza Rice admitted in late October that the DPRK's diplomatic initiatives hadn't gone unnoticed – and indicated that she also knew why. 'North Korea has been signalling and saying that it wants to break out of its economic isolation. This is a regime that in terms of its economic condition is going down for the third time. Its people are starving,' she told CNN, adding, 'It's not going to break out of that isolation while it's brandishing a nuclear weapon.'

Early October's visit to the DPRK by special US envoy James Kelly was reputedly about the country's missile programme, its human rights record and the inordinate size of its conventional forces. The DPRK foreign ministry denounced this 'arrogant' attempt to bring it to its knees and, only two weeks later, admitted it had not abandoned its nuclear programme. Secretary of State Colin Powell's statement that this came as a 'complete surprise' seems a little disingenuous, but it did make possible a joint statement from the US, Japan and the ROK calling on the DPRK to dismantle its programme in a prompt and verifiable manner as it was in violation not only of the Agreed Framework, but also of the Non-Proliferation Treaty, North Korea's IAEA safeguards agreement, and the South–North Joint Declaration on Denuclearisation of the Korean peninsula. The US is thought still to have nuclear weapons on the peninsula; Japan and the ROK have halted their weapons programmes but both countries maintain threshold capability.

But the rogue state must be tamed. Powell has outlined its way back into the fold: 'Our position with respect to North Korea is clear . . . if you will stop nuclear proliferation activities, if you will stop with these missile development activities, if you will do something about the large conventional force that hangs over the 38th Parallel, then there are great opportunities for you to benefit from a willing world that wants to help you get out of the economic distress you're in and the poverty that your people are suffering under.'

The large conventional force in question, the Korean People's Army, has a front-line strength of 1 million troops with support services and affiliated industries bringing the total to approximately 5 million people. The ROK has a fighting force of 500,000 plus 40,000 US troops. The standard and quality of the US trained force vastly exceeds that of the DPRK and, as everyone knows, the KPA hasn't the petrol to reach Seoul.

Soon they won't even have the fuel to keep warm. President Bush says he will cut off oil shipments to North Korea unless the regime dismantles its nuclear weapons programme. The ROK has protested, urging the US to continue shipments over the winter and regretting that the US had not consulted its allies on the matter. As far as the Bush administration is concerned, however, the DPRK is reaping no more than it has sown. ❑

Robin Tudge *is a freelance writer who visited N Korea earlier this year*

INVISIBLE CITY

TADASHI TAMAKI

AS IN THE US FILM 'THE TRUMAN SHOW',
PYONGYANG SEEMS TO BE A CITY
POPULATED BY EXTRAS. A JAPANESE
REPORTER DESCRIBES A VISIT TO THE
NORTH KOREAN CAPITAL

I recently spent a week in Pyongyang. I landed at Sunan, the city's airport, under a crisp, clear sky. Though the presence of uniformed soldiers initially put me on edge, the entry formalities turned out to be surprisingly simple. Once out of the airport, I was presented with the smiling face of a guide. 'Welcome to the Democratic People's Republic of Korea,' he said.

The glass façade of my hotel was polished to perfection, the sheets were impeccably clean and hot water flowed abundantly from the taps. I could even get CNN on the television in my room. In the restaurant, the portions were never less than copious. Not far from the hotel there was a nine-hole golf course where an early morning game cost me only US$20. I even had a shot at karaoke in the evening. It has to be said that, as a foreigner, I was enjoying a most comfortable stay.

But I quickly began to suffer from an inexplicable sense of tiredness. First, there was the nervous fatigue that comes with permanent surveillance. For any foreign tourist is accompanied at all times by two minders: a 'guide' and a 'monitor'. Always smiling and friendly, they stay at your hotel and follow you wherever you go. Even when I got up at the crack of dawn to go for a walk, they appeared after just a few minutes with a polite, 'Good morning, sir!'

But what exhausted me most were the bizarre occurrences that punctuated my stay. Whenever I spoke to people in the street, they would reply sagely with formulas such as: 'It is good that the great general [Kim-Jong-il] has decided to improve relations with Japan.' (A reference to the decision taken by Japan and North Korea last September to resume talks with a view to normalising relations.) Or: 'Pyongyang is the most agreeable city to live in in the world.' And then I noticed that all the people I met – that is, all the people who were sufficiently near to me for me to be able to speak to them – had the same characteristics: they were tall and good-looking, they had pale skin and they were smiling.

One day, in front of a department store, I saw two pretty girls go by. I told my minders that I would like to take a photo of them, and they called the girls over. When they'd gone, after a long conversation, I thanked my 'chaperones'. And they replied, 'No problem – they're friends.' Friends? After they hadn't even said hello on bumping into each other?!

On another occasion, we went to visit one of the town's parks. 'There's been a fashion for pets lately,' one of my minders told me. And just like that, at the park gates, we saw a couple with a baby – and a Maltese lapdog.

One day a beer hall caught my attention and I insisted, like a spoilt child, that we go in. Eventually, one of the minders went into the establishment, came out a quarter of an hour later, and gave me the nod. Inside, I could feel the stares of all the clients upon me. But it was no good trying to start a conversation: no one wanted to answer my questions.

In fact, if you pay attention when walking in the street, it's easy to arrange the passers-by into two categories: those who immediately turn around or into a side street as soon as they realise you're foreign, and those who keep walking towards you quite happily. This led me to suspect that perhaps the only people with whom I'd been able to communicate were, if you like, 'extras'. Paranoia or reality? These were the questions that haunted my evenings at the hotel. No wonder I was exhausted. ❏

Tadashi Tamaki *is the South Korean correspondent for* Nihon Keizai Shimbun *(Tokyo)*

Translated from French by GC

TALKING FIGURES

Military spending, US$ (2001)

Iraq	1.4bn
Iran	7.5bn
North Korea	1.3bn
USA	343.2bn

IRAQ

Literacy male 65.6%; female 45.9%

Average life expectancy 66.5 years

Population 18.3 million

GDP (1989) US$75.5bn; per capita US$3,510
In 1995, per capita GDP was US$199, the tenth worst in the world, between Nepal (US$205) and Sierra Leone (US$182)

Inflation (2001) 60%

Mortality rate for under-fives (2001) 133 per 1,000 live births, almost trebled since 1990 with 50 per 1,000

Nourishment 32% of children under five (c1million) are chronically malnourished, a rise of 72% since 1991

49% of families do not earn enough money to meet their basic needs

the UN food programme distributes 300,000 tons of foodstuffs per month – 2,200 kilo-calories per person per day

two-thirds of the Iraqi population (14–16 million) depend solely on UN rations to survive

UN oil-for-food programme proceeds 72% to humanitarian relief
25% to war reparations
2.2% to UN costs
0.8% to weapons inspection

War reparations Iraq's payments to victims of the Gulf War are the highest post-war reparations ever recorded

Construction Since 1991, Saddam has spent US$2 billion on the construction of presidential palaces

Support for Palestinians Since 1991, Saddam has spent US$1 billion on support for the intifada

Biological weapons Nine of the ten biological materials suspected of being used in Iraqi biological warfare research were supplied by US companies

Mental health Attendance at centres 57,206 (1998), a 157% increase since 1990

Admissions to hospital for mental disorders 15,996 (1998), a 137% increase since 1990 with 6,736

Press and communications One ISP (internet provider); four daily newspapers (all state-owned); 83 televisions per 1,000 people

On 20 November 2002, the daily newspaper *Babel*, owned by Saddam's eldest son, Uday, was banned

IRAN

Literacy male 84%; female 70%
single mothers in rural areas 30%

Average life expectancy 70.25 years

Population 70 million

Demography 70% of the population is under 35; most are more concerned with pop music than with Islamic values

14% of the population is unemployed

Women make up 9% of the labour force; 72% are teachers or in educational centres

GDP (2000) US$99 billion; per capita US$7,400

Deprivation 29% of families below the poverty line are single-mother families

Mental health Female suicide is four times greater than male suicide

Prostitution The average age has dropped from 27 to 20

Girl runaways have increased 30% in the past decade

Death penalty 90% of known executions in the world took place in China, Iran, Saudi Arabia and the USA

Press and communications Eight ISPs; 31.8 PCs and 4.61 televisions per 1,000 inhabitants; 17 million radios; 265,000 mobile phones; 32 daily newspapers

Islamic traditions A new regulation relaxing the wearing of headscarves in schools was piloted in September 2002: 'You can't play basketball wearing a chador,' said a student

NORTH KOREA

Life expectancy male 66 years; female 73 years

Literacy 99% (government estimate)

City dwellers (1990) 67% of the population (22 million)

Aid (1995/1996) US provided over US$8 million in humanitarian aid, second only to China
(1996/97) US pledged US$6.2 million to the UN emergency appeal, 38.5% of the total requested

Mortality rate for under-fives increased from 31 to 58 per 1,000 between 1994 and 1996

Nourishment 45% of children under five are chronically malnourished

4 million schoolchildren are severely underfed

10% of the population (2–3 million) have died of hunger or famine-related disease since 1994

'Only 30% of the population need survive to reconstruct a victorious society' (Kim Jong-Il, 1996)

Defence spending 20–25% of annual GDP

Ideological production line The Ch'ollima movement of 1958, modelled on China's Great Leap Forward, demanded that writers produce 522 literary works; those who failed were accused of committing a 'crime against the people'

'The number of written works to be produced is an integral part of the country's overall economic strategy. Writers are therefore criticised if they fail to produce the amount assigned within the time limit prescribed. Objectionable matter is removed by the State Administration Council's General Publications Bureau.'

Press and communications 1.4 million telephones; 2 million televisions; 4.7 million radios ❏

Compiled by **Najlae Naaoumi**, **Jason Pollard** *and* **Andrew Smith**

Sources include: UNDP; Caritas; Dr Eric Herring; Médecin Sans Frontières; SF; www.penpress.org; US Senate Committee on Banking, Housing and Urban Affairs; Centre for Defence Information; World Health Organisation; Middle Eastern Review for International Affairs; UNICEF; www.peacewomen.org; Reutersalert.org; Association of Iranian Women; UN office of the Oil-for-Food programme; US State Department; The World Factbook 2002; www.polisci.com; University of Louisville; Library of Congress; Censorship: A World Encyclopaedia; *www.kurdishmedia.com; Agence France Presse; Amnesty International*

KEEPING UP APPEARANCES

GULLIVER CRAGG

ONE-TIME ROGUE STATE SUPREME,
CUBA IS TRYING TO TIGHTEN ITS GRIP
ON DISSENT WITHOUT SCANDALISING
THE WORLD OR ALIENATING THE
TOURISTS

You get the occasional foreigner who's prepared to pay US$20 for a glimpse, through binoculars, of a tiny sliver of the US naval base at Guantánamo. So they get a bit of money out of that. And nine Cubans still work at the base. Other than that, its presence interferes very little in the life of this workaday colonial town.

I met three of the naval base workers, and two agreed to speak to me. The first said he simply wasn't allowed. Neither of the other two would answer any questions about the base's current use: the most total silence is imposed by the Americans. It's less clear how far the Cuban authorities care what people do and don't say about this thorn in their proud independent side. My friend Omar scoffs at the workers for being paranoid.

Whether the risk is real or not, Cubans instinctively watch what they say, even about something as innocuous as the commemoration of that first independence from the US.

Four hours on the back of a truck across the mountains from Guantánamo is Baracoa, a pretty town of 50,000 inhabitants where tourism is really beginning to take off. I'm struggling to ask Rafael, my landlord, whether there have been any centenary celebrations in Cuba this year, when we pass a mural representing the country's history from Columbus to the revolution. Great! A visual aid! But Rafael keeps talking about different national holidays, avoiding the question, and then surrenders: 'They're going to celebrate that next year, so that the kids will be on holiday.' What? Oh, he doesn't know.

There's nothing strange about Cuba not celebrating 100 years of independence. For the revolutionary government, Cuba was a US puppet state until 1959. But why won't Rafael just tell me there aren't any celebrations? Surprised that I seem to care so much about it, he's opted for simply saying what I want to hear – maybe I'm not who I seem, why risk upsetting me?

Later, Rafael reminds me that 'no babies starve here, nobody can't read, nobody gets murdered'. It's probably truer of Cuba than of any other Latin American country. But looking at this 55-year-old man surrounded by his three unemployed nephews and second bottle of rum of the afternoon, I sense he's trying to convince himself as much as me. One often gets the feeling that Cuba in 2002 is seeking to perpetuate an illusion.

The romanticism of the Cuban Revolution is compelling, as the success of those Che T-shirts shows. Very real improvements – literacy and a road linking the town to the rest of Cuba – have planted it in the hearts of Baracoa's older generation. These people would find it hard to admit that the dream has gone rather sour, even without the efforts of the state to prevent them from doing so. Cuba, that society whose most conservative members are called revolutionaries, is often glibly described as a land of contradictions. Surely, living in a land of contradictions has psychological implications. There is a sense that truth has lost currency amid ever-sunny media, money-spinning tricks and favours that keep Cubans alive while they pretend to live on state salaries of US$15–25 a month, and walls that proudly declare '*Venceremos*' ('We shall overcome') and then fall down.

Baracoa's walls are covered in slogans. Diligently painted by members of the CDRs (Comités de Defensa de la Revolución, a combination of community centre and a rather more sinister form of neighbourhood watch), the lettering has that 1950s charm that pervades the whole island. One sign candidly declares '*Sembrar ideas es sembrar Revolución*' ('Sowing ideas is spreading the seed of Revolution'). Hence the Cuban media, and the lack of alternatives to it.

You could make up the Cuban TV news What springs to mind about communist Cuba? Great achievements in the fields of education and health-care. These are reported every single evening. Another thing? That the US embargo has stifled economic development. The embargo is known in Cuba as a blockade, virtually an act of war. It is never not mentioned. Good news happens despite the embargo; bad news because of it. Many, though, expect it to be lifted soon. Cuba trades freely with the rest of the world, and many US companies defy the embargo. On 26 September, Minnesota governor Jesse Ventura accompanied a group of US food exporters to an unprecedented Havana trade fair. Castro is reported to have confessed to Ventura that he would 'feel a certain nostalgia' when the embargo is lifted. To judge by the media, nostalgia may be too weak a word to describe Castro's alarm at the prospect of losing a scapegoat he uses so regularly.

I spoke to five journalists working within and outside the state in Cuba. The first, René, reads the news for Baracoa's provincial radio station. This October the main news concerned the Popular Power elections. Each constituency chooses between two candidates who are both party members. This elects a local government, which then sends three representatives to Havana. René is most proud that 'the candidates don't waste money on publicity like in other countries. Everyone knows their candidate personally.' The only information they have about them otherwise is an A4 sheet pinned up on the local noticeboard.

René's is the only radio station in Guantánamo province, though residents can apparently pick up Radio Martí, the Miami-based exile radio station that broadcasts to Cuba. 'They can if they want to! It's a pack of lies. If there were good things and bad things about your country, would you like to hear about the bad things?' René speaks with great sincerity. He is the only Cuban who tells me his salary in Cuban pesos, saying: 'In dollars it's not much, but in pesos it's plenty.'

He's also the only Cuban I've met who brings up unprompted the problem of prostitution. 'Tourism is good for Cuba, but as tourism increases, so does *jineterismo*.' *Jineterismo*, literally 'jockeying', is a term that encompasses everyone from outright prostitutes to hustlers and fixers. 'Once someone's earned US$20 in a night, it's hard to persuade them to go back to working for US$20 a month. They'll go looking for other tourists.' A more fundamental threat to the survival of the communist system is hard to imagine. René, however, will acknowledge but won't confront. 'Fidel himself has said this: prostitution and tourism go together.' Fidel used to claim the eradication of prostitution from Cuba as one of communism's greatest triumphs. Nowadays, things look dangerously like a return to the days when Cuba was 'the whorehouse of the Caribbean'. Baracoa teems with old European men, awkward smiles on their faces and slender young women on their arms. In reality, Cuba needs the money too much to launch any serious crackdown on sex tourism.

It's tempting to include Cuba's new, spruced-up appearance in this catalogue of falsehood. With sugar prices low and not enough money to develop other industries, the government has made tourist dollars its priority. Historical buildings have been repainted (in Havana as part of a UNESCO heritage programme) and hotels refurbished. Tourist facilities everywhere have proliferated. Ranks of brand new Citroën taxis wait outside luxury hotels such as Santiago's Casa Granda, while bands play that

*Centra Havana, October 2002: primary schoolchildren
on their way to the gym. Credit: Gulliver Cragg*

Buena Vista Social Club tune incessantly in the bar. Repair work is under
way all over the country.

A lot of this is only skin-deep. Bar the small class of Cubans who have
relatives abroad or money from guest-houses or private restaurants, only
foreigners can afford the new facilities. And much less has changed outside
the main tourist spots. Nevertheless, tourism has transformed the economy,
and not all the improvements are cosmetic. Brand new buses have restored
public transport to areas that had gone without it since the fuel shortages of
the 'Special Period' (the crisis that followed the fall of the Soviet Union).
The phones work. The trains run. A lot of the restored areas are residential
and, after buildings of historical significance, priority has been given to
schools: every primary school in Havana has been refurbished – thanks to
the all-important tourist dollar.

I visited one. The rooms were clean; there were drinking-water foun-
tains and computers. The children were all wearing the bandana of the
Pioneers and every single one of them recited to me the revolutionary
poem that laments '*La montaña está llorando, Porque mataron al Che*' ('The
mountain is crying because they killed Che'). Milagros Beatón, head of the
Oriente Free Press Agency and the first dissident journalist I met, told me
she had objected to her daughters' wearing the Pioneers' bandana, but that
they themselves had insisted. They didn't want to feel left out in class.
Indoctrination certainly has its role in Cuba's legendary education system.
'*Sembrar ideas . . .*'

The Oriente Free Press Agency is one of around 20 bodies getting 'real'
news out of Cuba and on to the internet. Milagros and her colleagues fax

CUBA'S OTHER ISLAND

A RELEASED 'TERRORIST' RECOUNTS
THE GUANTÁNAMO BAY EXPERIENCE

Mohammed Sanghir, a missionary preacher with the Tablighi Jamaat, a non-political organisation for the propagation of Islam with several million adherents around the world, returned to his village in Pakistan last November after more than a year's imprisonment in the US base at Guantánamo in Cuba. The first Pakistani to be released, he still wears the green plastic bracelet that bears his 'American' ID: US 9PK 0001 43 DP, plus his age (51), height, weight and a photograph.

Sanghir had been in Afghanistan around three months when war broke out and was taken prisoner in the chaos of the battle for Kunduz. 'Together with around 250 people, 50 of whom died,' he was loaded into a container to be taken to Uzbek leader General Rashid Dostom's notorious Sheberghan prison. 'They were screaming for water, they were banging their heads against the walls and there, right there beside me, they died,' says Sanghir of his companions.

After 45 days in Sheberghan 'they turned us over to some US soldiers who blindfolded us and took us by helicopter to Kandahar'. There he was finally interrogated. 'There was an American and a translator. They asked me where I was from, why I was in Afghanistan, if I had links with al-Qaida, if I knew people from al-Qaida, if I'd ever seen Osama bin Laden and if I'd be able to recognise him.'

After this one summary questioning, a doctor called for Sanghir. 'He took my fingerprints and one earprint,' he says. Eighteen days later, they came again. 'They shaved my head, my beard and my moustache, put a blindfold over my eyes and put me in a tent where I waited for two or three hours with some other people. Before they shaved us, an American woman who spoke a little Urdu said: "We're taking you to a place where you'll have better facilities and you'll be more comfortable."' The soldiers, he says, completely ignored his attempts to save his beard, which has religious significance. 'I protested physically, but they weren't having any of it and they just said, "It's not allowed."'

For the 22-hour flight to Cuba, Sanghir was tied to his seat, gagged, blindfolded and had earplugs in his ears. 'A woman gave us apples twice, and some bread and water,' he recalls.

The arrival at the Guantánamo base was rough. 'While we still had our hands tied behind our backs and our eyes blindfolded, I was thrown outside and beaten by some soldiers,' Sanghir says, showing his cheek. He was to spend the next three and a half months, dressed in red overalls, in a cage open to the winds, 'to the millions of mosquitoes and to the heat', and without even a minute's privacy.

'We were like animals. If we were men, why put us in a cage? In the beginning, they didn't let us pray or speak to each other, but after two days of hunger strike a superior officer came, allowed us to pray and gave us half an hour for lunch.

'Twice a week they took us out to walk, and they gave us a clean uniform once a week,' Sanghir explains, adding that a doctor was always on hand. After three and a half months, he was transferred to a new, more comfortable cage, with running water and a WC in the corner.

Over the ten months he spent at Guantánamo, Sanghir was interrogated around 20 times. 'The questions were always the same, just presented in different ways. First, they showed me photographs of members of al-Quaida to find out if I knew them; then they asked me if there were any al-Qaida members around me; they wanted to know if I'd met bin Laden and if I'd be able to recognise him. The photos were of people who looked like Afghans or Arabs.' Sanghir maintains he did not recognise anyone.

The only people whom he saw at Guantánamo – 'once, during a move' – were Mullah Abdul Salam Zaeef, the ex-Taliban ambassador to Pakistan handed over to the US by Islamabad, 'who looked very weak'; Khairallah Kwaiwa, ex-governor of Herat, arrested in Chaman on the Afghan–Pakistan border; Mullah Fazl, ex-commander of Kunduz; and another commander, Mullah Abdel Raouf.

'One day, a new general came and said to me, "You're going to have some good news next week,"' Mohammed explains, recalling his release. He is still shocked that not one US official expressed even the slightest remorse at the year he had lost and the humiliation he had suffered. 'They just said, "You are innocent." No one apologised.' Sanghir plans to claim damages from the US. 'At Guantánamo, the soldiers told me I would get US$400 for each month's detention, but I only got US$100 when I arrived in Islamabad.'

Sanghir makes his living using a machine for cutting wood, highly prized in this isolated and mountainous region. 'For a year, my family had to borrow in order to survive, and now, how am I going to repay the money?' he asks, indicating how his machine has rusted from lack of maintenance. 'What can I do against the United States? It is a great power,' he says, resignedly, when asked how he feels about the Americans. His fellow citizens, in this highly conservative region, are not always so reserved. Painted in black on the wall of the village school two Kalashnikovs frame an unambiguous call to arms: 'Jihad on those who deny the Quran.' ❑

Françoise Chipaux for Le Monde

Translated by GC

articles to Havana and then on to Miami via the US Embassy. She explains: 'I'm not a journalist, I'm a doctor. But because of the way I see things I'm not allowed to work as a doctor any more.'

Milagros coordinates the agency from her home – a tiny bungalow in a ramshackle suburb of Santiago whose streets turn into rivers of mud every time it rains. Everybody had stared at me as I went to knock on Milagros's door, so I was worried about arousing unwanted suspicion. But when a neighbour comes to ask to borrow a few potatoes, she laughs. 'She's spying. She knows I haven't got any.'

The threat to Milagros is not from the local CDR *vigilanza*. The authorities know all about her, as the catalogue of persecution she proceeds to describe makes clear. 'There is a lot of psychological intimidation,' she says. Still a potential addition to Bush's current list of rogue states, Cuba is trying to tighten its grip on dissent without scandalising the rest of the world and driving away tourists. Milagros and her daughters have received threats, been followed by police agents in slow-moving cars and told to meet family members in certain places, only to find cops waiting to interrogate them.

I ask her what part self-censorship and what part genuine belief will have played in the reluctance of the people I met in Baracoa to criticise the system; none of them had a bad word to say about the regime. 'There are people who love Fidel, who love the Revolution. Probably some of the people you met do. But a lot of others are just scared.' It's hard to gauge how dangerous it really is to speak freely in the street. Cubans seem unsure themselves. As it is the local CDRs whose *vigilanza* reports counter-revolutionary activities, there is a lot of local variation: the more committed communists there are, the more vigilant the *vigilanza*, the less room for alternative opinions . . . But Milagros thinks Cubans ought to be more courageous about facing the truth. 'You see how much these people really love their Revolution when they get lucky with a visa and shove off to North America,' she concludes. She herself has a US visa. Her husband, a physics professor, was granted asylum there after refusing to teach revolutionary politics.

After hearing about Milagros's situation I feel more sympathetic to journalists who keep their heads down, like René. But the Cuban Independent Journalists' Bureau in Havana has a different story. Israel Ortiz and Manuel Lopez run the office from a vast flat. They seem extremely relaxed compared with Milagros. 'Things are harder outside Havana. Here there are all the diplomats, and the government wants to pretend that there is a free press in this country, so they can't touch us. Though they've given us a lot of advice. The advice they give us is this: leave the country!' They both laugh. 'But I want to see how this film ends!' Then, more seriously: 'Is there freedom of expression in this country? Yes. I'm not going to prison for telling the truth. But are we legal? No. Can we use the internet? Can we publish in Cuba? No.'

Israel and Manuel are both professional journalists who worked in the state media until the early 1990s and still have friends there. Apparently, Cuba's main evening newsreader calls the bureau to get the real news. So even he doesn't believe the stuff he's reading? I ask Manuel what the state pays this man to keep him in his job. 'Not much. But they gave him a nice car and in the mornings he drives it as a taxi.'

It's a cliché that taxi drivers earn more than doctors in Cuba. Actually, practically no one lives off a state salary. Some, like waitresses and taxi drivers, receive tips. Private businesses and relatives abroad provide other legitimate sources of income. Then there's *jineterismo*. In between is a world of inventiveness in which Cubans make use of their workplace to earn money. 'Alongside the double [peso/dollar] economy, we have the *doble moral* [something like 'two-facedness'],' Israel says, and then explains how people actually make money from their jobs. Doctors, for instance. 'Well. You don't want to work for a month. I'm a doctor. I put your arm in plaster, I give you a note, you don't work for a month. Five dollars. You give me 100, you can retire – acute asthma!' I'd thought it was odd how many early retirees I'd met. Israel then brings out his electric iron. It's broken. 'A guy is coming tonight to fix it. If you go to try and get it fixed in the shop where he works, they haven't got the part. *No hay*. It's as simple as that.'

Manuel Sayes also used to be a state journalist. Now embittered against the whole profession, he takes a dim view even of the free press agencies. 'A lot of them have a very low standard of journalism. And much of it comes down to counter-propaganda.' Manuel feels he was deliberately given a particularly bad job after his dissident student days at Havana University during the early '90s. 'It was a different time.' He gestures to the fearsome traffic behind him on 23, modern Havana's main artery. 'No cars. No one in the street. It was terrible. So at the university, how could they expect us to carry on pretending it was OK, *then*? It was *obviously* terrible. Nowadays there is less tolerance than before.' He sums up his work as 'writing things that aren't true and nobody reads. Other journalists didn't understand why I didn't want to toe the line, win prizes, promotion. Be careful, they would say. Careful of what?'

Manuel is currently one of eight Cubans studying at the prestigious International School of Film and Television outside Havana. This means he has internet access. Could he print out and distribute web pages, if he wanted to? 'No. It's illegal.' As far as Manuel knows, nobody breaks the law. 'Cubans do not have internet access. I am one of maybe 10,000 out of 11 million It's nothing.'

Young Cubans with less information than Manuel are often even more angry. Exotic conspiracy theories abound among the Rastafarians in Central Park. Fidel is apparently the eighth richest man in the world, with bank accounts all over Switzerland, thanks to Jamaican drug deals. The wizened dealer who tells me this story is pretty convincing and the rumour is widely believed, despite resting on the absurd assumption that the drugs acquire value by being consumed by Cubans. Once people have realised that the government lies, they readily believe anyone who contradicts it. Young *Habañeros* get their news from tourists, and can easily get the impression that the whole of the rest of the world is middle class. 'Don't think we don't know how it is in other countries,' someone says to me. It didn't feel right to add 'for some people'. The Rastas' reaction when I told them I'd been to New York was in perfect keeping with that inescapable 1950s atmosphere: 'The city of dreams. You go there a pauper and wake up a millionaire.' 'Or a dead junkie,' I mutter. Quick as a flash: 'But at least you have the option.'

I met one young *Habañero* with a more balanced view of things. Jorge aims to write a book about what should happen when Castro dies. 'The Party, through the military, will try to hold on. The Miami Cubans will try to take over. But my book ends with the first free elections in this country. We don't want communism; we don't want capitalism. Social democracy.'

I find myself assuming, from Jorge's analytical approach and yearning for democracy, that he is anti-Castro. He isn't. 'Nobody is perfect. But in Mexico, mothers give their children drugs to stop them crying from hunger. In Nicaragua it's the same. In Guatemala, worse. Those are the countries that Cuba should be comparing itself with. And compared with those countries, Cuba is like Europe! Here, we have hygiene, basic nutrition, drinking water, medical care, electricity . . . we have peace. Cubans struggle, for sure. But someone who doesn't eat today will eat tomorrow.' There are echoes of what Rafael was saying in Baracoa, but none of the sadness that his bleary-eyed state of denial evoked. Jorge's position seems rationally optimistic in

*Santiago de Cuba, October 2002: 'There is no personality cult
surrounding Fidel Castro.' Credit: Gulliver Cragg*

comparison. Perhaps the greater sadness, though, lies in recognising that a
one-party state with near universal poverty and severe limits on personal
freedoms is the best place in Central America for the great mass of its population. 'Not as bad as Guatemala' doesn't have quite the same ring to it as
'*Hasta la victoria siempre*'.

Of course, Fidel is only 76 and could live another 15 years. But Cuba
certainly feels like it's about to change, to relinquish its exceptional status in
some way. I wonder how the culture of deceit and denial that has developed
to accommodate the failures of the Revolution will affect the country's transition away from it. Jorge's dream of social democracy may be a hard one to
achieve in a society where everyone accepts that things aren't what they
seem; where people don't trust their neighbours, let alone the government.

The taxi driver who takes me to the airport asks if I've liked Cuba. 'Some
aspects are hard to understand, perhaps,' he suggests. 'Like the economy.'

'I think I've understood something,' I reply. 'The official economy of
Cuba is not the economy of Cuba.' 'That's basically it,' he laughs, and then
asks if I prefer Aerosmith or Bon Jovi. ❏

Gulliver Cragg *is a volunteer researcher and translator at* Index

TRIUMPH OF THE CZAR

JUAN GOYTISOLO

THE RESOLUTION OF MOSCOW'S
THEATRE SIEGE SHOWED AS LITTLE
CONCERN FOR THE HOSTAGES AS
FOR THE CHECHEN 'TERRORISTS'

The brutal display of force that ended the imprisonment of more than 700 civilians taken hostage by Chechen guerrillas in Moscow's Dubrovka theatre earned Vladimir Putin the congratulations of governments the world over, from Bush and Sharon to Saddam Hussein.

For some it was a matter of self-interest; others showed a certain credulity. But almost no one seems to have thought twice about the manner of this 'liberation', or the huge number of victims claimed by the mysterious poison gas used by the master of the Kremlin.

Can a massacre which, in the name of saving hostages' lives, tries out a new toxic weapon whose capacity to kill has not yet been tested really be called a success? Doesn't such carnage typify the utter contempt successive czars of Russia have shown for their own people? And is the cold-blooded execution of the hostage-takers – including those women who were lying unconscious in the orchestra pit and who had already been widowed in the so-called clean-up operation – worthy of a democratic state, or one that calls itself civilised?

CAN A MASSACRE WHICH, IN THE NAME OF SAVING HOSTAGES' LIVES, TRIES OUT A NEW TOXIC WEAPON WHOSE CAPACITY TO KILL HAS NOT YET BEEN TESTED REALLY BE CALLED A SUCCESS?

In any European Union country actions such as these, plus the gassing of innocent theatregoers, would have provoked a major governmental crisis and the resignation of all those involved. No such thing has happened in Russia: indeed, Putin has apparently emerged strengthened from the affair. Under his yoke, as under those of Yeltsin, Brezhnev, Stalin and the czars of the past, the lives of the people do not matter, as the Kursk submarine disaster and the 1999 Moscow bombings – in all probability organised by Putin's own secret services – have already shown.

The argument used by Bush's sparkling new ally – 'No one shall bring Russia to her knees' – is as mendacious as it is cynical. No one is trying to bring Russia to its knees; all that is asked is that it end its policy of extermination and sit down to negotiate with Chechnya's democratically elected President Aslan Maskhadov, as the Chechen World Congress in Copenhagen had requested some days before.

The attempt by Bush and his media manipulators to link the mystery terrorists to the Iraqi dictator have found an apt accomplice in Putin. Last year, when the war in Afghanistan started, Moscow's propaganda services, unthinkingly relayed by the Western media, claimed not just that Chechens were active in the ranks of the Taliban, but that they constituted the hard core of their fighting forces.

For weeks on end, the supposed al-Qaida Chechens were presented as the most formidable menace. It didn't matter that no one with any understanding of the situation in the tiny north Caucasus republic would dream of believing such claptrap. Why would Chechen separatists go to war thousands of kilometres from their country when they had the Russians to fight on their own doorstep, in the throes of a pitiless war distinguished by killing, rape, torture, mass graves and all imaginable forms of extortion and pillage?

This truth was quickly proved by the facts. When the campaign in Afghanistan ended in the fall of Mullah Omar's obscurantist regime, the infamous Chechen volunteers disappeared. Not one prisoner or corpse was

AFTER THE 'SUCCESSFUL OUTCOME' OF THE HOSTAGE CRISIS, PUTIN'S AND BUSH'S STATEMENTS ON TERRORISM OVERLAP: 'UNTIL IT IS BEATEN, NO ONE WILL BE ABLE TO FEEL SAFE IN ANY PART OF THE WORLD.'

found to back up the Russian secret services' fantasy. But Putin, a brilliant leader of these services in his day, had achieved his objective: Bush's war on terrorism in Afghanistan was identical to his own in the Caucasus.

Now, after the 'successful outcome' of the hostage crisis, Putin's and Bush's statements on terrorism overlap: 'Until it is beaten, no one will be able to feel safe in any part of the world.' The two share a penchant for barefaced lies. In the Russian's case, it is compounded by a long tradition of despotism, unscrupulousness and an almost paranoid obsession with secrecy and opacity.

'Terrorism must and will be beaten.' How many times have we heard this high-sounding phrase in the mouths of the supposed defenders of order?

But which terrorism are they talking about? The term changes like a chameleon: its multiple meanings get applied to quite different, not to say opposing, situations and organisations. Terror imposed with tanks, helicopters, missiles and JCBs can dress itself up in shining democratic robes; but there is no excuse or mitigation for the terror of those who oppose it with the weapons of the poor or the weak (suicide bombs, bloody acts). The razing of Chechen cities and the gratuitous killing of those held in the sinister 'filtering points' I tried in vain to visit in 1996 does not worry the strategists of the New World Order too much: it is all reduced to a struggle between goodies and baddies, between democrats and murderous fanatics.

This is the same rhetoric we heard first in the Algerian and then in the Vietnam War. Its generalised usage since 11 September has managed so to pervert the words' meanings that the aggressor becomes the victim and vice versa. Who is this strong and powerful, cruel and inhuman enemy that Putin so portentously invokes? History and geography can answer that question. We need only look at a map to compare the vast Russian Federation with a tiny breakaway republic half the size of Wales and see who's strong and who's powerful; a quick history lesson in the successive Caucasian wars of conquest and Chechen rebellions over the course of the nineteenth and twentieth centuries, culminating in the last but one invasion – instigated by a quite patently drunken Yeltsin – should do away with any doubts as to where the cruelty and inhumanity are coming from.

It is undeniable that the Chechens failed to make good the September 1996 agreements that effectively accepted their country's independence. Disorder and sectarian strife, along with high levels of organised crime, undermined the authority of Aslan Maskhadov and favoured Shamil Basaiev's sinister Dagestani venture. The combined effects of Saudi money feeding extreme Islamic groups opposed to the Caucasus's religious traditions and the Russian secret services' destabilisation activities (the role played by the oligarch Boris Berezovskii in the Wahabi connection is yet to be clarified) finished off the moderates' independence plans.

Since the not-so-mysterious Moscow bombings that catapulted Putin to the head of the Russian Federation, his bellicose pronouncements and declarations of victory are regularly contradicted by the facts. Russia is getting embroiled in Chechnya once again. According to the Association of Soldiers' Mothers, 11,500 conscripts and volunteers have lost their lives. The horrors of summary executions, mutilations and bodies piled up in mass graves constitute a strong case for trying the Russian army in Chechnya for genocide (*Index* 2 and 3/1996).

To ignore such stark facts, to applaud the resolve of a president capable, like Saddam Hussein, of gassing his own people in the name of the struggle against international terrorism without examining or trying to solve the problems that feed it, is simply to perpetuate the barbaric tyranny so masterfully described by Tolstoy in his short novel *Hadji Murat*.

In a ruined Grozny street market someone furtively slipped me a poster printed in Turkey bearing the words, 'Life, Faith, Holy War'. It hangs on a wall in my house as a reminder The Chechen people have never given in to brute force and probably never will, short of being wiped off the face of the earth by the latest czar's new weapons of mass destruction.

Europe needs to return to the values of openness, generosity and enlightened thinking that the Spanish statesman Manuel Azaña asked of its political class. Only a strong mobilisation of public opinion behind those values can stop the advance of Putin's repressive machinery in the wake of this shameful manipulation of events, both in Chechnya itself and in the triumphant assault on Moscow's theatre of death. ❏

Juan Goytisolo is a Spanish writer. See also his earlier writings on Chechnya in Index *5/96. His most recent books are* Landscapes of War: From Sarajevo to Chechnya *(City Lights Books, USA 2000) and* A Cock-Eyed Comedy *(Serpent's Tail, UK 2002), both translated by Peter Bush.* © *El País*

Translated by GC

STRIP SEARCH by Martin Rowson

Are you confused by the new doctrine of Humanitarian war? Be not afeared! It's really *terribly simple!*

1. There are *lots & lots* of **BAD THINGS** (Fig. a) and **BAD PEOPLE** (Fig. b) in the world

Fig. a. Bad things, like Famine and pictures hanging crooked

Fig. b. Bad people with *dirty mouths!*

2. **LUCKILY** there are also quite a few slightly less bad people (Fig. c) who now and again find it in their own interests to sort out Figs. a. & b. Hooray!

Fig. c. The less bad people

3. In order to stop Fig. a they **KILL** Fig. b, —— but being slightly less bad than Fig. b, when they kill people they do it in a "Humanitarian" way, and thus prove themselves actually to be **GOOD** (cf. "How to use the U.S. Imperium to Establish International Socialism" by C. Hitchens)

(4) AND THEY ACHIEVE THEIR UTTERLY LAUDABLE AIMS BY BEING **RICH** AND USING THE "LATEST TECHNOLOGY"(Fig.d)

Fig.d: Lockheed Tristar's new "EDIBLE/COOKING" BOMB DOCTOR®™© — Having wrought its *collateral damage*, the Bomb Doctor's®™© fragments can be eaten by the survivors, and at the same time, on exploding it will COOK the surrounding rubble to match the dietary laws and culinary traditions of the country being bombed! Also contains *depleted uranium* enriched with *VACCINES* and *ANTIBIOTICS* to eradicate **ALL KNOWN DISEASES**! (Plays Barber's "*Adagio for Strings*", Theme from "*E.R.*", Band Aid's "*Feed The World*", Tony Blair's 2001 Conference Speech, etc.)

(5) WHICH MEANS YOU CAN NOW TELL THE DIFFERENCE BETWEEN Figs.e & f!

Fig.e.— Victim of Bad People

Fig.f.— Empowered Stakeholder in the New Humanitarian World Order of GOOD PEOPLE

PUTIN'S GESTURE TO FREE SPEECH

RUSSIAN PRESIDENT VLADIMIR PUTIN'S
DECISION TO VETO REPRESSIVE MEDIA
LEGISLATION PASSED BY PARLIAMENT AS
A PART OF THE STATE'S WAR ON 'CHECHEN
TERRORISM' DOES NOTHING TO REVERSE
THE STEADY DECLINE IN THE RIGHTS OF
INDEPENDENT JOURNALISTS ACROSS RUSSIA

Thanks may be due to President Putin for his decision to veto legislation that would have sharply restricted independent media coverage of terrorism issues, but that hardly makes him a champion of free expression. His veto was issued on 25 November in response to an unprecedented display of solidarity from the country's media and worldwide criticism of the bill.

Representatives of 30 of the country's major media organisations – including state-controlled TV and their fierce foes from the independent networks – plus the head of Putin's own human rights commission had all urged him to ditch the bill.

'No truly democratic power can exist without publicity and openness, which are provided by the mass media,' Putin conceded. But his honeyed words were accompanied by stinging criticism of Russia's press, TV and radio coverage of October's deadly Moscow theatre hostage crisis (Goytisolo p106), and a suggestion that such situations were best tackled well out of public view.

'The main weapon of terrorists is not grenades and sub-machine guns and bullets, but blackmail, and the best means of such blackmail is to turn a terrorist act into a public show,' he said during a meeting with major media bosses on 25 November.

When Russian special forces stormed the theatre, they killed all 41 hostage-takers – and at least 129 of the hostages, most of them killed by a narcotic gas used to knock out the rebels. Questions on how the heavily armed rebels were able to stage the operation unhindered by state security have gone unanswered. Criticism of the conduct of the operation, particularly the apparent misuse of the gas, has been stifled and calls for an independent parliamentary investigation rejected.

The vetoed legislation, amending the Law on the Struggle with Terrorism and the Law on Mass Media, would have prohibited reports adjudged to hinder counter-terrorist operations and banned the broadcast or publication of rebel statements or extremist 'propaganda'. Critics said the bill's language was deliberately vague and could be used to shut down news organisations that annoyed the authorities, especially in advance of parliamentary elections in 2003 and presidential elections in 2004. They also complained that the laws would only further restrict already tightly controlled coverage of the so-called 'counter-terrorist' war in Chechnya.

But regardless of the veto, the Russian press already works under adverse conditions and looks likely to remain so for the duration of the election years to come. As the Committee to Protect Journalists notes, 'Independent media outlets face excessive legal restrictions, economic impoverishment, political intimidation, and violent retribution for critical reporting on official corruption and human rights abuses in Chechnya.'

Foreign media have not escaped. On 20 November, Russian security agents seized four video cassettes from Hans-Wilhelm Steinfeld, Moscow correspondent for the Norwegian public TV station NRK, who was working on a report about Chechen refugees. The film was returned, but two cassettes were partly erased.

The CPJ said the Russian press played an extremely constructive role during the hostage crisis. 'At a time when the public was apprehensive and afraid, the media provided accurate and timely information about what was happening inside the theatre.' After the raid, added the CPJ, the press asked questions that the Russian public wanted asked, such as: 'Was every possible measure taken to protect the lives of the hostages?' 'Some of these questions may have made your administration uncomfortable,' said the CPJ, 'but it is the proper role of the press to take up such issues on behalf of the public.'

Putin's administration has been directly or indirectly responsible for a broad range of abuses, including the selective use of tax audits, prosecutions, and police raids to stifle independent media. Disputes over commercial debt and shareholders' rights have masked a wholesale takeover of private media seen as critical of Putin and the war in Chechnya. Security forces are stealthily amassing control over information and widespread violence against journalists continued in the face of general indifference from the police, particularly outside Russia. Changes in the system of state subsidy have reinforced the Kremlin's grip on the broadcast sector and the hands-on power of the Ministry of Press and Information and its chief, Mikhail Lesin. Putin's veto over the latest manifestation of this trend does nothing to reverse it. ❏

RJ

AFGHANISTAN

The Afghan Supreme Court dismissed judge **Marziya Basil** after she was pictured without a headscarf in a photo taken with President George W Bush during an official trip to Washington. The Kabul daily *Suhbat* said the delegation's US trip was a 'disgrace to the dignity of Afghanistan'. (RFE/RL)

Recent Publications: *All Our Hopes Are Crushed: Violence and Repression in Western Afghanistan* by Human Rights Watch, report Vol. 14, No. 7 (C), October 2002.

ALBANIA

Five days after the independent daily *Koha Jone* published a series of critical articles about Prime Minister Fatos Nano, five different state agencies sent inspectors to check its compliance with financial, labour and other regulations in what was seen as a deliberately intimidatory act. (HRW)

ALGERIA

On 12 September, the daily *Le Matin* (*Index* 3/02) reported new UK ambassador Graham Hand-Stewart as explaining British reluctance to sell arms to Algiers as due to the tendency of its security services 'to be brutal sometimes'. Hand-Stewart denied having made the remarks, despite *Le Matin*'s insistence. (BBC)

On 27 September, a French court threw out Algerian ex-defence minister Khaled Nezzer's suit against ex-army officer **Habib Souaidia** (*Index* 4/02), author of a book

about army atrocities. The court said it could not judge Algerian history and that Souaidia had repeated his allegations on French TV in good faith. (AFP)

Nationwide local elections ending on 11 October were marked by a record low turnout, partly because of another election boycott in the Berber minority region in Kabylia (*Index* 3/02). In Tizi Ouzou province participation was as low as 2.5 per cent and there were clashes between police and Berber militants. (*El País*, AFP)

ARGENTINA

On 18 September, a federal court subpoenaed the telephone records of **Thomas Catán**, Buenos Aires correspondent for the London *Financial Times*, after he reported that foreign bankers had complained to their embassies about legislators seeking bribes to defer a 2 per cent tax on banks. (Periodistas/IFEX)

On 20 September, **Miguel Armaleo** of the daily *Lo Nuestro* was sentenced to a one-year suspended jail term for libelling Ricardo Ortiz, president of a Buenos Aires district council. Armaleo had added Ortiz's face to a photomontage titled 'The Usual Suspects', alluding to corruption at the municipality. (IFEX)

ARMENIA

All 4,600 copies of the 31 October issue of the newspaper *Aravot* were bought up and taken away by an unknown buyer outside the state printing house. Editor **Aram Abrahamian** cited an article accusing associates of premier Andranik Markarian of blackmailing their way to buy a popular resort complex. (RFE/RL)

The Armenian government revised a draft media law withdrawn in March after it was criticised by both local journalists and the Council of Europe. The original bill proposed the creation of a state agency to oversee the media that could also revoke licences to publish. (*Index* 4/02, 3/02, 2/02) (RFE/RL)

On 14 September, the National Democratic Union (AZhM) resumed publication of its weekly *Ayzhm* under a new editor, National Press Club Chairwoman **Narine Mkrtchian**. Predecessor **Vigen Sargsian** was fired in September 1998 and the paper closed following disagreements with AZhM leadership over editorial policy. (RFE/RL)

Caucasus Media Institute deputy director **Mark Grigorian** was hospitalised on 22 October after a grenade exploded at his feet on the street in Yerevan. He was working on an article about the October 1999 attack on the Armenian parliament. The assailant was not identified. (RFE/RL, CPJ)

Education minister Levon Mkrtchian defended an order to schools to display the Armenian flag and portraits of President Robert Kocharian and the top Armenian churchman Catholicos Gagerin II. He said he aimed to strengthen young Armenians' patriotic readiness to defend their country against foreigners. (RFE/RL)

AUSTRALIA

An Australian government super-regulator may get jurisdiction over both the country's telecommunications industry and its electronic media. Radio and TV firms fear a single regulator will raise media licensing costs in line with the higher charges now imposed on telecom firms. (*The Age*)

AZERBAIJAN

Editor **Aydyn Guliev** and journalists from the Azerbaijani opposition newspaper *Khurriyet* (*Index* 1/02, 3/01), received death threats after exposing a petrol smugglers' racket. Callers claiming to be friends of implicated customs officials threatened to blow up the paper's offices if more articles appeared. (RSF, CJES, WAN)

Defending a decree requiring the media to check reports on security issues with officials before publication and to identify sources if required, President Heidar Aliev hinted on 6 September that he might recognise journalists' objections and revise it. (RSF, IWPR, RFE/RL)

BAHRAIN

The Discover Islam Centre, sponsors of a visit to Bahrain by US white supremacist David Duke, claimed US embassy staff had tried to persuade Bahrainis not to attend his lectures. Duke objects to what he calls the 'Zionist occupation of the US' and links Israel to the 11 September attacks. (*Gulf News*)

BANGLADESH

Ekushey TV (ETV) managing director **Simon Dring** was expelled from the country on the orders of the government, in conflict with ETV since taking power in October 2000 (*Index* 4/02). It accused Dring, a former London *Daily Telegraph* correspondent, of bias and senior ETV executives of fraud. (*Telegraph*)

Moniruzzaman Monir, correspondent for the newspaper *Dainik Juganator* (*Index* 3/02, 4/00) in the town of Nalchity, was arrested on 23 October after he alleged that a local Jamaat-e-Islami Party leader was corrupt. Monir was accused of extortion by the brother of the Islamist party's leader. (RSF)

On 30 October, **Saiful Islam**, of *Dainik Juganator*, **Omar Ali Sani**, of *Dainik Ittefaq*, and **Babu**, of the local *Dainik Gono Jagaron,* were arrested and later bailed in the town of Agailjhara, and also charged with extortion. Their arrest is linked to their reports on illegal tree-felling. (RSF)

A film once banned by the Bangladesh authorities has been officially entered for a best foreign language Oscar. *Matir Moyna*, directed by **Tareque Masud**, tells the story of a boy at an Islamic religious school. The government initially refused to allow its release, concerned for local Islamic sensitivities. (BBC)

BELARUS

On 29 August, the **Belarusian Association of Journalists** began a campaign to secure 50,000 signatures on a petition calling on the country's parliament to abolish the charge of 'criminal libel'. (RSF, BAJ)

On 15 October, **Viktor Ivaskevich**, editor of the weekly *Rabochy*, lost his appeal against a two-year sentence for defaming Belarusian president Alexander Lukashenka during the 2001 elections. He followed editor **Nikolai Markevich** and journalist **Pavel Mazheiko** of *Pahonya* (*Index* 3/02), sentenced on similar charges to a year and 18 months respectively a few days earlier, into a labour camp. (RSF, BAJ)

In November, the **Belarusian Association of Journalists** (*Index* 3/02) was awarded the 2003 Golden Pen of Freedom award for 'fighting bravely against what is probably the most repressive regime in Europe,' according to award organisers from the World Association of Newspapers. (WAN)

On 3 October, Belarus's law on religion (*Index* 3/02) was amended to restrict minority religious groups' right to publish in a bid, the government said, to stop the spread of 'destructive sects and occultism'. There are over 2,900 officially registered religious groups in Belarus. (*Prima News*, A19)

On 5 November, opposition United Civic Party leader **Anatol Lyabedzka** was detained by police as he left the US Embassy in Minsk and warned against contacts with foreigners and 'dependence on Western sponsors'. Lyabedzka accused the police of 'political schizophrenia'. (RFE/RL)

Recent Publications: *Uncovering the fate of Belarus' 'Disappeared'* by Amnesty International, September 2002.

BOTSWANA

Reporter **Alice Banda**, of the independent daily *The Voice*, received 15 threats after her October investigation into illegal abortions. Posing as a pregnant woman she found that five out of seven registered doctors in Francistown, Botswana's second city, offered illegal terminations for fees between $133 and $533. Abortion is illegal in Botswana. (MISA)

BRAZIL

The Inter American Press Association called on the Brazilian government to continue its hunt for the killers of Globo TV reporter **Tim Lopes** (*Index* 4/02) after the August deaths of several suspects. The IAPA also criticised police 'insinuations' that Lopes' own negligence may have caused his death. (IAPA)

Domingos Sávio Brandão Lima Júnior, owner of the daily *Folha do Estado*, was murdered on 1 October in Cuiabá, central Brazil, allegedly at the behest of local mafiosi. Military policemen Célio Alves de Souza and Hércules Araújo Coutinho were arrested in connection with the killing. (*Folha do Estado*)

On 5 October, **Felipe Santolia**, a journalist with Radio Chibata in the town of Esperantina, was found shot and tied to a tree with barbed wire. Santolia, who recovered in hospital, had claimed to have video evidence of a candidate buying votes ahead of 6 October parliamentary elections. (RSF/IFEX)

BURMA

Four prisoners of conscience, **Aye Thar Aung, Htwe Myint** (*Index* 2/02), doctor **Than Nyein** and veteran dissident **Win Tin**, began a 'hospital strike' on 11 August, demanding that the authorities return them to prison from Rangoon Hospital unless they were treated like 'normal patients'. Secret policemen took photos of them daily, during medical examinations, meals and while they slept. After his release on 16 August, Aye Thar told the dissident radio Democratic Voice of Burma that Win Tin's heart problems and blood pressure had worsened in July. Win Tin was finally returned to Insein Prison on 6 September. He is 13 years into a 25-year sentence on subversion charges and informing UN agencies about ill-treatment and poor prison conditions. (RSF, AI)

The Burmese junta ordered the month-long closure of two magazines, *Han Thit* and *Beauty Magazine*, after the former quoted a poem that mentioned the banned poet **Ko Lay** by **Maung Chaw Nwe**, who died in September. *Beauty Magazine* had broken a ban on printing adverts for Thai companies, applied after a diplomatic dispute between Burma and Thailand. (RSF)

Some 30 dissidents, mostly former political prisoners, were arrested on 25 September for possessing opposition publications, notably the newspaper *Khit Pyaing*, published in Thailand. Some 12 of them were subsequently detained in undisclosed locations for more than ten days. (RSF, CPJ)

Recent Publications: *'My Gun Was As Tall As Me'* – *Child Soldiers in Burma* by Human Rights Watch, October 2002.

CAMEROON

Cameroonian cartoonist **Paul Nyemb Ntoogue**, pen name 'Popoli', was stopped at a police checkpoint on 30 November and told by a policeman that 'all he was doing in the country was insulting people'. Ntoogue, of the daily *Le Messager*, was then beaten for ten minutes by the police, suffering head and back injuries. (CRN)

CANADA

Invoking the need to preserve journalistic integrity, Canadian media withdrew an agency photo taken of a streaker – a person who runs naked through public events as a prank – later found to have been computer manipulated by the photographer to obscure the streaker's genitalia. (www.waymore-sports.com)

On 8 October, Canadian monarchists demanded that deputy prime minister **John Manley** be barred from meeting Britain's Queen Elizabeth during her tour of the country. He had jokingly suggested that multimillionaire Canadian singer Celine Dion could replace her as Canada's titular head of state. (*Telegraph*)

CHILE

On 29 October, a Santiago court ruled that **Eduardo Yáñez** (*Index* 2/02) should be charged with insult. During a November 2001 TV debate he had called Chile's courts 'immoral, cowardly and corrupt' in the handling of the case of a woman accused of murder and detained for three years before the case was thrown out. (*Periodistas*/IFEX)

When a hearse carrying the body of one Nelson Contreras was hit by a truck in the town of Eistein, police and passers-by left his coffin and flowers in the street, believing it to be an art installation in homage to the Chilean surrealist artist Roberto Matta Echaurren who had died that day. (*Ananova*)

Chile's senate approved a bill to replace the panel of soldiers and judges that has censored more than 1,000 films deemed immoral, unethical or an affront to public order since 1974. The new panel of educationalists, film critics and film makers will instead assign ratings based on the moviegoers' age. (*Periodistas*)

CHINA

The two months prior to the 16th National Congress of the Chinese Communist Party (CCP) held in Beijing from 8–16 November witnessed determined efforts in China to target publications and media deemed to threaten the image of the party. Shi Zongyuan, director of the State Press and Publications Administration (SPPA), said at a conference of publishers in October, 'All possible

measures should be taken to ensure that the publication market will not air voices that challenge the party's policies and unity,' and he warned publishers of severe penalties including forced closure, for 'providing a venue for wrong views'. An official from SPPA said on 11 September that dozens of titles from 10 publishing houses throughout China had been banned. (CNA, SCMP, *Xinhua*)

Two known dissidents, **Fang Jue** and **Xu Wanping**, were detained by police in Beijing and Chongqing respectively on 5 November, just ahead of the party congress. Fang, a former government official and vocal critic of the CCP, was released from prison in July 2002 having served a four-year prison term on charges of business malpractice. Xu was a prominent participant in the 1989 Tiananmen protests. Their whereabouts are unknown. (AP)

The US internet search engine **Google** was blocked by Chinese authorities on 31 August ahead of the CCP National Congress. The block was lifted on 12 September, but access to sites sourced via Google were severely limited. Analysts estimate the Chinese state employs 30,000 people to monitor and control information (*Index* 4/02 & *passim*) on the internet. (AP, CPJ, SCMP, *Xinhua*)

Chen Shaowen, a writer from Hunan province, was reported on 25 September to be facing charges of subversion for writing more than 70 articles and 40 essays since 2001 for 'foreign reactionary' websites, and 'falsifying information and slandering the CCP'. (CPJ, SCMP)

New controls on internet cafés in Jiangxi province were reported on 3 November (*Index* 4/02 & *passim*). Users must swipe a card with detailed personal information through a unit attached to the computer before going online, allowing police to monitor their web-browsing habits. (AP, CPJ, SCMP, *Xinhua*)

Dr Wan Yanhai, co-ordinator of the Beijing-based Aids Action Project, was detained incommunicado between 24 August and 20 September after publishing a report on the internet about neglected children orphaned by Aids. State media alleged that his report 'illegally provided foreign sources with state secrets' but that he had been released uncharged because he confessed and identified his sources. Dr Wan was key to the exposure of corruption and bad medical practice at state blood clinics in Henan province between 1994 and 1997, which led to around 150,000 people becoming infected with HIV. (SCMP, HRIC, *Xinhua*)

Seven police officers raided the home of **Yeo Shi-dong**, Beijing correspondent for South Korea's *Chusom Ilop* newspaper, on 31 August. Officers took away Yeo's passport, ID papers and documents on North Korean defectors and refugees in China. (*Yonhap*)

Wang Fei, **Wu Sisheng** and **Chen Ren**, members of the Christian 'Shouters' sect in Fujian province, were

reported on 3 September to be serving 're-education through labour' terms of one, two and three years respectively. They were arrested on 2 June with 31 others when police raided their congregation and charged them with illegal assembly. (AP, ICHRD, SCMP)

In an unusual step, on 10 October five members of the **South China Church** centred in Hubei province had their December 2001 death sentences commuted to prison terms ranging from 15 years to life. All five were sentenced for 'using an evil cult to obstruct the law', assault and rape. **Gong Shengliang**, the founder of the church, **Xu Fuming** and **Hu Yong** were sentenced to life. **Li Ying** and **Gong Bangkun** were sentenced to 15 years. Twelve others jailed with them also had their sentences reduced on appeal, with four of the 12 being released. (AP, ICHRD, SCMP)

It was reported on 26 September that **Yao Zhenxiang**, a Shanghai-based dissident linked to the outlawed **China Democracy Party** (CDP), had been sentenced to three years 're-education through labour' on 2 September on charges of 'visiting prostitutes'. Yao was released in March 2002 after two years in jail on similar charges. (AFP, Reuters)

The BBC protested 'in the strongest possible terms' to China in October over the jamming of Uzbek-language radio signals into Xinjiang province (*Index* 2/01). The BBC said the jamming started on 1 September and is affect-

ing signals into Uzbekistan itself. Uzbeki is similar to the Uighur language, spoken by the Islamic majority in the province which has a large pro-separatist community. (BBC)

Chinese authorities briefly blacked out CNN and BBC broadcasts relayed to satellite feeds to hotels and foreign compounds in Beijing on 10 November in apparent response to coverage of the party congress. Authorities blocked CNN file footage of an interview with dissident **Fang Jue** and a brief mention of Falun Gong, during a feature about the search among Chinese for spiritual solace, said CNN Beijing bureau chief, Jaime FlorCruz. (CNN)

The Chinese government has ordered local modifications to a new TV satellite built by the French that will allow Beijing to block efforts by the banned Falun Gong movement to use it for their protests. Falun Gong supporters broke into state and cable television networks this year (*Index* 3/02) to broadcast videos protesting against the state's clampdown against the group. (BBC)

On 17 October, Hong Kong Secretary for Justice Elsie Leung told the region's Newspaper Society that publication of unauthorised or sensitive information would contravene the proposed law unless an acceptable defence could be produced. Citing Watergate, she said public interest was a strong defence, 'But people should think carefully if they consider it is their duty as journalists to publish some information at the risk of violation of law.' (AP, SCMP)

Two critics of Hong Kong's public assembly laws were arrested six months after a minor offence – apparently to keep them in custody during an October visit by Chinese Premier Zhu Rongji. **Lau San Ching** and pro-democracy activist **Andrew To** were arrested for staging an 'unauthorised rally' on 11 May. (BBC)

Former monk **Lobsang Dhargyal** died on 18 November in a 'reform through labour' camp, 19 months after being reimprisoned on spying and separatist charges during a visit to his sick mother. Jailed in 1992 for publishing pro-independence posters, he had fled to India in 1997 after his sentence. (TCHRD)

Recent Publications: *State Control of the Internet in China* by Amnesty International, November 2002; *Selection of Cases from the Criminal Law* by the Dui Ha Foundation, October 2002; *News Review – Reports from Tibet 2001* by Tibet Information Network, October 2002; *The Invisible Exodus: North Koreans in the People's Republic of China* by Human Rights Watch, report Vol. 14, No. 8 (C), November 2002.

COLOMBIA

The Colombian government now requires foreign journalists to seek official permission to visit state-run security zones, citing fears that foreigners were training armed rebels there. Foreigners found in the zone without permission will be deported. Colombian journalists are exempt. (CPJ/IFEX)

Trades unionist **Adolfo de Jesus Munera** was murdered on 31 August, just after a court cleared him to sue Coca-Cola for unfair dismissal. He was fired from Coca-Cola's Barranquilla plant in April 1997 after his boss claimed he was a rebel sympathiser, forcing him into hiding from rightist paramilitaries. (*Indymedia*)

Less than a month after ratifying the International Criminal Court convention, Colombia cited its article 124 to deny the court jurisdiction over war crimes committed on its territory or by its citizens for seven years. Some 40 journalists have been killed in Colombia over the past 10 years (*Index* 3/01 & *passim*). (RSF/IFEX)

CÔTE D'IVOIRE

There has been a spate of attacks against the media in Côte d'Ivoire since 19 September and the start of an insurgency. The Mayama Editions press house was attacked on 16 October, and the private Radio Nostalgie on 17 October. Both are owned by an associate of opposition leader **Alassane Dramane Ouattara**. (RSF/IFEX)

Police also raided two opposition daily papers published by Mayama Editions, *Le Patriote* and *Tassouman*, after the latter reported the theft of a car used by Interior Minister Emile Boga Doudou. The newspaper had cited the theft as evidence of the regime's 'impotence' in the face of urban crime. (RSF/IFEX)

CUBA

Cuban authorities' confiscated French journalist **Catherine David**'s files and photographs after she was discovered to have entered Cuba on a tourist visa to report on dissidents and the human rights situation. Cuba routinely denies visas to journalists, while Law 88 of March 1999 provides for up to eight years' imprisonment for any person assisting the foreign news media. (RSF)

Congressional supporters of US relations with Cuba are seeking a presidential 'veto-proof' majority to lift a ban on US tourism to the island, says Democrat Massachusetts representative William Delahunt. 'It is our goal and purpose to repeal the travel ban . . . so that American citizens can exercise their constitutional right to travel anywhere,' Delahunt said during a visit to Havana on 14 December. (Reuters)

CYPRUS

On 8 August, editor-in-chief **Sener Levent** and **Memduh Ener** of the daily *Afrika* were sentenced to six months' jail for libelling Turkish Cypriot leader Rauf Denktash in a July 1999 article titled 'Who is the number one traitor?' On 6 October, their sentences were reduced on appeal to six weeks, and they were released. (IFJ)

Police evicted a group of Cypriot and Spanish journalists from the Turkish occupied part of Nicosia on 7 October. The group had crossed the Green Line for an European Union sponsored meeting of NGOs and Turkish Cypriot journalists. The meeting had just started when police broke it up. (IFJ)

CZECH REPUBLIC

Former communist official Karel Hoffman was charged with treason on 1 November for allegedly ordering the closure of state broadcasting to silence his own government during the 1968 Warsaw Pact invasion of Czechoslovakia. If convicted, Hoffman faces up to 15 years in prison. (RFE/RL)

Correspondent **Ivan Bonfanti** of the Italian leftist newspaper *Liberazione*, sent to cover the NATO summit in Prague, was refused entry to the Czech Republic on 18 November at Prague airport and told that his presence was 'undesirable' and 'could cause disturbance'. The Italian government refused to intervene. (*Il Manifesto*)

DENMARK

It was revealed on 28 August that **Stig Mathiessen**, a reporter on Denmark's second-largest newspaper, *Jyllands-Posten*, had his phone bugged and the tape played back in court, where he was required to reveal his sources for a report that extremist Arabs had created a deathlist of Jews in the Åarhus region. (IFJ)

EGYPT

Two brothers of **Yasser al-Siri**, the London-based director of the Islamic Observation Centre, were arrested on 7 August in a dawn raid on their homes in Suez. The raid came a week after a British court decided not to extradite Mr al-Siri to the US to face charges that he helped finance al-Qaida. (*Cairo Times*)

On 5 September, student **Mohammed Ahmed Abdo Hegazy** was arrested by State Security Investigation agents and charged with 'spreading rumours that disrupt public security', following the publication of his poetry. He was ordered to be detained until 2 October. (EOHR)

On 8 October, an **Amnesty International** fact-finding team left Egypt, having been refused permission to visit a list of 'prisoners of conscience' including academic **Dr Saad Eddin Ibrahim** and three Britons arrested on 1 April in connection with the banned Islamic Liberation Party (*Index* 3/02). (AI)

On 14 October, web designer **Shohdy Surur** (*Index* 1/02, 2/02, 3/02) had a one-year prison sentence confirmed by the appeals court. Surur, currently residing in Russia, was convicted for posting on the internet a political poem, famous for its crude street Arabic, written by his late father. (RSF)

On 4 November, **Dream TV** was officially warned that discussing female masturbation in a 'provocative way' would result in 'strict measures against the channel'. The warning against the privately owned channel relates to a programme broadcast in mid-October which tackled this and other taboo sexual issues. (*Cairo Times*)

A 41-episode TV series, made to coincide with the high viewing figures of the month of Ramadan, drew international protests for incorporating elements of the so-called 'Protocols of the Elders of Zion', a Russian Tsarist-era fake document supposed to outline a plan for Zionist world domination. (*Times*)

In November, the Egyptian authorities dropped its undeclared local ban on the Lebanese Arab literary and cultural review *al-Adab*, its apparent response to the magazine's recent extensive report on censorship in Egypt. (EOHR)

ERITREA

Zemenfes Haile, founder of the weekly *Tsigenay*, journalist **Ghebrehiwet Keleta**, reporter **Selamyinghes Beyene** of the weekly *Me Qaleh* and **Binyam Haile** of the pro-government *Haddas Eritrea*, who disappeared between 1999 and 2001, were confirmed as being among 18 journalists (*Index* 3/02) held incommunicado in state jails. (CPJ)

EUROPEAN UNION

Privacy campaigners have slammed a EU plan (*Index* 3/02) to require the storage of records of personal communications, including all emails and telephone calls, for at least a year, possibly two. The information would be held in central computer systems and made available to all EU governments. (*Statewatch*)

FRANCE

Rhône-Alpes regional council funders withdrew a US$64,000 grant from a jazz festival in the town of Vienne in south-west France after objecting to the event poster, which shows a white baby devil being suckled by a black woman. They judged it to be an attack on the beliefs of Christians. (BBC)

The Paris offices of the **Damoclès network** of **Reporters sans Frontières**, tasked to investigate and prosecute people who persecute journalists, were broken into on the night of 7 October. Nothing was stolen but computers were tampered with and threatening phrases were scrawled on the wall. (RSF)

Novelist **Michel Houellebecq** was cleared on 22 October of incitement to racial hatred in his anti-Islamic outbursts in interviews and recent novel *Platform*. A Paris judge ruled that the comments did not constitute an incitement to discrimination against Muslims. (*Guardian*)

GABON

On 6 September, the weeklies *Misamu* and *Gabaon* were suspended for three months by order of the National Communication Council, which accused them of 'undermining confidence in the state and the dignity of those responsible for the republic's institutions'. *Misamu* had investigated the reported disappearance of $4.4 million from the public treasury and *Gabaon* was punished for a 'violent' opinion article about Senate President Georges Rawiri in its 9 August edition. (RSF)

GEORGIA

On 27 September, TV journalists from an independent TV station in the western town of Zugdidi broadcast an item criticising police for beating up demonstrators at a protest at the city. About 30 police officers took offence, went down to the station and beat up the journalists as well. (RSF, RFE/RL)

GERMANY

Publishing giant Bertelsmann admitted that it had faked its claim to have been closed down for 'subversion' by the Nazis. In fact it was the wartime German army's main printer. It made up the subversion story to pass post-war tests applied by British occupation forces, allowing it to rebuild its empire. (*Times*)

A Munich court stopped German sales of US historian **Daniel Goldhagen**'s book *A Moral Reckoning: The Role of the Catholic Church in the Holocaust and Its Unfulfilled Duty of Repair*, which criticises the Church's activities during World War II, after claims by church officials that the book was inaccurate. (*Times*)

English words and phrases like 'ranking', 'pole position' and 'factory outlet' were replaced by German equivalents in the regional daily *Stuttgarter Zeitung* on 21 September in a bid to defend the German language from unnecessary 'anglicisms' – at least for one day. (www.expatica.com)

A group of mobile phone users discovered they were being bugged by German intelligence after the costs of the buggers' intercept calls were added to their bills. When the users of the mmO$_2$ network checked odd phone numbers on their bills, they turned out to belong to German secret services. (*IT Register*)

The online version of the German left-wing daily *Tageszeitung* shut down its online forum after failing to find a way to keep debate free and open without tolerating abusive and racist comment. A special 'anger zone' on the site failed to improve things, so the paper's staff decided to pull the plug. (www.taz.de)

GREECE

On 2 October, an organised gang of helmeted men, apparently supporters of the November 17 armed group, attacked the Athens offices of the daily *Apogevmatini* with Molotov cocktails. The paper's founder **Nikos Momfertos** was murdered by the group in 1985, and the title strongly supported its suppressions. (RSF)

GUINEA-BISSAU

On 1 December, the Portuguese public broadcaster **Radiotelevisão Portuguesa** (RTP) was barred from operating in Guinea-Bissau for an unspecified period. The state had criticised RTP for its coverage of the second anniversary of the death of coup plotter General Ansumane Mané, killed in November 2000. (RSF)

GULF STATES

Information ministers from the Gulf Cooperation Council states meeting in Oman on 9 October, warned the **al-Jazeera** satellite TV station to make its programmes more 'respectful', or face loss of official cooperation. If not, the GCC said it would call on advertisers in their countries to stop using the channel. (CNN)

HONDURAS

Hospital director **Gaspar Vallecillo** was fired by the Honduran health ministry after he wrote a opinion article for the daily *El Heraldo* criticising levels of state support for his hospital. He was subsequently informed that he was being dismissed from his post, 'following an order by President Ricardo Maduro'. (PFC)

HONG KONG

Tens of thousands of Hong Kong residents rallied against a proposed anti-subversion law on 15 December, the biggest public march since the mainland retook control of the former British colony. Organisers claimed more than 60,000 marchers turned out for the four-hour march, while police estimated the crowd at up to 12,000. (BBC Online, SCMP)

HUNGARY

Karoly Szadai, chairman of the board of trustees of *Hungarian Radio*, is to quiz President Ferenc Madl and parliamentary speaker Katalin Szili over fears that government control of funding will lead to unwarranted political pressure on the state-owned radio network. (RFE/RL)

INDIA

On 12 September, the Supreme Court rejected a public interest petition opposing the country's new schools curriculum. The petition accused the Hindu-nationalist government of undermining India's secular constitution with a biased account of Hindu and Muslim contributions to Indian history. (Reuters, *Frontline*)

On 24 October, the investigative news website **tehelka.com** temporarily suspended operations. Since its landmark March 2001 exposé of corruption in the defence ministry (*Index* 3/01, 2/02, 4/02), police and government have used every pretext to harass the website and its financial backers. (*Financial Times*)

P Neduraman, president of the Tamil Nationalist Movement, and **Vaiko**, leader of the Marumalarchi Dravida Kazhagam party, made court challenges to their detention under the Prevention of Terrorism Act for expressing support for Sri Lanka's Liberation Tigers of Tamil Eelam (*Index* 4/02). Neduraman claimed that he was wrongly denied bail and Vaiko says his detention is an illegal breach of his constitutional right to free expression. (*The Hindu*)

Editor **Ram Chander Chaterpatti** of the *Poora Sach* newspaper in Sirsa died on 22 November from gunshot wounds received in October. He had reported alleged fraud and sex scandals in the Dera Sacha Sauda religious cult. Three people, including a senior member of the group, were arrested. (*Times of India*)

Editor **Ghulam Mohammad Sofi** was shot in the hand in Srinagar, in India-controlled Jammu and Kashmir, by two unknown gunmen on 18 September. His bodyguard was also wounded. The attack was one of several surrounding legislative elections in the disputed territory held in September. (CPJ)

INDONESIA

Two journalists, **Anton Perdana** and **Rizal Ardiansyah**, were assulted by a Pontianak member of parliament and his associates at the Pontianak Regional House of Representatives compound on 7 November. Ardiansyah, a journalist from Radio Volare, was attacked when he tried to intervene. (SEAPA)

Academic **Lesley McCulloch**, former health worker **Joy Lee Sadler** and a translator were arrested in Aceh on 11 September. Police claimed they had videos and photos linked to the separatist Free Aceh Movement, charging them with 'activities incompatible with tourist visas'. McCulloch may also face spying charges. (NEAR)

Indonesia has delayed a decision on its new broadcast bill (*Index* 2/02), which would limit the right of radio and TV stations to relay foreign programming, a proposal that media rights groups view as a bid to limit uncensored news coverage from the BBC, Voice of America and CNN. (SEAPA)

Recent Publications: *Grave Human Rights violations in Wasior, Papua* by Amnesty International, September 2002; *Analysis of Indonesian Anti-Terrorism Bill*, Article 19, Forum Asia and the Alliance of Independent Journalists, November 2002.

INTERNATIONAL

A new report by the World Bank co-launched by the World Association of Newspapers concluded that a free press can spur economic development when its independence, quality and ability to reach a wide audience are guaranteed and help build public consensus to bring about change. (WAN)

IRAN

It was reported on 21 November that Ayatollah Ali Khamenei, Iran's supreme leader, had ordered a review of the death sentence passed on **Hashem Aghajari**, a liberal academic accused of blasphemy. Aghajari had called in June for a 'religious renewal' of Shi'ite Islam and that Muslims 'should not blindly follow religious leaders'. (AP, AFP, *IranMania*)

On 29 September, two Aghajari supporters, **Hossein Mojahed**, a senior member of the Islamic Iran Participation Front, and **Mojtaba Heydari**, of the Islamic Revolution Mujahedin Organisation, were jailed for two and a half years with 74 lashes and six months and 74 lashes respectively for 'inciting public contempt' for the judiciary. (AFP)

Tehran's Press Court suspended two more newspapers in September, bringing to 54 the total number of publications since April 2000 (*Index* 4/00 & *passim*). The newly opened daily *Golestan-e-Iran* was accused of publishing 'lies and rumours' and the weekly *Vaqt* for publishing photos and articles considered to be 'immoral.' (AFP)

Iranian official **Mohammad Ali Pakdel** was himself arrested on 2 October for failing to arrest actress **Gowhar Kheirandish** for giving a public kiss on the cheek to actor **Ali Zamani** at a film festival. Pakdel denied the charge and said the order to arrest the pair only came after they had both left town. (AFP)

In October, reformist cleric **Hasan Yusefi Eshkevari** (*Index* 5/00, 1/01, 3/01) had his death sentence commuted to seven years in jail. He was said to have defended the right of women to go out in public without head covering at an April 2000 conference in Berlin. Several of those who attended the meeting were later jailed. (AFP)

Polling institute director **Behrouz Gheranpayeh** was charged with selling 'secret classified information to foreigners' and his centre closed down after it published a poll commissioned by Iran's parliament that found 74.4 per cent of the populace supported normalisation of relations with the US. (AFP)

Ayatollah Ali Khamenei waived the remaining two years of reformist **Abdollah Nouri's** (*Index* 1/00, 2/00) five-year jail term in November after Nouri's brother, Alireza, a reformist parliamentarian, was killed in a car accident. Nouri remains banned from political activity. (RFE/RL)

The conservative Guardians Council used its veto powers in November to reject a fifth attempt by the reformist parliament to pass a law requiring political and media trials to be held openly and in front of a jury. Iran's closed courts have jailed dozens of reformist journalists and closed their papers. (AFP)

A Tehran appeals court lifted a ten-year sentence on US-based Iranian folk dancer **Mohammad Khordadian** in November. Arrested during his first home visit since 1979 and charged with 'promoting depravity' at his California dance school, he spent two months in jail before being allowed to leave Iran. (AFP)

Iranian secret services were accused of assassinating **Mansour Mairoufi** in the mainly Iranian Kurdish city of Bokan on 6 November, the sixth member of the Kurdish Democratic Party of Iran to die in mysterious circumstances in recent months. (www.kurdishmedia.com)

IRAQ

The Egyptian magazine *al-Usbou* published Iraqi President Saddam Hussein's first interview in 12 years on 4 November. Saddam said the US objective was to break up the Arab world into small emirates, none larger that Israel, so that their oil resources could be better controlled. He said the US had not targeted North Korea's nuclear weapons programme because North Korea is not Israel's enemy. He also claimed: 'We believe in the importance of public opinion and its effects, and learn from our experiences.' No Iraqi newspaper was allowed to report that the interview had taken place. (MEMRI)

The daily *Babel* newspaper was banned on 20 November, despite the fact that it is owned by Saddam's eldest son, Uday. *Babel* has recently reprinted some foreign news

MOVING PICTURES

BAHMAN GHOBADI

I'm an Iranian Kurd and proud of it. Any problems in Iran are shared
by all. There are difficulties for everyone, not just for me as a Kurd. Due
to restrictions under Islamic law, film-makers have been forced to create
a new style of film-making; to imply, rather than to explicitly show sex or
violence, for example. It is hard making movies, but the government has
never forbidden me from making a Kurdish movie; it actually helped me.
Today in Kurdistan more than 200 young Kurdish boys and girls are busy
learning the art of film-making. A friend of mine recently sold his taxi and
bought a film camera. Iran's Kurdistan is in the top flight of short film-
making.

I'm from Baneh, about 15 miles across the border from Iraq, and
until the age of 11 all I can remember is fighting in my area.

We had to flee to Sanandaj, the capital of Kurdistan province. Two
uncles and three cousins were killed, my sister and grandmother were
injured in Saddam's war. All these things formed me and pushed me
towards film-making.

Another thing was that I really, really loved sandwiches as a boy. I
wasn't a big fan of films, but the only sandwich place in Baneh was the
local cinema, and that's why I started going to watch films. I got such
pleasure from eating this wonderful sandwich while watching a film.
The owner of the sandwich shop was also the owner of the cinema,
and I thought that was a great combination.

My father had a major influence on me. When I was 15 he encouraged
me to take up Pahlavani wrestling [a style of wrestling popular in Iran], a
very traditional sport. He got me involved so that I wouldn't get into bad
habits, like smoking or drinking. I really got into it, so I used to hang
around before the training centre opened, and I became friendly with
a photographer who worked next door.

He was the same age as me and we began to go around together, taking
photographs. He encouraged me to do more.

I bought a book on animation for beginners and made my first animated film with my mother. We sent the film to a festival in Iran and it won the Best Animated Film award. But animation took too much energy, so I changed over to documentaries, fiction and other types of film. I never had enough money for 35mm so I shot in 8mm and VHS, low-budget films. I used my family and the neighbours as actors. I was 16 when my parents separated, which was unusual, so I had to work to support my family. At 21 I went to the Iranian University of Television in Tehran – I never learned anything there. I was working on other films as an assistant so I left without my qualification.

It is a shame that a hundred years after the birth of cinema, we don't have a branch called Kurdish cinema. We only have a few films at the moment, with some of them made by non-Kurdish directors. Once we have 15 or 20 movies a year, with Kurdish directors, in the Kurdish language, then Kurdish cinema will emerge. It is important to show a variety of Kurdish experiences, in different styles – it's not good to have, say, ten naive, political films that almost cancel each other out.

My films are a mixture of documentary and fiction. I don't want the viewer to be aware of any particular camera style, of the technical aspects. I want the viewer to feel the reality. I prefer to work with non-professional actors – I can help them create something and they help me too, so part of the story is created by the actors, I include things I learn from them, like feeding alcohol to the horses in my first film.

My aim is not political, but to show Kurdish traditions and culture. I don't want to see borders, to differentiate between Kurds from Turkey or Kurds from Iran, Iraq or Syria. I want to show all Kurdish culture. I don't like to talk about the possibility of war in our region. We haven't forgotten the weariness of previous wars. I hope that Saddam goes without war. My struggle is a different struggle, not through the gun but through the camera lens. ❏

Bahman Ghobadi won the Camera d'Or in Cannes for his Kurdish-language feature A Time For Drunken Horses *and played the lead role in* Blackboards. *His second feature,* Marooned in Iraq, *was premiered at the 2nd London Kurdish Film Festival. Interviewed by Gill Newsham*

CLERICAL CLASS WARFARE
HASHEM AGHAJARI

In Islam, we never had a class of clergy; some clerical titles were created as recently as 50 or 60 years ago. Where did we have a clerical class in the Safavid dynasty? Today's titles for Islamic clergy are like the (Christian) Church hierarchy – bishops, cardinals, priests. This type of hierarchy in (contemporary Shi'ite Islam) is an imitation of the Church. Today this clerical hierarchy is headed by the Ayatollah Ozma (the 'Grand Ayatollah') . . . And a level down you have an Ayatollah, Hujjat ul Islam, Thaqqat ul Islam (junior ranks of religious scholars) and so on.

In the past few years, the religious institutions have become a sort of government institution, and the issue has become more sensitive. Is there anyone in our society who understands the distinction between a Hujjat ul Islam and an Ayatollah?

Shari'ati* said that in Islam we do not have a class of religious leaders. This is not the 'core Islam'. It is a development of historical Islam and, fortunately, we have not yet seen in Iran the establishment of a single central apparatus based on the ranks of clerical titles. For years, there were many parallel Marja-e Taqlid institutions (bodies led by men with the right to issue fatwas) and each Marja-e Taqlid had his own structure.

Today, the ruling clergy in Iran wants to consolidate all the Ayatollah Ozma organisations under a single rule. [*The audience applauds wildly.*] Shari'ati said that in Iran we have never had a true clerical class. This is what they want to do in our country. I doubt whether they will succeed because of our independence and the elements that we have in Shi'ite Islam.

The divisions and the hierarchies they wanted to create are Catholic (and not Islamic) . . . Some of the clergy are so engrossed in what they are trying to do that they start thinking of themselves as icons . . .

*Shari'ati (b. 1933) was a political activist who argued that the solution for the oppressed peoples of the Middle East was 'Islamic humanism'. He attacked the traditionalist clergy and their fatalism towards and appeasement of the Shah's regime. He died in 1977 under mysterious circumstances. ❏

Excerpted from a speech by **Dr Hashem Aghajari**, *a University of Hamedan history lecturer, journalist, disabled veteran of the Iran–Iraq war and active member of the reformist Islamic Revolution's Mujahedin Organisation (IRMO). As a result of this speech he was sentenced to death in November by a Hamedan court for blaspheming the Prophet Muhammad, insulting the Shi'ite imams, and insulting top state religious authorities.*
Translated by the Middle East Media Information Institute (MEMRI) and used with permission

For the full translation, with an analysis by Ayelet Savyon, director of the Iranian Media Project ⇨ www.memri.org

reports including a British story alleging that Saddam was ready to pay Libya billions of dollars to guarantee political asylum for his family. (AFP)

Nizar Al-Khazraji, the highest-ranking Iraqi officer to defect, was detained on suspicion of war crimes in Denmark, where he sought asylum in 1999. He is linked to the 1988 chemical weapons attack on Halabja and led the Iraqi army during the Anfal operations, said to have claimed 182,000 civilian lives. (www.kurdishmedia.com)

Iraq expelled CNN Baghdad bureau chief **Jane Arraf** and correspondents **Nic Robertson** and **Rym Brahimi**, plus ABC News' **David Wright** and NBC's **Ned Colt**, apparently in response to their reports on a public protest by the families of political prisoners left out of a recent mass amnesty. (AP, CNN)

Supported in part by UNICEF, Salahadeen University in the Iraqi Kurdish-controlled city of Irbil is producing a pictorial sign language dictionary in Kurdish for the deaf and mute. It will be rendered in the main southern Kurdish dialects of Sorani and Bahdine, Arabic and English. (www.kurdishmedia.com)

Saddam Hussein's son **Uday Hussein** was forced to change email addresses after Yahoo closed his email account at the behest of the US Treasury Department, according to a report in Uday's own paper, *Babel*. The paper said the account was cancelled although the newspaper had paid for it. (WorldNetDaily)

IRELAND

Irish justice minister Michael McDowell announced the establishment of an expert group to examine and report on possible changes in libel law; a press council, including statutory press regulation, and other reforms. The expert group is to report by the end of the year. (www.indexonline.org)

Ireland took the UK to a special tribunal in The Hague on 21 October, demanding the release of two private reports on the Sellafield nuclear reprocessing plant in northwest England. Dublin says the reports will substantiate its case for the plant's closure, which it links to pollution in the Irish Sea. (*Guardian*)

ISRAEL

Israel released Reuters TV soundman **Youssry al-Jamal** on October 9 after detaining him without charge since 30 April. **Kamel Jbeil**, a journalist with the Palestinian newspaper *al-Quds*, was released on 15 September after being held without charge since 18 April. At least one journalist remained in Israeli custody, **Hussam Abu Alan**, a Hebron-based photographer with Agence France-Presse, detained on 24 April in Hebron. All three were accused by Israeli officials of having contacts with militant groups. They provided no details to support their allegations. (CPJ)

In its 2002 annual report, Reporters Sans Frontières put the Palestinian Authority ahead of Israel in a 'league table' of the relative freedom of the press in the world's countries. The Authority

came in at number 82, and Israel was placed at 92. (RSF)

Recent Publications: *Shielded from Scrutiny: IDF violence in Jenin and Nablus* by Amnesty International, November 2002.

ITALY

Former prime minister Giulio Andreotti was jailed for 24 years on 17 November for conspiring with Mafia assassins to murder journalist **Mino Pecorelli** in 1979. It has been claimed that Pecorelli planned to publish damaging revelations about the 1978 murder of Andreotti's party chairman, Aldo Moro. (CPJ, RSF)

Twenty anti-globalisation activists from self-proclaimed non-violent groups were arrested on 15 November in midnight raids across Italy and charged with 'subversive association'. 'With these arrests they want to show us that even campaigning is going to be dangerous,' said film-maker Luca Bigazzi. (Indymedia)

State-owned RAI TV (*Index* 3/02) banned an edition of the satirical show *Blob* dedicated to Italian Prime Minister Silvio Berlusconi, solely comprising video clips of his public mannerisms aired without comment. RAI 3 director-general Agostino Saccà said too much focus on one person was 'not good satire'. (*La Repubblica*)

Italy's Constitutional Court ordered the terrestrial TV station Rete 4, owned by Silvio Berlusconi's Mediaset company (*Index* 3/01), to surrender its licence by end

PUBLIC, ORDER, ISSUES
FRANCESCO CARUSO

A million people demonstrated in Florence in November for democracy, justice and dignity, values that seem pretty meaningless from behind the bars of this cell. How can we even talk about democracy, justice and dignity in a country that persecutes political dissidents?

If the charges proposed in Cosenza hold, every activist in the movement could be pursued as a dangerous and violent subversive. The implications are absurdly obvious.

But behind the ambiguous and inconsistent nature of the actual charges hides a clumsy attempt to reduce the richness and vitality of the movement of movements to the status of simple public order problem. Within the political and cultural establishment, there is a tendency to see social movements as dangerous viruses to be nipped in the bud in order to preserve order and discipline and the elites' own power.

With the rise of the movement, certain sections of the Italian policing and judicial systems, inspired by fear of activism and its potential to transform the status quo, have abandoned their nominal impartiality for obsessive political persecution, culminating in the violence of Genoa 2001 and in the murder of Carlo Giuliani.

And now we have the absurd Cosenza investigation, headed, once again, by the ROS [the Special Operative Division of the Carabinieri], supported this time by a few overzealous magistrates they've managed to dig up in the deepest South.

These magistrates' dream is to deal with the movement, with these 'noisy, troublesome' young people, on their own, using their own methods and strategies of systematic repression. As far as they're concerned, there is no need to investigate whether the anti-globalisation movement harbours criminal and violent activity: it just does.

And yet, in fact, you have to go right back to the fascist era in order to find anyone else on trial for what we're accused of! Or even beyond that, to the nineteenth-century Carbonari! If anyone seriously wants to compare our social and political engagement with that of our anti-fascist grandfathers or our Romantic ancestors, they flatter us.

What they don't realise is they're wasting their time. They'll lose this battle and the next. Because we are not an army of stragglers, but of dreamers.

(Signed) Francesco Caruso, Mammagialla, Viterbo, Italy, Europe, 25 November 2002, second year of the Permanent Global War ❏

Excerpted from a letter to the No Global Network in Naples from **Francesco Caruso***, one of 22 anti-globalisation protestors arrested in Cosenza on 15 November. He wrote the letter from prison*

2003. The broadcast rights will be given to another independent station in line with recent rulings to limit Berlusconi's grip on Italian media. (www.corriere.it)

Following an 11 December appeal by journalists at the *Corriere Della Sera*, the country's biggest-selling daily, for action to protect editorial independence at the paper, the International Federation of Journalists warned that corporate changes may give Prime Minister Silvio Berlusconi and his media empire new and unwanted influence over the newspaper. (IFJ)

An Italian 'anti-capitalist group' calling itself the Five Cs (Cell against Capitalism, Prisons, their Jailers and their Prison Cells) has been blamed for a series of parcel bomb attacks. The first was on the *El País* newspaper office in Barcelona, then the Rome and Milan offices of the Spanish airline **Iberia** on 13 December and, on 16 December, the Rome offices of the Italian national broadcaster **RAI**, the only bomb to explode before it could be defused. No one was hurt. (RSF, *La Repubblica*)

JORDAN

Jordan protested to Qatar after a guest on Doha-based al-Jazeera satellite TV said Jordan was a 'historic traitor' to the Palestinian cause. But when a Jordanian paper replied with a disparaging article about Qatar, its senior editors **Sakher Abu Anza** and **Ma'mun Russan** were charged with slander. (MEI)

Jordanian engineers union boss **Ali Abu Sukkar** was arrested for a third time on 8 October for publishing leaflets opposed to normalisation with Israel. Prime Minister Ali Abu Ragheb has repeatedly urged the unions to stay away from political activity and to dedicate themselves to 'union work'. (AFP)

KAZAKHSTAN

Journalist **Sergei Duganov**, author of an online critique of the policies of Kazakh President Nursultan Nazarbayev, was attacked on 28 August. He had been arrested on 9 July and charged with 'insulting the honour and dignity of the President', and though freed, the charge remains open against him. (HRW, RSF)

The Kazakhstan National Security Ministry reported that the newly launched dissident **Radio DAT** – which describes itself as 'the voice of democratic forces in Kazakhstan' – was not broadcasting on short wave from the west, as first thought, but from an unnamed town in the Russian Federation. (RFE/RL)

On 4 September, three top ministers and the chairman of Kazakhstan's National Security Committee met with the heads of the independent media to respond to recent attacks on journalists (*Index* 3/02). In reply, they accused the press of distortion, unverified errors and ascribing political motives to simple crimes. (RFE/RL)

On 18 September, editor **Saghynghaliy Khafizov** of the *Altyn ghazyr* was found not guilty of insulting President Nursultan Nazarbaev. Earlier this year, Khafizov rejected a presidential award arguing he could not accept an award from someone 'who is culpable of taking bribes'. (RFE/RL)

The *Ekonomika Finansy Rynki* continued to face official harassment. On 10 October, the paper reported that court bailiffs seized all copies of the paper at its printworks under the terms of a 12 August conviction of former editor **Askar Darimbet**. The paper is already banned from sale in public kiosks. (CJES)

KENYA

State-controlled Kenya Broadcasting Corporation (KBC) was censured by the Electoral Commission of Kenya and the Kenya Domestic Observation Programme, whose chairman, Archbishop John Njenga, said KBC was denying Kenyans a chance to make informed decisions on which candidate to support. (*East African Standard*)

Journalist **Ekuwam Adou** of *The Nation* was stabbed at a KANU Party parliamentary candidates selection meeting in September. The attack was linked to a *Nation* report that the official supervising the vote was an associate of incumbent MP Charfano Guyo Mokku. Mokku subsequently lost the candidacy. (*The Nation*)

KOSOVO

A package containing a large Russian-made grenade was delivered to the Zurich office of the Kosovo Albanian-language newspaper *Bota Sot* on 27 September. The grenade failed to detonate when the package was opened. One of the newspaper's reporters, **Bekim Kastrati**, was murdered in Kosovo in 2001 (*Index* 1/02). (RSF)

KUWAIT

On 3 November, Kuwait ordered the closure of the local offices of **al-Jazeera**, claiming a 'lack of professionalism and neutrality when dealing with Kuwaiti issues' on the part of the satellite TV station (*Index* 2/02). It was not clear at the time whether the ban was temporary or permanent. (BBC Online)

The first phase of Iraq's handover to Kuwait of documents looted during the 1990–91 occupation of the emirate was completed on 29 October. (AFP)

KYRGYZSTAN

An **independent media trade union** was set up in Kyrgyzstan on 21 September with a starting membership of 167 journalists from across the country. Two days later, as President Askar Akaev met George W Bush, Human Rights Watch urged the US to press for human rights in Kyrgyzstan, a key US ally in the region. (CJES, HRW)

Samidin Stambekov, editor of *Akyikat*, the official daily of the Dzhalal-Abad regional administration, ordered his staff on 8 October not to join the new independent union over the paper's officially recognised Cultural Workers Trade Union. Several staff were reported to have defied the order. (CJES)

On 28 September, a journalist from Osh, whose name was withheld for his own protection, suffered two broken ribs when he was detained and beaten at a customs post between Kyrgyzstan and Uzbekistan. He was returning home from attending a conference organised by the OSCE and the Open Society Institute. (CJES)

LEBANON

State security officers forcibly closed down the private **Murr TV** channel and **Mount Lebanon Radio Station** on 4 September. A Beirut court order ruled that Murr TV had broken election broadcast rules. Both stations are owned by MP **Gabriel Murr**, a critic of Syrian influence in Lebanon. (CPJ)

Gedeon Kouts, a journalist with dual French-Israeli citizenship, was barred from reporting the 9th Francophonie summit in Beirut after Lebanese journalists claimed that he was a reporter for Israeli Channel 2 news. He had accredited to the conference as a reporter with a French Jewish community newspaper. (UPI)

LIBERIA

Hassan Bility, editor of the privately owned weekly *The Analyst* (*Index* 3/02), was freed in November from four months' detention incommunicado. However, the release order came on the strict condition that he and other released prisoners of conscience would be rearrested 'in the event of any [unspecified] violations'. (CPJ, RSF)

LIBYA

On 30 August, 65 political prisoners were reported as having been released ahead of Moammer Qaddafi's 33rd anniversary as national leader. The authorities said they had been members of secular opposition movements such as communists and 'defenders of political pluralism' but had 'now repented'. (BBC)

On 26 October, Libya closed its airports and cut international phone links with the outside world for a 'Day of Mourning' to mark crimes committed by Italian colonial forces between 1911 and 1943. Italy says it settled its obligations in a one-off payment of $6.7 million in 1956 and a 1998 peace accord. (BBC Online)

MACEDONIA

Two days after Interior Minister Ljube Boshkovski (*Index* 3/02) warned the independent media against defaming the government, he brought criminal libel charges against **Marjan Djurovski** of the weekly *Start*, who allegedly claimed that the government planned to start a war to delay 15 September parliamentary polls. (CPJ, IWPR)

MALAWI

On 21 August, senior *Malawi News* reporter **Bright Sonani** (*Index* 6/98) was assaulted by three unidentified men who accused him of criticising the government. The ruling United Democratic Front is widely alleged to be plotting to 'deal' with investigative reporters, despite the party's strong denials. (MISA)

The editor of the *Malawi Standard* **Brian Ligomeka** received death threats after publishing two articles in November about deputy parliament speaker Beston Majoni and National Democratic Alliance leader Brown Mpinganjira, entitled 'Deputy Speaker in Sex Scandal' and 'Mpinganjira Diverts Donor Funds'. (www.allAfrica.com)

MALDIVES

Activist and former MP **Mohamed Nasheed** (*Index* 2/02, 3/02, 4/02), jailed for the supposed theft of state property, was released on 29 August. He is a leading figure in a campaign to found an opposition political party in the Maldives and make the government accountable to the public. (www.maldives-culture.com)

MAURITANIA

The 19 August edition of the Nouakchott daily *al-Qalem* (*Index* 4/02) was banned without official explanation. Editor-in-chief **Riadh Ould Mohamed Elhadi** said the government's action may have been related to an article that criticised political Islam. (IPI)

MOLDOVA

Supporters of **Sergiu Afanasiu**, editor of the investigative weekly *Accente,* say the state has falsely charged him with blackmail in a bid to silence his paper. The government say he demanded $1,500 to drop a story about a businessman. The paper was immediately banned after his arrest on 9 October. (RFE/RL)

A law supposed to turn state Teleradio Moldova into a 'national public institution' went into effect in August, despite the opposition's insistence that the law disregarded Council of Europe guidelines on media independence (*Index* 4/02). All staff will be dismissed and must reapply for their old jobs. (RFE/RL)

MOROCCO

On 30 August, King Mohammed VI announced plans to end a state monopoly on broadcasting, the first Maghrebi nation to consider private TV and radio licensing. According to the proposals, an audiovisual commission will be responsible for the granting of licences to potential broadcasters. (*El País*)

Managing editor **Ali Amar** and reporter **Mouaad Rhandy** of the weekly *Journal Hebdomadaire* (*Index* 3/01), were detained on 13 October at the border with the Spanish enclave of Ceuta. Security services quizzed them for three hours about their report on the management of a company named in a parliamentary investigation. (RSF)

MOZAMBIQUE

Mozambique's judicial authorities say they will question Nymphine Chissano, son of President Joaquim Chissano, as part of their investigation into the murder of journalist **Carlos Cardoso**, Mozambique's leading investigative reporter, assassinated in November 2000 (*Index* 4/01, 3/01, 2/01). (RSF)

NAMIBIA

On 30 September, Prime Minister Sam Nujoma ordered state NBC TV to stop broadcasting imported programmes, believing them to be corrupting the country's youth. US soap operas were replaced with reruns of coverage of Nujoma's party congress, local documentaries and news programming. (BBC)

NEPAL

Between 4 and 5 November editor **Ishwor Chandra Gyawali** and office worker **Manarishi Dhital** of the pro-Maoist monthly *Dishabodh,* plus typist **Ram Bhakta Maharjan**, reporter **Deepak Sapkota**, assistant **Dipendra Rokaya** and photographer **Dhana Bahadur Thapa Magar**, all of *Janadesh*, and editor **Mina Sharma** of the monthly *Aikyabaddata,* were all released from Kathmandu's central prison. All seven were detained for between six months and a year on suspicion of supporting the Maoist guerrilla insurrection. Sharma was allegedly beaten during interrogation. (RSF)

Tikaram Rai, editor of the Nepali-language daily *Aparahana,* was arrested in Kathmandu on 12 November after a complaint by a senior police officer accused of bribery in his newspaper. (CPJ)

On 17 November, journalists, human rights activists and lawyers founded a 13-member Press Freedom Grand Jury Nepal under the leadership of International Press Institute Nepal national committee chairperson **Puskar Lal Shrestha**. The jury will provide legal assistance to victimised journalists. (*Nepal News*)

NEW ZEALAND

The government has tabled a bill to require telecoms firms to help security agencies snoop on email and bug mobile phone calls. Green MP Keith Locke said the bill, and an amendment allowing police to hack into computers and intercept email, meant his party was unlikely to support it. (*New Zealand Herald*)

Censors at New Zealand's Office of Film and Literature Classification have been given $500 a year to spend on activities such as piano lessons or aerobics to ease the stress of dealing with the 'psychological pollution' caused by their work. Staff are also entitled to counselling sessions. (*Dominion Post*)

NICARAGUA

A proposal before Nicaragua's Congress aims to increase the penalty for offending government agencies or the president to five years in jail from a current maximum of four years. Criminal insult laws have been repealed in Argentina, Costa Rica and Paraguay in line with free speech conventions. (IAPA)

NIGER

Elhadji Bagnou Bonkoukou, 75-year-old president of the Niger Human Rights League (LNDH), was arrested on 14 August and held for nearly a month before being charge with disseminating 'false news'. He had been interviewed on local radio stations and the BBC, and cast doubts on the official death tolls given for clashes between army mutineers and forces loyal to the government. (A19)

NIGERIA

On 15 November, a bomber targeted the *National Pilot* newspaper in the regional capital of Ilorin, severely injuring five people. Publisher **Bukola Saraki** accuses state governor Mohammed Lawal of involvement in the attack and has called on President Olusegun Obasanjo to order an inquiry. (www.allAfrica.com)

Fashion journalist **Isioma Daniel** of the newspaper *This Day*, whose 16 November article on the Miss World pageant sparked deadly riots across the country, sought refuge in the US after Islamic authorities and local officials in the northern state of Zamfara endorsed a call for her murder, despite a retraction and several front-page apologies for Daniel's article, which suggested that the Prophet Muhammad would have approved of the botched beauty pageant. The federal government promised to punish the paper and detained editor **Simon Kolawole**, editor of *This Day*'s Saturday edition, for questioning. Zamfara was one of the first Nigerian states to adopt Islamic law, or sharia, in January 2000. At least 11 more of Nigeria's 36 states have followed suit, heightening tensions in the nominally secular federal republic, which is divided between a predominantly Muslim north and a mostly Christian south. (CPJ)

Recent Publications: *Nigeria – The Niger Delta: No Democratic Dividend* by Human Rights Watch, report Vol. 14, No. 7 (A), October 2002.

PAKISTAN

Amir Mateen, Islamabad correspondent for *The News* daily, was cornered by security services in September after speculating that the military planned to rig the 10 October general election. Mateen said that the agents told him that, with his heart condition, he would 'not be able to bear a day's torture'. (RSF)

In the runup to the election, General Pervez Musharraf barred former premiers **Benazir Bhutto** and **Nawaz Sharif** from taking part (*Index* 4/02) and facilitated self-censorship by the media by strengthening defamation laws, to allow up to three months' jail for 'ridicule, unjust criticism, dislike, contempt or hatred' and fines of up to 50,000 rupees ($850). He also openly and illegally used state resources for campaigning purposes and limited the freedom of movement for political parties to campaign legally in the streets. Despite this, the pro-military Pakistan Muslim League (Quaid-e-Azam) finished well short of a majority, winning only 73 seats, and the Pakistan People's Party (PPP), led by Bhutto from exile, won 62 seats. The balance of power is now held by an alliance of six anti-US and pro-Islamic groups called the Muttahida Majlis-e-Amal, which won 52 seats. (*Dawn, Guardian*, www.heraldelections.com, EU Election Observer Mission to Pakistan)

Shahid Soomro, Kandhkot correspondent for the Hyderabad-based daily *Kawish*, died from a gunshot wound on 20 October. Soomro's articles had allegedly angered the family of provincial assembly member Mir Mehboob Bijarani, whose brother Mohammad Ali was arrested. Another man was sought by police in connection with the killing. (RSF, PPF)

The blasphemy conviction of editor **Zahoor Ansari** and columnist **Ayub Khoso** of the Sindhi daily *Alakh* has been set aside. Both were sentenced to 17 years in prison in November 1999, but the High Court ruled that the original case should not have been heard by an Anti-Terrorism Court (*Index* 1/00). (PPF)

On 2 November, the authorities banned the reprinting of reports from the US-based online *South Asian Tribune*, threatening transgressors with the new penalties for defamation. Launched in July, the bulletin's charges of corruption and rights abuse by the military have been widely picked up by Pakistani media. (RSF)

Recent Publication: *Pakistan: The Tribal Justice System* (AI, August 2002, 40 pp).

PALESTINE

Voice of Palestine radio journalist and presenter **Esam al-Tellawe** was fatally shot in the back of the head, apparently by an Israeli army sniper, as he was reporting on a Palestinian demonstration in Ramallah during the night of 21-22 September. (IFJ, RSF)

Israeli police arrested Mufti of Jerusalem **Ikrema Sabri** on 15 October on charges of incitement to terrorism, citing an interview in which he

reportedly defended suicide bombings. But Sabri's family said he was charged for sermons criticising Israel's ban on men under 40 from praying at the al-Aqsa mosque. (*Ha'aretz*)

Recent Publications: *Erased In A Moment: Suicide Bombing Attacks Against Israeli Civilians* by Human Rights Watch, October 2002.

PERU

On 3 November police arrested Pedro Roberto Villacorta Cotrina, in connection with the murder of US journalist **Todd Smith** of the *Tampa Tribune* in 1989. Villacorta Cotrina is believed to have been a member of the Shining Path guerrillas at the time of Smith's kidnapping and subsequent murder. (IPYS)

On 5 and 6 September, journalist **Nancy Villacorta Pérez** of Radio 10 in Loreto province received death threats after she raised the past terrorism convictions of 17 members of the Unidos por Loreto political party. She had previously been threatened by another group, Arriba Loreto, in July (*Index* 4/02). (IPYS)

On 24 October, about a dozen journalists were assaulted by police with batons and tear gas outside Peru's Congress as they sought to cover the meeting of Mauricio Diez Canseco, former National Food Assistance Programme chief and MP Jorge Del Castillo, whom he had earlier challenged to a fist fight. (IPYS)

POLAND

Polish authorities have brought 12 criminal lawsuits against *Rzeczpospolita* newspaper in what one expert said was a bid to bring the paper under the influence of the ruling party. Three members of the paper's board were deprived of their passports for four months and put under police surveillance (*Index* 3/02). (WAN)

Catholic primate Cardinal Josef Glemp ordered popular Church-run Radio Maryja station to close its operations. The station, the fifth most popular in Poland, owns a national newspaper and its director, Fr Tadeusz Rydzyk, has been accused of using both for political purposes and for fomenting prejudice. (*The Tablet*)

Still resisting Church criticism, Radio Maryja applied to Polish media regulators in December for a licence to launch a satellite television channel called Trwam ('I abide'). The application specifies that Trwam is to be a commercial station and, in contrast to Radio Maryja, will air advertisements. (RFE/RL)

PORTUGAL

A Portuguese court charged journalist **José Luis Manso Preto** of the weekly *Expresso* with 'refusing to obey the law', after he refused to reveal his sources in his paper's exposé of drug smuggling to Portugal from Morocco. (RSF)

ROMANIA

Romania plans to amend a draft law governing the country's Rompres National News Agency that would give prosecutors the authority to order journalists to disclose their sources without reference to the courts and the need to demonstrate an overriding public interest in making such orders. (A19)

RUSSIA

One journalist has disappeared, another been murdered and six more beaten in a wave of violence against journalists in the Russian region of Penza, 700 km south-east of Moscow. **Igor Salikov**, head of security at the newspaper *Moskovsky Komsomolets v Penze* (*Index* 3/02) in the town of Arbekov, was shot dead on 20 September. **Yuri Frolov**, deputy head of the paper's printers, also received death threats, but after telling friends he disappeared and has not been seen since. The paper had run several articles criticising Penza's mayor, Alexander Kalashnikov. Thugs also beat up **Anton Sharonov**, editor of the Communist opposition newspaper *Lyubimyi Gorod* on 11 September, along with colleagues **Denis Abramov**, **Natalia Sisova** and **Nadezhda Gorshkova**. The paper is a frequent critic of Penza governor Grigorii Bochkarev and his government. *Pensenskaya Pravda* crime reporter **Victor Shamayev** was kidnapped on 14 September and beaten up by unknown attackers who warned him to leave town. His colleague, **Alexander Kizlov**, was similarly assaulted nine days later. (RSF, BBC)

Soviet activist **Tatyana M Velikanova**, a key editor of

the samizdat *Chronicle of Current Events* human rights bulletin died of cancer on 19 September. Arrested in 1979 on charges of 'anti-Soviet propaganda' she spent four years in a prison camp before being exiled to Kazakhstan. (www.indexonline.org)

Russia refused a visa to the **Dalai Lama** in August, dashing his hopes of visiting the federation's three Buddhist republics in 2002. Officials cited the tour's possible 'political orientation' and the need to 'take account of the position of China'. More than one million Buddhists live in the three republics. The Dali Lama last visited Russia in 1992. (*Times of India*)

In November President Vladimir Putin vetoed legislation that would have sharply restricted independent media coverage of terrorism issues, but failed to reverse the downward trend in media rights in Russia. The catalyst was a special forces raid on a Moscow theatre held by Chechen rebels in October. All 41 hostage takers were killed – and more than 125 hostages, most by a narcotic gas used to knock out the rebels. During the 23–26 October siege, information minister Mikhail Lesin clamped down on the media, threatening to shut down the radio station Moscow Echo's website after it posted an interview with the kidnappers. After the disastrous raid the offices of the weekly *Versia* were searched by FSB secret police on 2 November, the day before it ran an article on the bungled rescue bid. **Irek Murtazin**, head of state regional broadcaster Tatarstan

TV says Moscow forced his resignation after he hosted a 24 October talk show on the crisis which included comments from participants calling for an end to the war in Chechnya and criticising Moscow strategy. Questions on how the heavily armed rebels were able to stage the operation unhindered by state security have gone unanswered. Criticism of the conduct of the operation, particularly the apparent misuse of the gas, has been stifled and calls for an independent parliamentary investigation rejected. The vetoed legislation would have prohibited reports adjudged to hinder counter-terrorist operations and banned the broadcast or publication of rebel statements or extremist 'propaganda'. The vague language of the bill could have been used to shut down media that annoyed the authorities, especially in advance of parliamentary elections in 2003 and presidential elections in 2004. Putin's administration has been directly or indirectly responsible for a broad range of abuses, including the selective use of tax audits, prosecutions and police raids to stifle independent media. Disputes over commercial debt and shareholders' rights have masked a wholesale takeover of private media seen as critical of Putin and the war in Chechnya. Security forces are stealthily amassing control over information and widespread violence against journalists continued in the face of general indifference from the police, particularly outside Russia. Changes in the system of state subsidy have reinforced the Kremlin's grip on the broadcast sector and the hands-on power of minister

Lesin. (RFE/RL, www.index online.org)

A government directive signed on 11 October is being used to keep foreign journalists out of Chechnya. Its list of territories and establishments that require special permission to visit includes 'zones where anti-terrorist operations are being conducted'. (CJES)

Moscow spokesman Sergei Yastrzhembsky described the death of British TV journalist **Roddy Scott** on 25 September in a clash between Russian military and rebels on the Chechen border as 'regrettable' but also as 'evidence of the dangers of the region'. Calls for an investigation into the true circumstances of his death have been rebuffed. (UPI, CPJ)

On 20 November, Russian security seized four videotapes from **Hans-Wilhelm Steinfeld**, Moscow correspondent for the Norwegian public TV station NRK, who was working on a report about Chechen refugees. The film was returned, but two cassettes were partly erased. (RFR/RL)

Recent Publications: *Recommendations to the Russian Federation Government* by Amnesty International, October 2002; *Conscription Through Detention In Russia's Armed Forces* by Human Rights Watch, report Vol. 14, No. 8 (D), November 2002.

SAUDI ARABIA

On 25 October, it was reported that an edition of the London-based newspaper *al-Hayat* was banned because it printed an open letter from 67 American intellectuals defending the US campaign against terrorism and calling on Saudi intellectuals to denounce 'militant jihadism' as un-Islamic. (*Washington Post*)

SERBIA

NATO Assistant Secretary General Edgar Buckley defended the April 1999 attack on Radio TV Serbia in a 7 October meeting with Reporters Sans Frontières. 'The RTS building was chosen solely for military reasons,' he said, adding, 'a NATO military target is not necessarily a target of a military nature'. (RSF)

SOMALIA

Officials in the self-declared autonomous region of Puntland sought to ban two journalists from reporting for the BBC Somali service on 19 August. The two, **Ahmad Muhammad Kismayo** and **Muhammad Khalif Gir**, rejected official claims that they 'have not been and are not objective'. (IRIN)

Somali journalists went on strike on 1 October to protest the country's new media law drafted by President Abdulkassim Salat Hassan's transitional government. The new media bill was reportedly passed without MPs being given a copy of the document to study before debating or voting on the bill. (IRIN)

SOUTH AFRICA

In the early hours of 20 October, at least five intruders, one armed with a pistol, broke into the offices of the **South African Press Association** (SAPA) and stole equipment. The cost of the damage is reported to be in the region of $19,300. (MISA)

Draft amendments to broadcasting laws could legally require that South African Broadcasting Corporation (SABC) news be accurate, accountable and fairly reported and that its staff should act in SABC's best interests. The bill would also enhance state powers to pick SABC management board members. (A19)

On 27 September, the *Mail & Guardian* scored a key victory in a defamation suit filed by housing minister Sankie Mthembi-Mahanyele (*Index* 1/02). It was argued that since parliamentary privilege protected ministers from defamation actions, they had not legal right to sue over comments relating to their official duties. (MISA)

SOUTH KOREA

On 21 August, the Seoul city council cancelled a public award ceremony for an essay-writing competition when it was realised that winner **Xu Bo** was an exiled Chinese dissident and vocal critic of the Beijing government, one of South Korea's largest trading partners. Xu was handed his prize in private. (AP)

SPAIN

A law introduced on 12 October obliges Spanish website operators and internet service providers to sever access to any foreign-hosted site that the authorities deem threatening to public order, national defence or consumer rights in Spain. (www.dfn. org)

TOWARDS A TOTALITARIAN PEACE?
UNIVERSITY TEACHERS FOR HUMAN RIGHTS (JAFFNA)

We [in Sri Lanka] are today the dubious beneficiaries of a technocratic approach to peace that dandles the community with pledges of development. The process relies on selective memory, doctored history and myths to entrench a force (the Liberation Tigers of Tamil Eelam, or LTTE) that would inevitably impose further tragedy on the [Tamil] people. While the conflict was being neglected for decades, politicians in the South . . . proved singularly inept in building a national consensus founded on broader principles and values. Manipulation has become the substitute for courage to face up to the darker side of recent history, which governs today's political outlook.

However, the people of this country know well that there can be no decent future, until this conflict is behind us. They are also eminently capable of rising up to the call for truth and reconciliation. But whether the politicians who have invested and thriven on lies and manipulation can face this challenge remains in question. The same applies to leaders of the militant groups, especially the LTTE, which invested in a cult of the leader underpinned by terror.

The challenge is before the people and civil society organisations to make those seeking power face up to their past, irrespective of whether they are prepared. The [present] demand for institutions and structures is essential, but they would have little value if the overarching values and culture remain moribund . . .

Hence, it is not sufficient to demand monitoring mechanisms and programmes to instil respect for human rights as an integral part of the peace process. But we must also develop the ability to monitor and coordinate campaigns to expose violations and the hidden agendas of the various actors. We are faced with today the government's cynical attitudes to child conscription and abduction (by the LTTE) in the north–east, and its manipulative approach to law enforcement.

No less cynical and dangerous are its moves to appropriate opposition members in parliament. This is not being done by appealing to principles or programmes, but rather to individual greed and insecurity. The confusion along with the failure to act with decision on these concerns is an indictment on a civil society that has shown itself weak and ineffective.

False notions of development and peace in the absence of a qualitative shift in political and social mores may in the short term lead to complacent hope, but would in reality entrench a dangerously authoritarian and volatile political future. ❑

Excerpted from the October report, In the Shadows of Sattahip: The Many Faces of Peace, *by the Tamil human rights organisation UTHR-J, published following the first round of peace talks in Sattahip, Thailand in September*

SRI LANKA

After opening talks between the government and the Liberation Tigers of Tamil Eelam in Thailand in September, the National Peace Council and the Peace Support Group urged both sides not to remain silent on human rights, political pluralism and efforts to protect these rights in the country's north and east. (NPC, PSG)

Paul Harris of the *Daily Telegraph* of London and *Jane's Intelligence Review* was forced to leave Sri Lanka on 8 November after the government refused him a new work visa. Harris had critically reported the Norwegian-facilitated peace process and had contacts with the opposition People's Alliance Party. (RSF, AP)

Journalist **Uvidu Kurukulasuriya** of the *Ravaya* newspaper was arrested and charged with obstruction when he stopped to investigate the beating of two men on his way home. After he tried to note the ID numbers of the officers, he announced himself as a journalist and was arrested. (AHRC)

Sri Lankan officials sought to establish whether the LTTE was involved in the making of **Rajesh Touchriver's** debut film *In the Name of Buddha*, premiered in Oslo on 17 November. Others asked if the film, about a Tamil boy forced to seek refuge in Britain, could be deemed blasphemous. (*Lanka Academic, Sunday Leader*)

Recent Publications: *The Meaning of 'People's Action' and the Consequences of Prolonged Negotiations — Information*

Bulletin No. 29 by University Teachers for Human Rights, Jaffna (UTHR (J), 26 October 2002); *In the Shadows of Sattahip: The Many Faces of Peace* by University Teachers For Human Rights (Jaffna) (UTHR (J), 4 October 2002, 47 pp).

SUDAN

Journalist **Faisal el-Bagir** of the Sudan Organisation Against Torture was detained for five hours in Khartoum on 7 October. He had not long returned from Dakar, where he attended the annual meeting of members of the International Freedom of Expression Exchange (IFEX) network. (IPI)

Editor **Sidahmed Khalifa** and his journalist son **Adil**, of the daily *el-Watan*, were arrested for questioning on 19 November after publicly condemning the seizure of his paper and two others, *al-Sahafa* and *al-Horriya*. The papers reported clashes between students and police despite state security orders not to do so. (CPJ)

Columnist **Osman Merghani** of the daily *al-Rai al-Aam* was detained for questioning after he appeared on a debate on al-Jazeera satellite on 2 September and reportedly criticised Sudanese government handling of peace talks with southern rebel groups. (CPJ)

SWAZILAND

The country saw its first political protest for ten years on 30 September when protestors from the **Swaziland Democratic Alliance** petitioned the offices of Prime Minister Sibusiso Dlamini, calling for the King to promote a new democratic constitution. (*Mail & Guardian*)

On 9 October, police raided private Channel S TV and seized a recording of a September sermon by pastor **Justice Dlamini** of the Swaziland Association of Christian Ministries that suggested that Incwala, the annual festival celebrating the King, could be considered ungodly. (MISA)

SYRIA

Haytham al-Maleh, head of the Human Rights Association of Syria, fled to Jordan in late August to escape arrest over the publication of the magazine *Tayyarat* (*Currents*). It was reported that all the contributors to the first issue, published in Beirut in August, had been held for questioning. (MEI)

TAJIKISTAN

Akram Azivov, Nasim Rahimov and **Yusuf Yunusuv** of SMI TV, were arrested at a training course on 28 October in Khujand, northern Tajikistan, and accused of evading conscription. Army officers had threatened SMI TV boss **Mahmujan Dadabayev** with death and his station with closure on 5 November. (RFE/RL)

On 28 August, the Tajik government granted the independent news agency **Asia-Plus** (*Index* 4/02) a radio licence to broadcast in the capital. It reversed an April refusal on the grounds that the capital 'only needed one radio station'. Two other new stations, Asia FM and Vatan, also benefited from the decision. (IRIN, RFE/RL)

TANZANIA

Tanzanian officials issued a four-page statement on 20 August condemning 'unethical media practices', threatening to punish tabloids that publish material deemed pornographic or sensationalist photos of the dead. Nine weeklies and three tabloids were banned or suspended in July for such offences. (MISA)

THAILAND

Thailand's leading newspapers and media associations called on the government to abolish the 1941 Printing Act, which gives authorities the power to shut down publications considered 'detrimental to national security', without a court order. The law has already been ruled unconstitutional. (SEAPA)

TOGO

Publisher **Julien Ayi** of *Nouvel Echo* was jailed on 13 September for four months for 'attacking the honour' of President Gnassingbé Eyadéma by alleging that he had a personal fortune of $4.5 billion (*Index* 4/02). Editor **Alphonse Névamé Klu**, who went into hiding after the case, was sentenced to six months in absentia. (RSF)

TUNISIA

On 23 August, **Abdallah Zouari** (*Index* 4/02), formerly of the banned weekly *al-Fajr*, was jailed for failing to obey a court order banishing

him to the south of the country applied after he was freed from an 11-year sentence for 'membership of illegal organisations'. He was released pending appeal on 6 November. (RSF)

Communist Workers' Party leader **Hamma Hammami** and colleagues **Samir Taamallah**, **Abdeljabbar Madouri** and **Ammar Amroussia** were conditionally released on 4–5 November on humanitarian grounds. They were jailed in February 2002 (*Index* 2/02) for membership of banned groups and 'inciting rebellion'. (BBC, OMCT)

Rights groups raised concerns for the health of jailed online journalist **Zouhair Yahyaoui** (*Index* 4/02). Known to have a kidney problem, Yahyaoui was on hunger strike and refused the medication offered because he could not identify the medicine. On 13 September, he was reportedly transferred to hospital. (PEN)

TURKEY

Journalist **Emin Karaca** and editor **Mehmet Emin Sert** of *Türkiye'de ve Avrupa'da Yazi* magazine went on trial on 26 November on charges of insulting the military in articles marking the 30th anniversary of the murder of three leftist youth leaders and the army's role in the killings. A warrant has been issued for the arrest of a third writer, **Dogan Ozgüden**, chief editor of the Info-Türk news agency, exiled to Belgium since the 1971 Turkish military coup. (RSF)

Writer **Ahmet Altan** (*Index* 1/97, 2/01) and weekly *Aktuel* magazine's director **Murat Tunali** (*Index* 2/01) were acquitted of writing and publishing four articles that insulted the military. The articles were published in the 22–28 July 2000 and 22 February 2001 editions of *Aktuel*. (BIA)

On 7 October, Istanbul state security court started to hear the case of publisher **Sanar Yurdatapan** (*Index* 3/02, 1/02, 4/01, 2/99, 5/98, 3/97) and **Yilmaz Çamlibel** in connection with the booklet *Freedom of Thought – 2001*. They are charged with publishing material declared a crime by law and holding publishers responsible in line with authors and translators. Only two of the 11 people who signed the booklet as publishers, including US writer **Noam Chomsky** and Turkish human rights activist and lawyer **Eren Keskin** (*Index* 6/2000), in a deliberate attempt to challenge the court have been prosecuted. On 6 November, the court began separate hearings in the case against the publication's supporters, taking advantage of recent elections in which MPs supporting the book lost their seats and their parliamentary immunity, including ex-MPs **Sacit Günbey**, **Mustafa Yanmaz**, **Mustafa Geçer**, **Mustafa Kamalak**, **Latif Öztek**, **Ali Gören**, **Zeki Ünal**, **Zeki Çelik**, **Yasin Hatipoglu**, **Mehmet Bekâroglu**, **Fethullah Erbas** and **Ali Oguz**. No charges will be brought against MPs who also accredited themselves as publishers of the book but were re-elected. (Info-Türk)

The Supreme Board of Police reported on its handling of rights allegations over the past seven years, saying that 9,174 police officers were investigated on charges of ill treatment and 975 on torture allegations. Between 1 January 1995 and 31 January 2002, 210 police officers were found guilty of ill treatment. Thirty-one officers were found guilty of torture. (NTV)

Later cases included the landmark sentencing of ten police officers in October for the torture of the 'Manisa children' – 16 young people aged 14 to 26 tortured at police headquarters in Manisa, western Turkey, between December 1995 and January 1996. The victims reported being stripped naked, sexually assaulted, hung by the arms and subjected to electric shocks. (AI)

Asiye Güzel Zeybek (Index 1/02), a former editor of a radical newspaper, was sentenced on 6 October to 12 and a half years in prison for involvement in an 'illegal' organisation. Zeybek, who was released in June pending the court decision, remains free pending an appeal. When the sentence was announced, Zeybek was in Sweden to receive the PEN Tucholsky Award for writers who have been persecuted, threatened or are in exile. Zeybek's book on her experiences in prison is reportedly under investigation by security services. (WiPC, Info-Türk)

Turkey's long-awaited regulations allowing broadcasts in Kurdish were unveiled on 20 November. However, TV broadcasts in different regional languages and dialects may not exceed 30 minutes a day and a total of two hours a week. The radio broadcasts in different regional languages and dialects may not exceed 45 minutes a day and a total of four hours a week. (AFP)

Similarly motivated by Turkish desires for a better hearing on its EU membership bid, the Department of Religious Affairs in Turkey gave permission for Muslim imans to use Kurdish in religious activities. (AFP)

Meanwhile, the country's education ministry said it would permit private teaching in Kurdish for 12–18-year-olds only, outside school hours. Students must produce a medical certificate proving that they are neither mentally or physically handicapped and the wearing of 'ethnic' clothing, however defined, is prohibited; rules that the teachers' union in Diyarbakir said rendered Kurdish courses 'simply impossible' in practice. (MHA, www.kurdishmedia.com, Neue Zuricher Zeitung, AFP)

The rector of Dicle University in Diyarbakir dismissed seven students in September for up to a term after they had tried to present petitions for Kurdish as an elective course, but were detained before they could reach the office. (Cumhuriyet, Info-Türk)

Journalist Nevzat Bingol, former owner of Gun TV in Diyarbakir, was convicted and fined the equivalent of $1,700 on 14 October for broadcasting the songs, 'Where is My Mother', 'Happy Birthday', and 'Everyone Mind Their Own Business', by Kurdish singer Ahmet Kaya. On 28 October, police raided a wedding and arrested band member Ismail Ayhan for singing in Kurdish. (www.kurdishmedia.com)

The Turkish authorities are investigating parliamentary candidate Orhan Ekmen from the Republican People's Party. He allegedly used a Kurdish proverb in a speech, thereby 'propagating separatism'. Ekmen said he used the proverb in Kurdish because he could not quickly translate it into Turkish. (Radikal)

The Supervisory Council for Cinema, Video and Music in the justice ministry banned the short film Pardon by Vedat Özdemir, after it won a special prize at Turkey's Golden Orange film festival. The film narrates the problems of a juvenile, detained over a confusion in names. (Cumhuriyet)

The public prosecutor in Eyüp began an investigation into allegations that three unnamed transvestites detained in July on suspicion of breaking into cars had been raped by nine prison staff, witnessed by political prisoners who informed their families. The three have been moved to another prison. (Hürriyet)

Environmentalist Oktay Konyar, famous for his campaign against cyanide pollution by local gold extractors in the town of Bergama, was fined about $1,000 for insulting police officers at a teachers' union event in April. (Cumhuriyet)

Pablo Neruda's poem 'Song to mothers whose sons have died', a tribute to the bereaved of the Spanish Civil War, became the subject of a Turkish State Security Court prosecution in September after it was published in Turkey in a magazine called *Stance on Cultural Living*. The magazine was banned and owner **Muharrem Cengiz** and editor **Ahu Zeynep Gorgun** are now accused of 'spreading terrorist propaganda'. (*Ozgurpolitika*)

Recent Publications: *Turkey: Systematic Torture continues in 2002* (AI, September 2002, 14pp); *Newsline, Issue 19* (Kurdish Human rights Project, Autumn 2002, 16pp); *Displaced and Disregarded: Turkey's Failing Village Return Programme* (Human Rights Watch, 30 October 2002).

UGANDA

President Yoweri Museveni warned radio stations in Uganda they may be banned for putting exiled dissidents on air, including former presidential candidate **Kizza Besigye**. Speaking on independent Radio West he said stations would only be spared if the exiles denounced terrorism and subversion. (*New Vision*)

The daily *Monitor* was raided by police and missed a day's issue on 11 October after journalist **Frank Nyakairu** reported that rebels downed two army helicopters piloted by foreigners, thought to be South African or Russian. The army denies the claim and Nyakairu has since been charged by police. (www.all africa.com)

Some 20 members of the Ugandan rebel Lord's Resistance Army used axes to force their way into the premises of Radio Wa, a Roman Catholic Church-sponsored radio station on 27 September. The LRA forces used grenades to set off a fire that destroyed the whole building, in the northern Ugandan town of Lira. (RSF)

Ugandan minister of information Basoga Nsadhu warned that even jokes made by journalists were recorded as they may make points that warranted investigation. He was speaking at a November seminar titled 'A Legal Balance Between Freedom of Expression, Preservation of Public Order and State Security'. (*Monitor*)

UKRAINE

Mykhailo Kolomiyets, director of the Ukrainski Novyny financial news agency in Kiev was found hanged on 18 November in Belarus. He had gone missing on 21 October. Kolomiyets is the third prominent Ukrainian journalist to die in two years. Murder has not been ruled out by some of his friends. (RSF)

Journalists from across the Ukrainian media plan to create an independent journalists' trade union in response to increasing state pressure. On 5 October the group said it would tackle censorship through negotiation and provide support for journalists who lose their jobs under official pressure. (RFE/RL)

Petro Kobevko, editor-in-chief of the opposition news-paper *Chas* in the western town of Chernivtsi, was beaten up on 14 September. Kobevko said he did not rule out the possibility that the attack was aimed at intimidating the staff of *Chas* in the light of autumn anti-government protests. (RFE/RL)

On 14 September, about 15,000 demonstrators marched in Kiev and tens of thousands of others in public squares around the country in defence of an independent media and in memory of investigative journalist **Georgii Gongadze** (*Index* 2/02, 1/02, 2/01, 1/01) allegedly killed by associates of President Leonid Kuchma. (RFE/RL)

UNITED KINGDOM

Former MI5 agent **David Shayler** (*Index* 2/02, 3/01, 5/00) received a six-month sentence on 5 November for breaking the Official Secrets Act. He was legally denied the right to argue that his leaking of documents regarding alleged British security service malpractice to the British media had been in the public interest. Justice Alan Moses ruled on 7 October that the media would be restricted from reporting parts of the trial relating to sensitive security and intelligence matters. The identities of MI5 agents giving testimony also remained secret. (*Guardian*, BBC)

Four British newspapers called on 12 November for greater rights for financial journalists who want to protect their sources from the government's Financial Services Agency as it investigates criminal manipulation of financial markets. The call followed an attempt by a Belgian brewing conglomerate (*Index* 4/02) to make them hand over copies of a leaked document about a possible takeover bid. (*Guardian*)

An appeal court ruled on 25 September that foreign suspects may be held indefinitely without trial under new anti-terrorism laws. Two days earlier Muslim cleric **Abu Qatada** had been arrested under the act. He is not accused of any crimes in the UK but Spanish and French authorities link him to al-Qaida. (*Guardian*)

On 21 November, Labour peer and human rights lawyer Helena Kennedy said the government had abandoned the rule of law by allowing such detention without trial and warned that British judges were being compelled to make decisions under pressure from outside forces. (*Financial Times*, BBC, *Guardian*)

Journalist **Rod Liddle** stood down as editor of BBC Radio 4's flagship *Today* news programme. In his part-time job as a *Guardian* newspaper columnist he criticised a protest march in London in support of rural issues, which the BBC said was a 'serious error of judgement' that broke its rules on impartiality. (*Guardian*)

The British internet industry told the country's Home Office that it would not voluntarily stockpile records of their customers' web usage for the future use of British security services. Industry representatives said that it was not convinced that it was

truly necessary in the fight against terrorism. (*Guardian*)

Lord Chief Justice Lord Woolf, Britain's top judge, said people who thought the country's two-year-old Human Rights act was 'intrinsically objectionable' were entitled to their view. 'But I am also entitled to freedom of speech and to be candid I find their attitude unacceptable in the 21st century.' (*Guardian*)

Channel 4 TV broadcast the country's first public autopsy in 170 years on 20 November, conducted by German performance anatomist **Gunther von Hagens**. He had been told by Britain's inspector of anatomy that he did not have a licence to carry out postmortems, nor was the venue licensed to hold them. (*Guardian*)

Oxford City Council banned visiting Dutch performance artist **Sonja van Kerkhoff** from reading poetry to drivers waiting at traffic lights in October, after concluding that reading the chosen anti-colonialist works could provoke road users to violence. (*Oxford Mail*)

In November, Manchester University banned a calendar featuring scantily clad female students from being sold in its students' union shop, ruling it 'offensive' – but allowed the sale of a more 'humorous' Students' Union charity calendar featuring naked union staff. (*Manchester Evening News*)

Scots columnist **John MacLeod** was fired after complaints about his published view that child murder

victims Holly Wells and Jessica Chapman would still be alive if their parents had observed the Sabbath. His union voiced concern that a columnist could be fired for views cleared by his editors. (*Observer*)

Afghan asylum seekers **Farid** and **Fariba Ahmadi** were barred by a High Court ruling from returning to the UK to argue their case against deportation and must give testimony via video instead. The court had earlier ruled that their forced extradition from their refuge in a mosque was illegal. (*Telegraph*)

Sudanese citizen **Mende Nazer**, who claimed in a German book that she was kept as a slave in the London home of a Sudanese diplomat, had her request for asylum refused on 17 October. The Home Office said Nazer's allegations, even if true, did not constitute sufficient grounds for asylum. She will appeal. (*Guardian*)

The British Board of Film Classification decided on 22 October to allow the uncut release of the French film *Irreversible*. Critics of the film objected to the inclusion of a nine-minute rape sequence and a depiction of man's head being beaten to a pulp. (*Telegraph*)

Reporters Sans Frontières released a ranked index of countries in terms of press freedom on 23 October, listing the UK behind Hong Kong, Ecuador and Benin. The UK ranked 21, in part due to the slow pace of the investigation into last year's murder of journalist **Martin O'Hagan** in Northern Ireland. (RSF)

A group of Orthodox rabbis called on Chief Rabbi **Dr Jonathan Sacks** to withdraw his book *The Dignity of Difference* on grounds of heresy. Sacks agreed to remove or clarify text in future editions. Controversial phrases included the view that 'no one creed has a monopoly on spiritual truth'. (*Jewish Chronicle*)

An atheist rights campaigner is threatening to take the BBC to court if it refuses to open up a religious opinion spot to non-believers. The former National Secular Society president **Barbara Smoker** claims that the three-minute daily 'Thought for the Day' slot breaches her human rights because it is allocated exclusively to religious contributors. (Ananova)

UNITED STATES

Outgoing UN high commissioner for human rights **Mary Robinson** has warned of the erosion of civil liberties in the US in the name of the war on terror. Speaking before stepping down on 14 September, she cited the 'ripple' effects these new US policies had in less democratic countries. (*New York Times*)

Author and scientist **Haluk Gerger** (*Index* 5/1998, 1/1996, 6/1995, 5/1995, 1/1995) was refused entry into the US on arrival at New York; his 10-year visa was cancelled; he was photographed, fingerprinted and deported on the next flight. A founding member of the Human Rights Association of Turkey and a respected writer on nuclear strategy, his arrest in Turkey in 1994 and 1995 was once cited by the US State Department as an example of how Ankara misused anti-terror laws to violate the free speech rights of writers and academics. (PEN)

Abbas Kiarostami, the Iranian film-maker failed even to get a visa to visit the US at the invitation of the New York Film Festival and lecture at Harvard. Winner of the Palme d'Or at the Cannes Film Festival for his 1997 film *A Taste of Cherry*, he has visited the US at least seven times in the past decade. Officials at the embassy told the festival that they would require at least 90 days to investigate Kiarostami's background. (www.salon.com)

A federal appeals court in Ohio declared the secrecy of immigration hearings since 21 September to be unconstitutional in a ruling in the case of **Rabih Haddad**, an activist charged with overstaying a tourist visa and suspected of links to al-Qaida. (*Herald Tribune*)

Schools across the US are increasing the use of web filters to block websites containing pornography or other material deemed inappropriate for children. But critics say they are inadvertently blocking sites that students use for lessons and research. The schools must comply with the federal Children's Internet Protection Act before they can be eligible for technology grants administered by the federal government. (www.ncac.org)

Harvard University president Lawrence Summers warned on 23 September that 'profoundly anti-Israeli' views were no longer the preserve of the 'poorly educated', but are 'finding support in progressive intellectual communities'. He described anti-Israeli views as 'anti-Semitic in their effect if not in their intent'. (www.ncac.org)

An annual survey by the US First Amendment Center found a further drop in support for the constitutional guarantee, with 49 per cent of respondents believing that it offers too much protection. 'Many Americans view these fundamental freedoms as possible obstacles in the war on terrorism', conceded centre director Ken Paulson. (www.ncac.org)

A federal appeals court upheld a law banning the sale or rental of sexual explicit material on US military bases on 13 September, rejecting a challenge from magazine distributors on the grounds that was, among other things, a violation of First Amendment rights to free speech. A US Defense Department agency decides what products to allow for sale, including *Playboy* and *Celebrity Skin*, but not *Penthouse*, *Hustler* and *Playgirl*. In 1998 it was reported that 12.6 million porn magazines were sold on US bases, making the US government the largest single distributor of pornography in the world. (AP)

Mormons in Arizona have presented a petition to a department store to ask them to stock more 'modest' clothes for teenagers that cover 'the midriff, bust, shoulder, back, legs to the knee and any clothing that shows respect for the body'. (*Arizona Republic*)

Sami al-Haj, a Sudanese TV journalist with Arab satellite channel al-Jazeera, remained in detention at the Guantámano Bay US naval base in Cuba despite appeals by his employers. Sent to cover the US military operation in Afghanistan for the Qatar-based TV station, he was arrested near the Pakistan border in December 2001. (RSF)

The American Library Association marked its 21st annual Banned Books Week by reporting a reduction in the number of complaints about banned publications. The number of times a book was removed from school reading lists or libraries dropped to an estimated 20–25 last year, far below the estimated 200 or higher of the early 1980s, when the ALA started its programme. (ALA)

A 61-year-old man convicted for making obscene comments to a 13-year-old girl has appealed against the judgement, claiming that the Missouri state law under which he was sentenced was an unconstititional restriction on his First Amendment free speech rights. **Charles E Moore** of Springfield was convicted of third-degree sexual misconduct in June 2001. He was given two years' probation and was required to register as a sex offender. (AP)

NASA experts are reportedly trying to develop an airport security screen that will monitor and analyse brain-wave and heartbeat patterns in a bid to identify terrorists. One critic said that flagging anyone who 'goes ballistic after hours of ineptitude and patro-nising contempt from the airline industry' as a terrorist will mean the end of all air traffic. (*IT Register*)

The global sports shoemaker **Nike Inc.** says its free speech rights will be denied if anti-globalisation campaigners are allowed to make use of a California state legal ruling allowing them to sue the company under the state's false advertising laws. The company is appealing to the US Supreme Court to over-rule the ruling that Nike's publicity material in defence of working conditions in its foreign plants broke California's laws against misleading advertising. (AP)

On 8 October, the **American Association of University sity Professors** and nine other groups wrote a letter asking the University of California at San Diego to abandon threats of disciplinary action against the **Che Café Collective** to remove links to a site supporting the Revolutionary Armed Forces of Colombia, which the US government has designated as a terrorist group. (AP)

Recent Publications: *United States — Ignorance Only: HIV/ Aids, Human Rights and Federally Funded Abstinence-Only Programs In The United States* by Human Rights Watch, report Vol. 14, No. 5 (G), October 2002; *'We Are Not The Enemy'. Hate Crimes Against Arabs, Muslims and Those Perceived to be Arab or Muslim after September 11* by Human Rights Watch, report Vol. 14, No. 6 (G), November 2002.

URUGUAY

Journalist **Daniel Cancela** of Canal 10 TV received death threats after his reports on corruption in Uruguayan prisons led to the prosecution of three top officials. Threats were also made against presiding Judge **Pablo Eguren**, investigator **Luisa Scelza** and two prisoners who testified. (PFC/IFEX)

A legislative bill on the right to public information was passed in the Uruguayan lower house of Congress on 8 October. When finally introduced it will allow citizens free access to all government documents and the right to receive and distribute such information. (IAPA)

UZBEKISTAN

On 17 September, **Yuldash Rasulov** of the Human Rights Movement of Uzbekistan was jailed for seven years for disseminating anti-government propaganda and recruiting for the banned Islamist group Hizb ut-Tahrir. The group said the prosecution produced no evidence to substantiate the charges. (RFE/RL, AP)

On 27 October, **Tashpulat Rakhmatullayev**, editor of the banned daily *Samarkand*, warned a conference of Central Asian journalists that true media freedom in the country still needed rule of law, independent courts, private media and opposition parties – despite the nominal abolition of censorship in May. (CJES)

THE VATICAN

Catholic circles denounced the Venice film festival's 8 September award to a drama about homes for 'fallen women' run by Irish nuns. The Vatican newspaper *L'Osservatore Romano* said the film, *The Magdalene Sisters*, by the Scots Catholic director **Peter Mullan**, was an 'angry and rancorous provocation'. (BBC)

VENEZUELA

The Inter American Press Association and the International Press Institute have criticised President Hugo Chávez for encouraging a climate of intimidation towards independent journalists. Attacks on journalists are often the work of groups close to the government (*Index* 3/02). (IAPA, IPI)

The regional Promar TV station in Barquisimeto City was hit by a bomb on 13 September after a series of anonymous threats and attacks on its reporters. Owner **Jorge Kossosky** said he would not pull the news and debate programmes believed to have drawn the attack. No one was injured by the bomb. (IPYS/IFEX)

Speaking at the 16 September opening of a so-called Bolivarian school, restored under army leadership, President Hugo Chávez accused the media of only publishing 'trash, lies, perversion and immoralities'. He said the media had distorted reports on the financing of the Bolivarian school system. (IFJ/IFEX)

VIETNAM

Vietnam issued new rules on 14 October requiring new websites to get state permission to go online. The penal-

ties for breaking them were not divulged. Owners of the country's estimated 4,000 internet cafés are already held responsible for controlling their clients' Web surfing. (CPJ)

On 8 November, Vietnamese cyber-dissident **Le Chi Quang** (*Index* 4/02) was jailed for four years followed by three years' house arrest for 'criticism of the government on the internet'. He had criticised Sino-Vietnamese border agreements between China and Vietnam and praised dissidents **Nguyen Thanh Giang** and **Vu Cao Quan**. (CPJ)

An essay on Sino-Vietnamese border talks was also thought to be behind the rearrest of writer **Nguyen Vu Binh** (*Index* 4/02) on 25 September. In late July, Binh was briefly detained after submitting written testimony to a US Congressional Human Rights Caucus briefing on freedom of expression in Vietnam. (CPJ)

Recent Publications: *Vietnam – a Human Rights review based on the International Covenant on Civil & Political Rights* by Amnesty International, October 2002.

YUGOSLAVIA

The Swedish section of writers' support group PEN awarded one of its Tucholsky awards to Roma poet **Rajko Djuric**, presently living in exile in Berlin. Yugoslavia-born poet Djuric writes on the culture and history of the Roma and its preservation over centuries of displacement and persecution. (PEN Sweden)

A court in the central Serbian city of Kragujevac convicted and fined journalist **Gordana Bozic** for libel on 25 September following a complaint by town mayor Vlatko Rajkovich about her investigation into allegations of criminality in the operation of local youth organisations. (ANEM)

ZAMBIA

On 12 November, the Supreme Court dismissed contempt charges against editor **Arthur Simuchoba** and chief reporter **Chali Nondo** (*Index* 2/01) of the *Monitor* newspaper, but did not rule out later prosecution. The paper had suggested that President Levy Mwanawasa had raised judges' salaries to 'soften them' ahead of a court hearing into alleged malpractice during his December 2001 election campaign. (MISA)

ZIMBABWE

The Zimbabwean government conceded that Section 80 of the Access to Information and Protection of Privacy Act (AIPPA) is unconstitutional and has introduced an amendment bill to the act to close this 'loophole'. The cases of **Geoff Nyarota**, editor-in-chief of the *Daily News*, and **Lloyd Mudiwa**, the newspaper's municipal reporter, charged under Section 80 of the AIPPA for publishing 'falsehoods' (*Index* 3/02, 1/02, 4/01, 3/01) have been remanded until 27 February 2003 while the state organises the amendment. (*Daily News*)

A senior member of the Zimbabwe Union of Journalists

(ZUJ) says government is sowing the seeds of genocide in the country by continuing, through the national broadcaster, to fill the minds of the nation with anti-white, anti-opposition propaganda. Presenting a paper on the new Broadcasting Services Act (BSA) on the weekend of 24/25 November, **Kelvin Jakachira**, a ZUJ national executive member, said that referring to Movement for Democratic Change (MDC) members 'as terrorists can actually give other people the excuse to attack them. Genocide starts on a small scale,' he warned. 'We do not want what happened in Rwanda to be repeated here.' (IFJ)

Blessing Zulu, a reporter with the *Zimbabwe Independent*, and **Pedzisai Ruhanya**, chief reporter of the *Daily News*, were threatened by police when they went to cover the funeral of opposition member of parliament **Learnmore Jongwe** in Harare. Jongwe died in remand prison on 22 October. An inspector told them: 'If you write anything about what has transpired here, I will not hesitate to arrest you and shoot you afterwards.' (*Daily News*)

Medical director **Dr Frances Lovemore** of the *Amani Trust* was arrested in Harare on 28 August and charged with 'publishing or communicating false statements prejudicial to the state'. She had been quoted in a British paper on the Trust's work with victims of torture and politically motivated rape at the hands of pro-government supporters. On 30 August, all charges were dropped because of insufficient evidence. (AI)

On 14 September, another foreign correspondent, **Griffin Shea** of Agence France-Presse, left the country after the renewal of his work permit was refused. The information minister, Jonathan Moyo, stated that: 'No foreigner should be resident here as a journalist.' Moyo reportedly accused Shea of working for the US government in a plot to overthrow Mugabe's regime. (*Guardian*, MISA)

It has been estimated that 698 out of the 1,397 Movement for Democratic Change candidates who intended to stand in the local elections have withdrawn as a result of murder, intimidation and violence inflicted by government authorities and state-sponsored 'militia'. (AI)

Mark Chavunduka (*Index* 3/99, 4/00, 3/01, 4/01 & *passim*), the founding editor of the *Standard* newspaper, died in Harare on 13 November after a long illness. At the time of his death, he was the chief executive officer of Thomson Publications, the publishers of *Parade* magazine. He was a victim of government brutality when, together with his then chief writer at the *Standard*, **Ray Choto** (*Index* 3/01), he exposed a foiled military coup attempt in 1999. The two were arrested and later tortured by the army. (MISA, CPJ)

Compiled by: James Badcock (North Africa); Ben Carrdus (East Asia); Gulliver Cragg (Western Europe, Northern America, Pacific and Australasia); Avery Davis-Roberts (Western Africa); Ioli Delivani (Eastern Europe); Hanna Gezelius (South-East Asia); Monica Gonzalez Correa (Central Asia and Caucasus); Frances Harvey (Southern Africa); Andrew Kendle (India and subcontinent); Agustina Lattanzi (South and Central America); Najlae Naaoumi (Russia, Poland, Ukraine and Baltic States); Gill Newsham (Turkey and Kurdish areas); Ben Owen (UK and Ireland); Shifa Rahman (East Africa); Neil Sammonds (Gulf States and Middle East); Mike Yeoman (Central America and Caribbean)

Edited by Rohan Jayasekera and coordinated by Natasha Schmidt

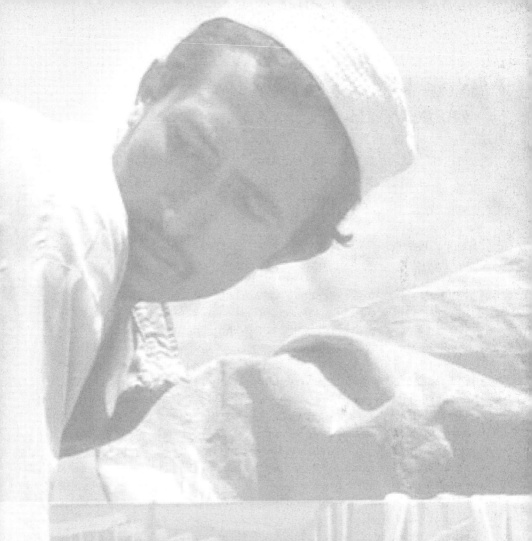

NEW HUMANITARIAN WARS . . .

. . . OF WORDS, THAT IS, AS GOVERNMENTS AND NGOS DEBATE THE ETHICS OF HUMANITARIAN AID AND INTERVENTION

Near Kabul, 14 July 2002: the return. Some 1.2 million Afghans have returned since the fall of the Taliban, the fastest refugee influx ever. Credit: AP Photo / Sergei Grits

AT THE LIMITS OF AID

CAROLINE MOOREHEAD

FROM BEING A RELATIVELY SIMPLE
PHILANTHROPIC ENDEAVOUR, THE DELIVERY
OF HUMANITARIAN AID HAS BECOME AN
ETHICAL AND LEGAL MINEFIELD THROUGH
WHICH DONORS AND AGENCIES MUST WEAVE
A PRECARIOUS PATH

Not long ago, a man working for the United Nations in Afghanistan went to oversee the arrival of provisions for refugees returning home after the years of war and drought. A small boy from the local village was standing watching the delivery. The UN expert asked him what he wanted to be when he grew up. Most children in Afghanistan today, alert to the nuances of friendly foreign aid workers, reply instantly that they intend to be doctors, engineers and, sometimes, teachers. This small boy paused. Then he said, eyeing the trucks lumbering their way up the dirt track under their heavy loads: 'When I grow up, I want to be a refugee.'

Around 1.6 million Afghan refugees have come home in the last eight months, over 1.25 million of them from the villages and camps over the Pakistani border. They arrive at dawn at the reception centres set up by the UN High Commission for Refugees just outside Kabul and at a small number of other places. They travel crammed into buses and rented lorries, brightly and busily decorated with peacocks, birds in cages, camels and palm trees, their belongings piled high on the roof. A little over 200,000 have returned from camps in Iran. UNHCR had been expecting 800,000 people for the whole year, evenly divided between the two countries, but refugees do not always move as expected. New arrivals report increasing hostility by Pakistani police, who are stopping the Afghans in the streets and demanding bribes, and later taking more money before they reach the frontier. As camps empty, so those hesitating about return are beginning to pack up, fearful of what may happen to them if they are left behind.

The returning refugees, whose numbers are soon expected to reach 2 million, are being greeted by the Afghans and the aid community with some ambivalence. President Hamid Karzai announced not long ago that he hopes to have welcomed every refugee home by the end of his transitional government in 12 months' time: the 2 million still left in Pakistan, the 1 million in Iran, the 300,000–500,000 scattered between Western Europe, the United States, India and the Gulf. With a quarter of its population in exile, Afghanistan has for many years held the record of having more refugees than any other country in the world. Western countries, meanwhile, are lining up behind UNHCR in encouraging voluntary repatriation, though where these returning families will go and how they will live has not been spelled out. The small Afghan boy was right in suspecting that the refugees returning from exile may fare better in terms of relief – a little wheat, a bucket, a blanket or two, some soap, a few dollars – than those who endured at home through the years of fighting; but there will be very little in it. The winter is bringing considerable hardship to everyone.

Afghanistan holds another record. It lies near the bottom of the world league for such economic indicators as literacy, child mortality and nutrition. One Afghan child in four dies before the age of five. Outside Kabul, the country may be as much as 90 per cent illiterate. The ten-year war against the Soviets, the mujahedin civil war, the Taliban occupation and the recent three-year drought, which only partially lifted in 2002 – 23 years of violence, displacement and extreme poverty – have left the country destitute. The capital alone is three-quarters destroyed. Eighty per cent of the country depends on agriculture but drought and the war have between them reduced many areas to well below subsistence levels. The water supply, once the delight of Afghanistan, flowing in a vast network of underground canals and irrigating wheat fields, orchards and vineyards, has collapsed under mines and shelling. The towns have sporadic electricity. There is no national postal system or telephone and there never was a railway. There are said to be up to 10 million unexploded landmines – down wells, in fields, among the ruined houses. Afghanistan was once self-sufficient: it is hard to imagine it will ever be so again.

Afghanistan is only the most recent in the series of major international humanitarian interventions of the last decade. It has followed, swiftly, as crises do these days, in the wake of Bosnia, Rwanda, Somalia, East Timor and Kosovo. It is also, in many ways, the most worrying. The sheer immensity of its needs, in terms of food, water, roads, schools, hospitals, government offices, equipment, cars, tractors, seed, hospitals and drugs, is matched only by the difficulty in providing them. Security, for Afghans and international aid workers alike, is poor, while warlords continue to control most of the country (in size the equivalent of Texas) outside Kabul. After one aid worker was raped in the summer of 2002, and others attacked and robbed, some organisations decided to employ guards or confine their employees to the capital. In any case, the warlords feel that since they won the war against the Taliban and al-Qaida – albeit with US help – it should be they who rule the peace, and not the fragile central government of President Karzai, to whom they are extremely reluctant to yield taxes. Afghanistan's many problems are not helped by the fact that, when not curtailed by the Taliban, the warlords have always fuelled their war economy from the harvest of opium poppies. In 2002 the harvest reached unprecedented levels.

In Bonn, in December 2001, the international community agreed to help rebuild Afghanistan and turn it into a democracy; in Tokyo, in January 2002, it pledged US$1.8bn for the first year, and US$5.2bn over the next four. Since then, it has reaffirmed these pledges. In November 2001, when the first experts flew cautiously in to scout out the lie of the land, they found the capital silent, empty and eerie. By February 2002, the UN agencies and the NGOs were frantically shifting their operations from Peshawar to Kabul. In keeping with a report drafted by Lakhdar Brahimi, the UN special representative, advocating integration of UN humanitarian and peacekeeping activities, Afghanistan is to be regarded as a model for a more coordinated and sensitive approach to UN assistance, drawing heavily on the wishes and resources of local inhabitants, and attempting to get away from the protectorate-like mandate in Kosovo and East Timor. Consultation, involvement, a 'light footprint' have become the catchphrases of foreign involvement. In and around the UN agencies flourish the NGOs – the old and long-established ones, such as the International Committee of the Red Cross, along with the new and highly specific – offering everything from training for democracy to new computer systems. There are said to be 109 international NGOs at work in Afghanistan today, and some 400 national ones, all but a handful fully funded from abroad. The experts work extremely hard, speeding between their offices and the World Bank, which has cleverly taken over a former ministerial palace and in the summer conducted its meetings in the gardens, under the shade of the mulberry trees.

Kabul 2002: queuing for Red Cross winter supplies – food, blankets and medicine.
Credit: Carlos Reyes-Manzo / Andes Press Agency

The arrival of the aid circus has brought traffic jams of gleaming white Toyota landcruisers, with their logos painted on the side, to the centre of Kabul. It has also brought exorbitant rents – houses are being leased out as offices for up to US$8,000 a month – and a marked and growing feeling of resentment in government circles that their best employees are being poached at inflated salaries by international organisations in need of inter-preters and local partnerships. In February, Kabul was a city of hopes. At last, after so many years of isolation, brutality and hardship, there was to be peace, a country to rebuild and the money and the people apparently flowing in with which to do so. Much of this spirit of hope has now gone. Within the UN, there are real fears that Brahimi's fine model of cooperation and consultation is not going to work, as UN agencies bicker and slip back into pursuing their own goals and the NGOs go their own way.

Within the Afghan community, the talk is mostly about money. No one can say precisely how much of the pledged money has been received and spent – the best guess seems be around US$1 billion – but it is clear that the Afghans consider the sums very disappointing. Most of this has gone on paying salaries and on the international community itself. Within Kabul there is little to show for the dollars: no housing developments to accom-modate the refugees who flocked back home in high summer at the rate of 10,000 a day into the city alone, or to replace the acres of Kabul flattened in successive waves of fighting; no new hospitals; no schools. Government offices remain without computers or even typewriters, without filing cabinets, without enough chairs. The slow approach, say the foreigners, is to be encouraged, for by taking proper stock of priorities and proper assess-ment of projects the pitfalls that accompanied earlier efforts at reconstruc-tion in Bosnia and elsewhere will be avoided. Afghans, looking at the banks of computers in the foreign offices, watching the speeding Toyotas, envying those with properties now able to fetch fairy-tale rents, do not see it that way. Rumours of greed, exploitation, corruption and straightforward ineffi-ciency abound.

When, in spring 2002, the UN agreed to provide the ministries and high-ranking officials with a mobile telephone system, they contracted a Swedish company to provide it. What they failed to do was to ensure that this system was compatible with their own, which links the UN and many of the major international organisations. But they also failed to find out that the system was extremely expensive. After five months, in which govern-ment employees were able to talk to other government employees but not to anyone else, the bill was sent in. It came, so it is said, to US$50 million. The UN cancelled the system, but paid the bill, out of the reconstruction account for Afghanistan. For US$12 million, apparently, Kabul could have had a 9,000-unit mobile system serving all. 'The UN', says one Afghan businessman, who returned to Kabul in the spring to do what he could to help in his country's reconstruction, 'is turning out to be a lousy procurement agent. They don't seem to care what prices they are charged – after all, it's not their money and there seems to be plenty of it.' How true this is – whether the UN is as ineffectual as it is perceived to be, or whether it has simply become a scapegoat, the focus for general discontent – is impossible to say. But the perceptions, and the feelings, are intense.

And even then, the money itself is not coming in the amounts that were promised and expected. UNHCR's budget for 2002 in Afghanistan was put at US$271 million, based on a projected figure of 800,000 returnees. Not only has no provision been made for the fact that the figure of returnees is now likely to double before the end of the first year, but UNHCR has still not been able to raise a quarter of its original target. The first returnees received, together with their small amount of cash, 150 kilos of wheat per family and transport to their former homes. Today, there is no transport and a single 50-kilo sack. In the devastated areas of Kabul and its surroundings, returnees are to be seen digging through the ruins of their former houses to recover such bricks as are still intact, in order to put up some kind of structure against the winter.

However, the picture is not all bleak. Some of Brahimi's insistence on building from the bottom up, on coordination and consultation, is paying off. Much effort is going into helping Afghans rewrite their criminal code, eroded by years of war and the Taliban fundamentalists, into training prosecutors and judges, and into building up libraries of law books, thrown away or burned by the Taliban. Outside Kabul, for all the power of the local warlords, real efforts at small-scale reconstruction are proceeding, in the form of mending roads destroyed by years of neglect and fighting, while grass-roots community organisations are being coaxed into assuming responsibility for local enterprises. The Loya Jirga, the gathering of the grand council in June, was widely regarded as a success if for no other reason than the fact that it happened at all. Some candidates were beaten up; others were intimidated; but 1,501 people, women as well as men, did meet and did agree on broad outlines for a new Afghanistan, and a constitution is being prepared in anticipation of elections next year.

Wars, as the economist Mary Kaldor remarked not long ago, are not what they used to be. There may not be more actual fighting and the weapons used may not have changed all that much, but the widespread conflict of the last decade has come to be seen as far more threatening to world security. The landscape of war is different, not just in Afghanistan, but everywhere; different, and changing all the time. Humanitarian work, like war, is not what it used to be; and it, too, is adapting and developing all the time.

Aid workers, once respected as neutral players, are now made targets for attack by rebel armies indifferent to or ignorant of any protecting Red Cross emblem or rules of war. The old distinction between war zone and zone of relief has largely disappeared. Security haunts all players in the humanitarian world today, and nowhere more than in the Red Cross movement, where the once universally recognised and respected emblem is now widely acknowledged to have become a target in wars in which none of the old rules apply. (Once the best-known sign in the world, it has now dropped to third place, behind Coca-Cola and Nike.) According to Michel Cagnieux, one of three full-time security delegates at the ICRC, 40 per cent of the incidents reported from the field in 2000 were the result of the direct targeting of the Red Cross; ten years ago, the figure was 3 per cent. Even the ICRC, which has gone to great lengths to do without military protection, has had to recognise that there are situations where aid cannot be delivered without it.

Since the end of the Cold War and the disengagement of the super-powers, violence has become more fragmented, and rebel forces reliant less on international funding than on the extraction and control of natural resources. The easy availability of small arms has encouraged the proliferation of armed groups, with little, or casual, patterns of leadership. Humanitarian intervention has become more uncertain, more precarious and more political, and it has been moving away from activities designed to mitigate the impact of war towards becoming an organising principle for international relations. Set against the backdrop of a continual debate about the balance between the rights of states to non-intervention and the rights of individuals to protection, the promotion of certain values, such as human rights, has become the reason for military interventions to redress the humanitarian effects of conflict and to stabilise countries like Somalia and Bosnia. Wherever civilians are harmed, wherever violence is targeted against aid workers or humanitarian supplies blocked, so has it become justified to send in the military.

Kabul 2002: child's play.
Credit: Carlos Reyes-Manzo / Andes Press Agency

This new face of war, with economic, political and natural disasters followed by massive displacements of people, has been matched by a clear shift in thinking by the UN Security Council, which has broadened its own security concerns to include not only the environment, water and Aids, but humanitarian issues. With modern wars breaking out within failed and weak states, rather than between states, humanitarian action has been adjusted to take into account such questions as whether protecting human rights supersedes the principle of sovereignty, what role should and can be played by the ever-present media, and where the peacekeeping forces fit into the spectrum of humanitarian assistance. As Hugo Slim, senior lecturer in International Humanitarianism at Oxford Brookes University, has noted, Boutros Boutros-Ghali's memorable phrase 'the time of absolute and exclusive sovereignty has passed' heralded an era of a new perceived relationship between the individual, the state and the rest of the world. It was also Boutros-Ghali who declared that conflicts, bringing in their wake death, destruction and regional instability, were to be seen first as emergencies, and then as

ONLY BY SEEING HUMANITARIANISM AS A THEORY OF RIGHTS CAN THERE BE REAL CHANGE

eligible for development programmes in their post-war phase. Systematic breaches of human rights and humanitarian law are now widely accepted as constituting threats to international peace and security. What Alex de Waal has called the 'humanitarian international', the cosy philanthropy that once dominated the charities and NGOs, is blamed for having failed to change the political systems that continue to permit famines and wars to break out. Only by seeing humanitarianism as a theory of rights – inviolable and fundamental, such as the right to life, food, health and physical well-being – and not as Victorian relief or assistance, it is argued, can there be real change and can hunger and violence become truly unacceptable. Argued, that is, but not yet enforced: eloquent on paper, the right to humanitarian aid remains subjective and ill-defined, while in many parts of the world the practice of sovereignty continues to constitute the greatest limitation to humanitarian assistance.

A subject once regarded as relatively straightforward – the delivery of aid in a disaster – has in fact now become fraught with moral dilemmas and complications. Donors today are forced to ask themselves whether they are doing good, and in some cases whether they are not in fact prolonging a conflict; whether, in short, they are right to intervene at all and on what terms. As Tricia Feeney, senior policy adviser at Oxfam, put it not long ago, humanitarian aid has become an 'ethical, geo-political and legal minefield' in which NGOs have to steer an uneasy course between effectiveness and safety in their search for a 'moral compass'. The funding itself has become immensely complicated, with money for any one emergency involving everything from multilateral and bilateral donors, private funders and foundations, subcontractors and the military, individuals and multinational companies. The question of where emergency ends and development begins hovers over every project. If money going to emergencies has risen dramatically in recent years, from US$600 million in 1985 to over US$3 billion in 2000, the percentage of Western budgets devoted to foreign aid has fallen steadily. Countries are not as willing as they once were to share their wealth. Only Denmark today devotes over 1 per cent of its GDP to aid, and only five countries scrape above 0.7 per cent, which is the target set by the UN. (The US famously lies near to the bottom, with 0.1 per cent.)

> BIAFRA WAS THE WAR THAT RAISED THE FIRST SERIOUS QUESTIONS. RWANDA WAS THE PLACE WHERE ACCOUNTABILITY WAS REALLY BORN

If Biafra was the war that brought the international community in force into a humanitarian catastrophe, and raised the first serious questions about the role of the media in such situations, then Rwanda was the place where the accountability of humanitarian players was really born. Rwanda, coming soon on the heels of the fiasco in Somalia, was a mess. The international community chose to ignore warnings from people on the spot, the UN pulled out their peacekeepers shortly before the genocide began, allowing the massacres to take place unchecked, while the non-governmental effort that followed was ill advised, uncoordinated and inefficient. Out of this came a new mood among NGOs: they must become more systematic and more professional. Starting at the top, among organisations like the International Committee of the Red Cross and the Federation of Red Cross and Red Crescent societies, and trickling down to the smallest of the NGOs, has come a new spirit of accountability, assessment and monitoring. A humanitarian charter has been drafted, with specified rules of conduct, while the Sphere project has drawn up minimum standards that now ground humanitarianism in international law and translate people's rights into specific duties by governments and NGOs. 'This gives humanitarianism,' writes Slim, 'an integrated political and legal framework for affirming universal human values.' Once floating around in the guise of charity and kindness, humanitarian acts are now anchored in political contracts, military duties, courts, tribunals, truth commissions and types of assistance. People with rights are harder to marginalise and harder to regard as victims. In the UK, the Disasters Emergency Committee, an umbrella of major charities that pool their fundraising at times of specific emergencies, is firmly committed to strict evaluations of performance. In Geneva, at the headquarters of the ICRC and the Red Cross Federation, the talk is all of coordination and cooperation. And in the wake of these new trends have come, not the gentlemen volunteers and willing spinsters of the early years, but hard-nosed administrators, backed up by teams of engineers, architects, epidemiologists, statisticians, economists and sanitation experts. 'To survive,' says Jean Michel Monod, deputy director of operations at the ICRC, 'you have to have a sophisticated act.' Donors, be they government or individuals, now insist on knowing where their money is going and how well it is being spent. There is a feeling of personal responsibility for creating a better world, and not simply acting as a Band Aid for its casualties.

And after Rwanda came 11 September. It fell at a moment of world economic retrenchment when donations from both governments and individuals were already declining after the more affluent mid-1990s. But it brought with it yet another shift in the perception of humanitarian work. At government level, it raised questions about how to rid the world of the terrorist threat, and how to address the conditions under which such threats develop. The debate moved from professionalism to the need to promote peace-building – either, as most European governments argue, by increasing development programmes or, as the US maintains, by focusing primarily on its own immediate security interests. Violent conflicts, which had once been seen as humanitarian crises, are now regarded as geostrategic threats. Conflict resolution, together with development, has become the order of the day.

Henri Dunant, founder of the Red Cross, trying to marshal half a dozen helpers from among the foreign tourists who happened to be sightseeing near the battlefield of Solferino on 24 June 1859, would indeed marvel today at the humanitarian movement he once helped to create. Appalled by the carnage he witnessed, Dunant saw, in his vision of introducing a spirit of humanity into warfare, two very different components: the care for those affected by conflict, and the drafting and monitoring of rules to govern the

Ghazni 2002: life among the ruins.
Credit: Carlos Reyes-Manzo / Andes Press Agency

conduct of those engaged in it. One hundred and fifty years later, in a world
in which there is no longer anything clear about warfare, in which conflict
and disaster feed on each other, in which internal conflicts run on for generations and victims are no longer soldiers but children who are mutilated by
landmines or women who are raped, the distinction between the two
becomes ever more blurred. It is as if the anarchic violence, the unending
conflicts, the natural disasters magnified by political manoeuvrings are all
combining to bring the humanitarian world to the very edge of what it can
cope with. It is what happens next – in Afghanistan, in the Middle East, in
some new place that no one currently has their eye on – that alarms those
who have the time to stop and think.

George Bush, while campaigning for the US presidency, made it clear
that he was opposed to using US soldiers for nation-building. But Afghanistan is posing a particular problem for the US and the rest of the world. To
prevent al-Qaida from returning to control the Afghan mountains once
again, the country must be made both strong and safe. It must have a democratic government and a basic infrastructure of roads, hospitals and schools.
It needs an army and a police force and telephones that work. At present,
Afghanistan has none of these. Even the 4,500 peacekeeping forces do not
venture far outside Kabul and, despite warnings that to achieve any real
degree of security peacekeepers need to be sent to the provinces, there is no
international will to find the men or the money this would take. Rebuilding
Afghanistan, say the economists, will take US$18 billion and at least ten
years. It cannot be done with less. With Bush set to take the war into Iraq,
with donors dragging their heels about future commitments and even past
promises, with the aid circus subject to crisis calls from other quarters, and
President Karzai vulnerable to sudden assassination attempts, the stability of
Afghanistan looks fragile indeed. And the humanitarian effort itself, under-
funded and faced by chronic problems, is faltering. Increasingly, people
wonder whether Brahimi's dream is achievable at all. They say, sadly, that
Afghanistan may turn out to be the place and the moment at which it
became finally clear that unless the UN system is radically overhauled,
perhaps even fused into a single entity without its rivalrous and uncoordinated agencies, then its future can only be bleak.

And it is easy to forget that it is not simply the country itself that is in
ruins. Its people have endured 23 years of deprivation and violence. When,
not long ago, UNICEF carried out a survey in Kabul on the effect of the

long-running war on children aged between eight and 18, they found that 41 per cent had lost a parent and over half had seen torture or violent death. Many had been forced by the Taliban to witness public executions and amputations. Asked about their view of their own futures, over 80 per cent of these children told the UNICEF researchers that they were not sure that life was worth living. For this generation, it is not simply a question of giving them enough to eat and an education. It is about restoring a sense of optimism and hope in a future not governed by violence and uncertainty. And this may be beyond the capability of any humanitarian endeavour. ❏

Caroline Moorehead *has recently returned from Afghanistan. She is completing a biography of Martha Gellhorn*

NOWHERE TO GO

Hassen Farah stands in a dry, sandy, 100-foot-wide river bed in south-eastern Ethiopia. 'Everywhere you look it is dry,' says the 54-year-old pastoralist, 'Everywhere.'

In Shinile, in Ethiopia's Somali region, they have already given a name to this current drought. They call it 'nowhere to go'. 'This is worse than before,' says Hassen. 'In the past we could travel with our animals to get water. Even in the worst times. But everywhere you go it is dry now. There is nothing for the animals to eat and without them we are nothing. We depend on our animals.'

The previous day, Ethiopian Prime Minister Meles Zenawi had made an international appeal to help 11.3 million people who face starvation next year unless aid is shipped in. The appeal has already sparked a response, but Hassen's plight goes far deeper than simply giving him food to keep his family alive. Like other pastoralists in the area, he has seen his flock diminish through several years of poor rains. With it his status falls and his ability to keep his family alive. It means that he becomes more and more reliant on food aid. There is at least a four-month wait before another drop of rain is likely to fall.

Three bare-chested men chant as they drop 20 feet into a tiny well, bringing up buckets of dirty brown water. This drought has meant the water table has fallen even further. The pastoralists gathered at this watering hole in the middle of the Harowe river bed have walked some 30km. They stop their desperately thirsty animals from over-watering as the long walk back can kill them if they are bloated.

The challenge facing humanitarian organisations now is to ensure that traditionally hardy pastoralists like Hassen can survive recurrent droughts, and to ensure any recovery is long-lasting and not a quick fix that would mean massive intervention at the next sign of trouble. Even so, immediate needs must still be met.

Hassen Abdullah, head of social affairs within the district, said government food aid to meet immediate needs had arrived but distribution was woefully inadequate. 'If these people are not helped now then in the future they will become more dependent,' he said from his office in Shinile district, from which he covers a population of 90,000. He estimates 70,000 of them are in need of food aid. The government estimates there are around 1 million people in acute need throughout the Somali region.

A second, more deadly factor has aggravated the situation: fighting between ethnic groups has reached an alarming scale. Dozens of Issas and Afar have been killed in clashes over scarce water resources.

A few kilometres away, the drought in Ethiopia is taking a different toll. Omer Hosh Maidane has taught the Quran to hundreds of children who have grown up in the village of Meto. But gradually, he says, the children are starting to drop out as the families move out in search of water. 'There is an obvious change in the children,' Omer adds. 'You can see the drought in their faces. They have lost weight, they look thin and their concentration is not the same because they are thinking about food.' He said one-third of his class had moved away and others would soon follow.

Mohamed Ahmed, head of Save the Children UK Eastern Region, says the cumulative effects of recurrent droughts in Ethiopia have taken an extraordinary toll. He reckons pastoralists need around 30 to 40 goats and sheep to be able to survive. Unlike farmers, their existence depends solely on their livestock, but recurrent droughts have depleted stocks.

Shinile epitomises the problems that need to be addressed by the international community and the Ethiopian government, both of which are now refocusing their aid efforts. Simply handing out food no longer works in places like Shinile. Pastoralists like Hassen must be able to recover their livestock and their livelihood so that they can cope during the droughts. 'We shall never get better by eating wheat,' says Hassen as he begins the long 30km walk back to his village with his goats. 'We survive by our animals. Without them we do not.' ❏

From a correspondent with the Addis Ababa-based Integrated Regional Information Networks (IRIN)

⇨ www.irinnews.org

ACCIDENTS AND EMERGENCIES: SOME FACTS AND FIGURES

'Complex emergencies' The UN has highlighted 22 countries of concern or 'complex emergencies' worldwide

Natural disasters The UN recorded 31 natural disasters between August and November 2002

Aid levels Levels of humanitarian assistance have fluctuated over the last decade: in 1991, aid totalled US$4.6bn; three years later, it peaked at US$5.7bn; by 1998 it was down to US$4.5bn. (Ted Turner of CNN has lost US$6.4bn since 11 September 2002)

DONORS

UN-controlled aid Fell from 45% of all aid in 1988 to 27% today. Richer countries have moved towards bilateral assistance rather than working through the UN; they now control 62%, the EU 11% and the UN 27% of all aid donations

OECD countries aid Total aid had fallen in real terms by one-third, from 0.3% to 0.2%, by 2000

Average per capita yearly income in OECD countries increased from US$21,000 to US$28,000 during the 1990s; just over US$5 per capita a year was given as aid

US aid to Central Africa The US was the largest single donor of aid to the Great Lakes region with US$36.9m; the EU was second with US$13.6m

Red Cross The International Committee of the Red Cross (ICRC) will need Swiss francs 788.8m to cover its field expenses in 2003. Its five largest operations worldwide will be in Afghanistan, Israel and the occupied Palestinian territories, the Russian Federation (in particular the northern Caucasus – Chechnya, Ingushetia, etc), the Democratic Republic of Congo and Sudan

UN World Food Programme Seeks US$150–200m for the first
quarter of 2003. In 2002, it assisted 77 million people worldwide

In Central America, 8.6 million people in live in a 'drought
corridor', and 690,000 people are dependent on food aid as
a result of collapsing global coffee prices and drought. WFP
needs US$55.1m to deal with the crisis

In Southern Africa, WFP is feeding 25 million of the 38 million
people currently at risk of famine

In the Horn of Africa, 10–15 million people face starvation over
the coming months as a result of widespread drought

AID WORKERS, REFUGEES, AIDS

UN civilian staff Between 1992 and 2000, 200 were killed during
humanitarian operations. In 1994, one of the worst years as a
result of operations in Rwanda and former Yugoslavia, 64 UN
workers were killed

By August 2000, only a handful of those responsible had been
brought to justice

Refugees At least 25 million people in 47 countries are refugees within
their own countries, displaced by violence and persecution

Aids in Southern Africa In 2001, 1.18 million people died from
HIV/Aids; South Africa had the largest death toll at c360,000

4.6 million children have lost their parents to HIV/Aids ❑

*Sources: Global Humanitarian Assistance report, 2000; ICRC; MSF; National
Intelligence Council; UNAIDS; UN Office of the Coordinator for Humanitarian
Affairs; WFP*

*Compiled by **Jason Pollard** and **Andrew Smith***

WELCOME TO THE PARTY

MARK THOMPSON

JOURNALISTS FIND THEMSELVES
ACTIVE PARTNERS IN FORGING
PEACE AS WELL AS WAR

In Mazar-e-Sharif, three competing local leaders – General Abdel Rashid Dostum, Ustad Atta and Haji Mohammad Mohaqiq – record their separate meetings with international organisations and diplomats. The local television station broadcasts them all.

This vignette from liberated Afghanistan suggests a litmus test for television news around the world. Wherever the programme showcases government leaders greeting international politicos or local A-list suits, with little if any effort to connect these meetings to the urgent issues of the day, then something is badly wrong. When the TV station in question is a national broadcaster, the country as a whole is probably suffering a democratic deficit. Chances are it is a more or less 'closed society' whose ruling elite sees control over segments of broadcasting and the press as a natural prerogative, and where the public is denied basic information about elite motives and intentions.

Such countries are much more likely to fall into conflict, or lesser forms of so-called 'complex [ie man-made] emergency' than their more open counterparts. This correlation should come as no surprise: freedom of expression is an attribute and pillar of democratic stability. Media outlets that are not controlled by governments or ruling cliques cannot readily be used to sow dissension and hatred as part of an expansionist strategy or (what often amounts to the same thing) a survivalist ploy. Yet, unfortunately, this observation is no more true than its opposite. Intra- and inter-state conflicts of the past decade, from south-eastern Europe to central Africa, bore indelible witness to the power of mass media to help tear countries apart.

The key democratic states – led by the US, UK, France, Germany, Italy, Japan and Canada – clearly failed to oppose the worst abuses of media in those instances, let alone prevent them. These failures have been offset to some extent by some path-breaking experiments in building democratic media in zones of actual or potential conflict. The attempt to forge new instruments of peace-building – sometimes called 'information intervention'

– deserves attention in its own right since these instruments will almost certainly be needed elsewhere, whether in Indonesia, Iraq, West Africa, or the great arc of territory between the Caucasus and the Chinese border.

What made the media a significant factor in conflict areas in the 1990s for Western foreign policy establishments was above all the problem of 'hate speech' in the Balkans and the African Great Lakes region. In both places, incendiary speech was directed and organised by the highest authorities in the land to encourage human rights abuses of the most heinous sort. What was more, the hate-mongering media clearly served a secondary political purpose: it provided an element of deniability for the responsible regime. 'These were not our instructions,' they could say disingenuously to critics, 'these were the free voices of the media. You don't want us to control the media, do you?'

The transparency of this stratagem did not prevent it from working pretty well with Western governments that did not, anyway, want to intervene effectively in Bosnia or Rwanda. When the US government was pressed to take action against Radio Mille Collines, which was explicitly inciting genocide, State Department lawyers warned against infringing international telecommunications law and freedom of speech norms. Pressed harder, they claimed that jamming would violate Rwandan sovereignty. Mille Collines duly retreated into the French-controlled zone of Rwanda, where it continued its work until Tutsi rebel forces drove it out of the country. At the end of the decade, several Hutu propagandists and a Belgian presenter were convicted for 'direct and public incitement to genocide' at the war crimes tribunal in Arusha (*Index* 4–5/94).

If the Western powers did shamefully little against hate media in 1994, then NATO's bombardment of Serbia's state broadcaster RTS in 1999 was a massive overreaction. On 23 April, a month into NATO's destructive campaign against the Serbian regime of Slobodan Milošević, the RTS centre in downtown Belgrade was hit, killing 16 civilians (*Index* 5/96).

In practical terms, the bombardment was futile at best. The network was back on air within hours, its prestige among Serbs greatly (though briefly) enhanced. Even worse, NATO may have perpetrated a war crime. Under the 1949 Geneva Conventions and additional protocols, 'Military objectives are limited to those objects which by their nature, location, purpose, or use make an effective contribution to military action and whose total or partial destruction, capture or neutralisation, in the circumstances ruling at the time, offers a definite military advantage' (Article 52 [2] of Additional

Protocol I). Organisations such as Amnesty International and Human Rights Watch do not believe RTS met this definition, rendering the attack illegal. Caught on the back foot, Alliance spokesmen were reduced to insisting that Serbian TV's propagandist role justified the attack. No one mentioned incitement as justification, presumably because NATO knew the case could not be made convincingly. In his memoirs, US General Wesley Clark, Alliance supreme commander at the time, ignored the subsequent furore, commenting lamely that the action demonstrated 'NATO's resolve'.

The watching world realised that NATO was going through the motions, making half-baked excuses for punishing a hostile television network that irritated them. Russia, Israel and then the US itself all seem to have drawn useful lessons. In August 1999, Russian forces bombarded media outlets in Dagestan on the ground that they were broadcasting 'open propaganda' with an Islamist slant.

On 12 October 2000, Israeli helicopter gunships rocketed the Palestinian Broadcasting Corporation's facilities in Ramallah. The Israeli government said the PBC had been inciting violence, and cited NATO's action against RTS in justification. The following month, a PBC television station in Gaza was bombed in retaliation for an attack on a school bus. Having tested the water and found it shark-free, the Israeli Defence Forces really went to town in April 2002. According to the US-based International Center for Journalists, *all* the Palestinians' indigenous television capacity was destroyed when 15 television stations in the Gaza Strip and West Bank were put out of action.

On 12 November 2001, the compound in Kabul that housed the Qatari satellite broadcaster, al-Jazeera, was destroyed by US missiles during the war against Afghanistan's Taliban regime. Claiming that the premises were used by al-Qaida and hence had a 'military significance' that made them a 'legitimate target', the US denied even knowing that al-Jazeera had been located there. The Pentagon refused subsequent requests from the BBC and the US-based Committee to Protect Journalists (CPJ) to explain what was meant by 'military significance'. It does not seem far-fetched to guess that NATO's embarrassment after the attack on RTS in April 1999 had convinced the US that it was futile to try to justify an attack on al-Jazeera, so it might as well tell an outright lie.

Writing well before the 11 September 2001 atrocities, Joel Simon of the Committee to Protect Journalists (CPJ) pointed out in the *Columbia Journalism Review* that 'international humanitarian law is clear that any attack on

Kabul 2002: post-Taliban free expression revived with NGO help.
Credit: IWPR

a broadcasting facility must be based on a careful determination that the station is serving a significant military function. If military commanders feel they can attack broadcasting facilities because they are offended or outraged by what they are putting on the air, then no journalist anywhere is safe and the ability of the press to cover conflict will be deeply compromised.' One year into the Orwellian-titled and prospectively interminable 'war against terrorism', this warning carries ever greater resonance.

These criminal actions by NATO members, Russia, Israel and the US against broadcasters who, however deplorable their output, should not have been demolished with munitions, form a sequence that will very likely extend into the future unless the leading democratic powers accept other ways of tackling incendiary media.

The most difficult challenge occurs where media are playing an incendiary role in a context where significant human rights abuses might readily occur. Here, the urgent priority is to *stop* the propaganda. Where a political crisis is simmering, every extra day's output of propaganda can make the difference between a potential conflict, where peaceful means of de-escalation still have a chance of success, and a spiral of violence triggered by a solitary incident that may – with the media's help – appear spontaneous ('the anger of the people', 'individual elements acting on their own') but rarely is so.

What then can be done? States are narrowly constrained in the sorts of intervention they can legally take against hate-mongering media. These constraints are given by the non-intervention norm in international law, the architecture of human rights treaties erected since World War II and, as mentioned above, the Geneva Conventions. They are monitored by inter-governmental organisations such as UNESCO and the Council of Europe, associations such as the International Federation of Journalists and media freedom NGOs such as Article 19, Reporters Sans Frontières, the World Press Freedom Committee and the CPJ.

There is, then, a high protective palisade around the free flow of information. This is as it should be. Liberals will surely feel that the free-flow model, which holds that regulation of the media should be minimal and voluntary wherever possible, is right in principle and, moreover, justified by results achieved during the decades of the Cold War. The Soviet authoritarian model of state-dominated media was not only rolled back, it was comprehensively discredited.

Yet the palisade is not unbroken. International human rights law does not defend speech that incites racial or ethnic hatred, but seems not to debar unilateral or multilateral intervention against media that promote such speech. For the worst cases, the Genocide Convention, which bans 'direct and public incitement to genocide', can be invoked as a warrant for suppression. Then there is Chapter VII of the United Nations Charter, which entitles the Security Council to determine measures against threats to international peace and security. (Article 41 conveniently provides that such measures may include 'complete or partial interruption of . . . postal, telegraphic, radio, and other means of communication'.)

There is scope, then, for the legal international suppression of media outlets in extreme situations. But these cannot be legally attacked unless they are serving directly military purposes – something that will very rarely occur. (Rwandan radio stations in 1994 were an exception that may never be repeated.) Or unless the UN Security Council judges they are guilty of direct incitement to genocide or other massive human rights abuses. Even in such clear-cut cases, outside powers should explore political and technical means of suppression before any resort to force. It should not be hard to agree a hierarchy of methods of intervention.

If the democratic powers have yet to adopt coherent strategies for tackling rogue media in conflict zones, their record at boosting alternative sources of information in such zones has been much better. A good many international organisations, both inter- and non-governmental, have spent many millions of pounds to support media outside the control of local regimes. Hundreds of journalists have taken part in training programmes. Computers and transmitters have been shipped, or sometimes slipped, to remote radio stations, and bales of newsprint delivered to paper-starved presses. Unofficial news agencies were set up using the internet. Experiences have been swapped at innumerable seminars and conferences. As a result, the public in war-torn parts of the Balkans and West Africa have benefited from independent information and views, presented by journalist-compatriots in their own languages. Stocks of skilled journalists were not entirely lost to emigration and a measure of professional honour was redeemed for the future.

When regimes refused to cooperate with media support projects, local journalists and outside donors found ways around them, often thanks to bold NGO activists from the UK, the US, Switzerland, The Netherlands and Sweden. Briefcases of cash were smuggled over borders. Radio masts were dismantled and loaded on to Land-Rovers.

While governments and intergovernmental organisations (IGOs) tend to be circumspect, there were splendid exceptions. UNESCO, not generally an acronym to conjure with, broke ground in 1994 by getting aid to media exempted from the international sanctions against Yugoslavia. Reclassifying this form of support as humanitarian assistance was a shift with major implications.

In Sierra Leone, the UK backed an ingenious response to the information dearth under the rebel junta in 1997–98. The key figure was High Commissioner Peter Penfold, who bought a mobile FM radio station and set it up beside the runway at the international airport, which the rebels did not control. Mixing news and music, 'Radio 98.1 – Radio Democracy' exasperated the junta by relaying insider news from Freetown, gathered through

a network of volunteer informants. The BBC World Service turned a blind eye when its programmes were pirated. People caught listening were liable to be shot, says Penfold. 'We needed to encourage those brave people in Freetown, above all,' he recalls. 'We supplied satellite phones, so the station could broadcast our messages live, telling people that the international community was determined to see the restoration of President Kabbah's legitimate government.' When Kabbah was restored, 'the two loudest chants in Freetown were for the Nigerian general who kicked out the junta – and the radio station!'

Elsewhere in West and Central Africa, the Swiss foundation Hirondelle does excellent work by setting up radio stations where one or two international staff work with local journalists. Operating in media-poor areas where the population is grossly under-informed, Hirondelle's stations in the Democratic Republic of Congo, Liberia, Burundi, Rwanda and the Central African Republic have quickly won large audiences. The US-based NGO Search for Common Ground runs similar projects in Liberia, Sierra Leone, Burundi and the former Yugoslav republic of Macedonia. Pound for pound, there cannot be many more economical ways of getting fresh information to the public while training local journalists.

The possibilities for media development multiply when executive authority rests with an international mission, as in Kosovo and East Timor, or is qualified by a very intrusive 'peace-building' mandate, as in Bosnia and Afghanistan. Those places have seen experiments in the restructuring of media sectors – including legislation, regulation and institutions – under international guidance, on a scale unknown since the post-war occupations of Germany and Japan. But the analogy does not stretch very far. The Nazi Party was banned; Radovan Karadzic's Serb Democratic Party, by contrast, became a fully legal member of Bosnia's government after the Dayton Agreement ended the war.

Today's 'humanitarian interventions' are bound by requirements of accountability and consensus-building under the sceptical gaze of the outside world (if it is watching at all). Default from the highest standards of human rights is swiftly publicised. These conditions can deter the interveners from taking the bold steps sometimes needed to establish democratic structures in undemocratic milieux. Returning from a big conference on

Kabul 2002: getting the news out to the people as part of post-war reconstruction.
Credit: IWPR

media development for Afghanistan last September, a veteran UK media activist called the situation there 'a bit surreal, because the international community is just here in an advisory capacity. We don't have any control, or even that much leverage. After fighting for 25 years, the Afghans are very stubborn. The ministry of information is being explicit that the next reform step is for them.'

In the longer term, this may be all to the good; new institutions can develop at a pace that suits the broader process of normalisation. Here and now, however, the sight of opportunities being lost as local interest groups – not always anti-Western extremists – outwit the well-meaning but often irresolute and uncoordinated efforts of international missions can be painful. (Would Mr Berlusconi be able to monopolise Italian media today if his country had been democratised like Germany and Japan in the 1940s?)

The goal of media development under a transitional administration is to establish laws and regulations in line with international norms, to ensure a plural press and a mixed broadcasting sector with a public service network in competition with private radio and television channels. This is hugely ambitious, and made even more difficult by economic conditions that usually mock the idea of a 'media market' in which professional media could sustain themselves commercially.

Nevertheless, in principle, it should be possible to get the right laws and regulations adopted, and to restructure the state broadcaster to function as more than the puppet of one or another political faction. In practice, the biggest stumbling block has been reform of state broadcasting. While there is no single explanation of this disappointing record, it does seem that public service broadcasting – the central feature in a mixed media landscape outside the Americas – cannot give birth to itself. The BBC, it has been said, is the child of parliamentary democracy. With the rider that this child has reached its majority, respectful of its parents but not bound by them, the same is true of all public service broadcasting worthy of the name.

In the words of Karol Jakubowicz, one of the wise men of European broadcasting: 'From both a conceptual and political point of view, it is hard to postulate the creation of a public service sector of broadcasting in a highly politicised society with a fundamentally unstable political and party system, where politics and a power struggle invade and subordinate practically every aspect of public life.' If this is the view from Warsaw, what can be expected in Sarajevo and Priština, let alone Kigali, Grozny, Dili or Kabul? Yet the effort must be made. The options – leaving the most powerful network in government hands, or sweeping deregulation – would very likely do the public a worse disservice than even botched reform.

One thing is clear: the best results are gained when intergovernmental bodies like UNESCO and the Council of Europe, backed by powerful Western states, collaborate with non-governmental groups. Together, they have brought effective pressures to bear in states that would never freely choose to democratise their media.

Around 1989, the age of ideology yielded to the age of human rights. Even those who are repelled by the Bush administration's opportunism since the atrocities of 11 September, and who doubt that Saddam Hussein today threatens anybody more than the Iraqis themselves, may wonder what form the Arab world's reckoning with liberal individualism will take. This returns us to Afghanistan, where we came in. Ahmed Rashid, author of a best-selling book on the Taliban, recently remarked that the potential knock-on benefits in other Islamic-majority states of building a democratic media sector in Afghanistan, and successfully transferring it to local control, could be immense. This was finely said; and, formidable as the obstacles are, a better opportunity may not come along. ❏

*Mark **Thompson***'s latest book is Forging Peace. Intervention, Human Rights and the Management of Media Space *jointly edited with Monroe F Price (Edinburgh University Press 2002)*

AIDS, AID AND FAMINE

ALEX DE WAAL

THERE IS NOTHING REMOTELY 'NORMAL'
ABOUT SOUTHERN AFRICA'S LATEST
FAMINE, AND NORMAL SOLUTIONS DO
NOT APPLY

Just as, over the millennia, humans have co-evolved mutual adaptation with
the commonest microbes, agrarian societies have developed responses to the
commonest collective threats to their survival. Notable among these threats
is famine, historically often brought about by aberrant weather.

Famine is the prototypical energy crisis: a society's production mechanisms – farming, gathering wild foods, fishing, livestock rearing – do not
generate sufficient calories to keep a society healthy. In these 'traditional'
famines, what we see is a series of adjustments that preserve the core of the
population so that it can quickly regenerate. As scarcity develops in a
community, one of the first signs of approaching distress is declining fertility.
Thus, when famine arrives, there are fewer young mouths to feed, and adult
women are freer to forage unencumbered by their infants. During a famine,
those who die are overwhelm-
ingly the very young and the
very old. Young adults are
scarcely affected at all. And, in a
well-documented but inadequately explained pattern that
recurs in virtually every recorded famine, women survive better than men.
By such means, a population under stress can use its depleted energies to
best effect. The resilience of African farmers, livestock herders and hunter-
gatherers when faced by food shortage has been admired by several generations of administrators and anthropologists. Livelihoods are adaptable and
diversified, coping mechanisms invaluable. Typically, a post-famine period
sees a quick rebound, with many babies born and food production rapidly
up to pre-famine levels. The smartest aid interventions are those that
support the existing skills and capacities of the real famine survival experts –
the affected people themselves.

THE SMARTEST AID INTERVENTIONS
ARE THOSE THAT SUPPORT THE
EXISTING SKILLS AND CAPACITIES OF
THE AFFECTED PEOPLE THEMSELVES

Starvation is actually rather rare in famines. Deaths hardly ever approach the huge totals so routinely predicted by journalists and aid agencies. Typically, overall mortality rates may double. A community of 1,000 people, which expects perhaps 15 deaths in a normal year, may experience 30 or 40. Most of these are due to infectious diseases, such as measles, dysentery and malaria, made more common by the social disruptions visited on a society by a food shortage (such as mass migration to find work), and made more life-threatening by malnutrition among children. If people are crowded into camps, these diseases may run riot and kill many more. When we see outright starvation, it is usually because men with guns have intruded and prevented a stricken community from following its well-established coping strategies – working, migrating, collecting roots and berries from the forests – and have also stolen their food. In such situations, the economic and nutritional temperature plummets and, in a metaphor favoured by an older school of practical emergency nutritionists, cold water turns to ice. At this point, death rates rocket by an order of magnitude. Among the people forced into some such famine camps in Ethiopia and Sudan in the 1980s, all the young children died.

LIKE WAR, STARVATION IS SOMETHING THAT PEOPLE DO TO ONE ANOTHER

The verb 'to starve' must be seen as transitive: someone does not merely starve, someone else needs to starve her. Like war, starvation is something that people do to one another. Fortunately, amid the depressing catalogue of recent African famines, there are very few in living memory in which frank starvation has happened.

But if we turn to the food shortage that steals across southern Africa today, we encounter some puzzles. The region is at peace for the first time in a generation. The barriers between the local economic superpower, South Africa, and its neighbours have been removed. By African standards, the subcontinent is relatively prosperous. The poorest economy, Mozambique, has been leading the world in its growth rates, admittedly from a very low base. Drought afflicts the area on a regular, predictable cycle of ten or 11 years, so that no one should be caught by surprise.

Yet governments and international agencies alike are bewildered by the scale of the food crisis and the relentlessly expanding numbers. If we examine more closely, we cannot be sanguine. There is a new factor at work in the form of the HIV/Aids pandemic. This is so profoundly affecting the societies of the region that none of the tried and tested rules hold good. Just as HIV is a pathogen that has not yet reached any form of equilibrium with its human host, the as-yet-nameless social catastrophe that it brings in its wake is one for which we have no measure and no remedy. Perhaps, like its cause, it needs an unwieldy acronym as a neologism: 'Aids-related national crisis' or ARNC.

The African pandemic of HIV/Aids subverts the logic of adaptation to a harsh and insecure environment. It kills adults in their twenties and thirties. Almost 30 million African adults are living with HIV and Aids; about 4 million died last year. It kills more women than men, and kills them younger. In some communities, fully one-fifth of young women are carrying HIV by the time they are 20. It has orphaned 11 million, a number that will probably treble inside ten years.

The mind grows numb trying to understand such statistics. But even these numbers do not tell the story of how the pandemic is altering the very structure of African societies. Aids strips households of their labour, both through the early death of breadwinners and through the protracted need for care during their illness. It erodes the lifetime accumulation of skill and wisdom and their intergenerational transmission. It threatens to erase the cultural archive, including essential survival skills, invariably possessed by older women, such as which wild berries and roots can safely be eaten in a time of famine. In the harshest famines in the Sahel and Sudan in the 1980s, rural people were impressively resilient, making tough but shrewd choices about how to husband their very scarce resources and use their working days to ensure their families' survival. Even the poorest farmers surprised many by managing to preserve sufficient seed to plant for the following year, enabling them to avoid perpetual pauperisation. Across southern Africa today, communities ground down by a decade of Aids deaths are stripped of that redeeming resourcefulness in adversity. Many have no assets left to sell or pawn, having sold all to pay for medicine, funerals and the upkeep of orphans. How can a 'sibling family' – the term used for orphans who live together under the premature leadership of an older sister or brother – plan and carry out the same complex 'survival strategies' that their parents or grandparents did one or a few decades ago? These children simply cannot know enough, or work hard enough, to see through the famine and build an economically viable household afterwards.

Throughout the subcontinent, the private sector and governments have quietly withdrawn social benefits, because of the escalating payroll costs associated with medical care and assistance to orphans. They have, in the jargon of Aids economists, 'shifted the burden' to wider society. But this 'wider society' has a name: it is mostly the village economy of smallholdings run on family labour. For a decade, this agrarian household economy has quietly borne this burden and, in doing so, has sold off its animals, ploughs, furniture and even its cooking pots. It has stopped growing nutritious and marketable but labour-intensive crops in favour of simple root crops such as cassava for subsistence. And now it can no longer shoulder this burden, and is facing starvation.

HIV/Aids has sent the historic processes of development into reverse. Alongside the reversion from cash cropping to bare subsistence, essential public services are in decline. Teachers and nurses are dying more quickly than they can be trained. Agricultural extension workers have been decimated. Hence the agrarian societies of southern Africa face an unexceptional drought in an exceptionally vulnerable condition.

All modern famines are accompanied by a 'shake-out' of the bottom tier of the poorest people and a 'bounce back' of the remainder. The shake-out is of those who can no longer make their way in a socially acceptable way as farmers or livestock herders or craftspeople, and are reduced to casual labour, begging or commercial sex work. Those who have retained key assets such as land and

WHAT THE CRUELTY OF WARLORDS AND GARRISON COMMANDERS ONCE IMPOSED UPON A FEW THOUSAND HIV/AIDS MAY NOW BE CREATING ACROSS HALF A DOZEN ENTIRE COUNTRIES

draught animals, and have retained seeds and managed to avoid sinking too far into debt, are generally able to rebound and recover their former livelihoods. But this recovery requires very hard work. Without the labour available – and most southern African countries have already undergone a workforce shrinkage of about 10 per cent, while the overall population continues to grow, albeit very slowly – that recovery is not in prospect. Southern Africans may be the victims of the continent's largest ever shake-out, condemned to indefinite immiseration.

What the cruelty of warlords and garrison commanders imposed upon a few thousand unfortunate famine refugees in the Horn of Africa a decade or so ago, HIV/Aids may now be creating across half a dozen entire countries.

Outright starvation may irrupt among the hundreds of thousands of people unable to cope. And, just as alarming, we are faced with the prospect that there will be no significant recovery; that what we say today is the harbinger of a new normality for southern Africa.

Humanitarians and economists alike are bewildered by the speed with which today's southern African food crisis has gathered momentum. This is a new and uniquely virulent variant of the familiar famine pathogen. It is as though, in the same way as HIV destroys the body's immune system, rendering it susceptible to 'normal' but strangely deadly infections, the HIV/Aids pandemic selectively annihilates a society's defences against social ills. Among the other distressing conditions that may emerge in this condition of diminished immunity are crime (perhaps related to the millions of orphans), urban unemployment (as businesses go bankrupt because of the increased payroll costs associated with staff illness and death) and

NOW WE ARE ON THE THRESHOLD OF NEW-VARIANT FAMINE – AIDS-RELATED FAMINE

political conflict (as military discipline breaks down). Economists' much-repeated prediction that a 10 per cent HIV rate among adults knocks 0.4 per cent off economic growth each year hardly does justice to the scale and nature of the regressive transformations that are probable. The US National Intelligence Council's depiction of HIV/Aids as a 'threat to security' cannot depict how such a threat may unfold. Now we are on the threshold of new-variant famine. The diagnosis of 'Aids-related famine' has already been made, though not in these exact words, by James Morris, head of the UN World Food Programme, and Stephen Lewis, the UN Secretary-General's Special Envoy for HIV/Aids in Africa.

For more than a decade, the more prescient social scientists in Africa have been warning that HIV/Aids threatens to unravel the social fabric of entire countries. The first predictions that it might contribute to 'food insecurity' were made by Tony Barnett and Piers Blaikie of the University of East Anglia in the late 1980s; the first whistle was blown on its likely macroeconomic impact in southern Africa by Alan Whiteside at the University of Natal shortly after. Most likely, the feared social and economic catastrophe is now with us. We have become so dulled to images of human misery in Africa, and so dismissive of humanitarians crying wolf about millions facing death before Christmas, that it has become easy to discount the predictions. But this time, even if the exact numbers of people in need and the time-scale of the unfolding crisis can be challenged, the disaster will be real and really on the scale feared.

Thus far, African governments and international aid donors have responded to HIV/Aids as another health challenge, albeit a rather large one. All the policies and programmes have been framed in terms of public health. The spiral of destitution in rural southern Africa compels us to examine the pandemic in the framework of its impact on political and economic systems. Teenagers in these countries now expect to live adult lives only half as long as their parents. Every aspect of life is changed by this fundamental redefinition of what constitutes a life. In turn this demands a level of resources and political energy rarely found in social policy, as well as a level of rethinking that is rarely found in political institutions of any kind. The humanitarians are in over their heads. Let them struggle on: their activities are far better than doing nothing. But let us not sleep easy in the delusion that this is a 'normal' famine for which 'normal' humanitarian responses will do. It will demand a humanitarian rethink that makes the 1990s advent of military humanitarianism look like a minor readjustment. Those, such as this author, who have long admired the skill and resilience of rural Africans faced with hardships such as drought, and criticised international welfarism, are now obliged to advocate a major international rescue package. The burden of HIV/Aids can only be borne by global philanthropy, if African societies are to survive. Watch this space. ❏

Alex de Waal is the director of Justice Africa

CAN BEGGARS BE CHOOSERS?

FACKSON BANDA

The policy dilemma confronting Zambia over whether or not to accept genetically modified maize, offered as food aid by the United States, has thrown up urgent questions over the way – and the extent to which – debate on the issue has been allowed in the country.

When the government rejected the US offer in August, many commentators described the move as a bold step aimed at asserting the country's national pride. But with the UN World Food Programme estimating that nearly 3 million people faced starvation in Zambia, the rejection was seen by some Western observers as unreasonable – the UK's *Financial Times* called it 'absurd'.

Now, following strong international pressure, a rethink is in the offing.

It is not as if there has been no public discussion about genetically modified organisms. On 12 August, the government organised a public debate in order to gauge the scientific evidence and other views. The debate highlighted deep divisions among Zambian scientists on the benefits of biotechnology.

The government voiced two concerns: the possibility of ill-health resulting from consumption of GM food and, later, its fears that GM crops might end up contaminating local non-GM crops and endanger Zambian agricultural exports to Europe, which maintain strict guidelines on GMOs. These discussions were given very little exposure in the local media coverage of GMOs: according to one media analyst, there were only four articles on the issue throughout 2000 and almost no discussion of the implications of imported GMOs on the local situation.

Focus group discussions organised by Panos in 2001, in conjunction with the Zambia National Farmers' Union (ZNFU), showed that farmers themselves were divided on the subject. While most small-scale farmers wanted more information, commercial farmers were opposed to GMOs, citing their fear of losing European markets for their existing non-GM exports.

The European Union accounts for 53 per cent of Zambian exports, mostly processed and refined foods, primary agricultural commodities and horticultural, animal and leather products. The ZNFU was among the

Livingstone, Zambia, September 2002: the first corn of the year – and it's not GM.
Credit: AP / Obed Zilwa

organisations that welcomed the government's rejection of the US food consignment. Others included the Organic Farming Association and the Jesuit Centre for Theological Reflection.

The scientific case for rejection is led by Dr Mwananyanda Mbikusita-Lewanika of the National Institute for Scientific and Industrial Research. He says there is compelling evidence that GMOs would have a negative impact on the local breeds such as millet, sorghum and traditional maize, and could cause ecological damage to farming generally. Lewanika says the government would do well to err on the side of caution by invoking the 'precautionary principle' clause of the Cartagena Protocol on Biosafety, arguing that there is convincing scientific evidence that GM plants have had adverse ecological effects on Mexican local maize varieties.

According to the precautionary principle, even if there is no clear scientific evidence that a seed type is dangerous, the government can decide to take the precaution of refusing it, if there is any likelihood that it might be harmful. Quoting research projects from around the world on potential ill effects such as toxicity, resistance to antibiotics, allergies, loss of biodiversity and resistance to pesticides, Lewanika builds the case against GMOs. He lays down two basic preconditions for allowing GMOs into the country. First, that there is a need to develop a national biosafety framework to regulate biotechnology and GMOs; and second, that the government must build the capacity to detect and monitor GMO substances in foodstuffs coming into Zambia.

Advocates of GMOs are largely drawn from University of Zambia scientists, among them some who have been working with South Africa's Muffy Koch, a senior microbiologist who is serving on the South African government's working group developing GMO regulations and drafting the country's position paper for the International Biosafety Protocol. Foremost among these are Dr Luke Mumba, dean of the School of Natural Sciences, and Dr Fastone Goma, a medical doctor in private practice and research scientist in the School of Medicine.

Mumba argues that 'in the developed world there is clear evidence that the use of GM crops has resulted in significant benefits', including higher crop yields, reduced farm costs, increased profits and improvements in the environment. He also asserts that research focusing on 'second-generation' transgenic crops has led to such beneficial products as iron- and vitamin-enriched rice, potatoes with higher starch content, edible vaccines in maize and potatoes and maize varieties able to grow in poor conditions.

In drought-prone Zambia, says Mumba, hardy, genetically modified maize would be a useful contribution to ensuring food security. 'Given the importance people place on the food they eat,' he adds, 'policies on GM crops must be based on an open and honest debate involving a wide cross-section of society.'

Both Mumba and Goma, as well as the ZNFU, argue that if it is indeed true that GM maize might contaminate local crop varieties, the GM maize should be milled and consumed now by the starving to ensure there is nothing left to store for planting next season.

Although most of the debate has been confined to scientific polemics, there has been some ideological-nationalistic opposition to GMOs. Led by Women for Change's executive director Emily Sikazwe, this argument suggests that the US government, pressured by huge seed transnational corporations, has an interest in establishing future markets on the African continent for its GM food exports. Sikazwe says the US is not willing to offer non-GM maize in place of GM food aid.

What is absent from the debate so far are the voices of the most affected people in rural areas. Bishop Peter Ndhlovu, head of the Bible Gospel Church in Africa, who has visited hunger-stricken villages, says: 'The food crisis in rural Zambia is more grave than can be imagined from an urban perspective.' His view articulates anxiety that the debate has been so urban-centred and elite-based that it has largely ignored the urgent needs of the rural poor. The emphasis on scientific evidence as a basis for policy-making has rendered the 'public debate' elitist. Apart from some vocal civil society organisations, those who are not schooled in science have been largely left on the sidelines.

While there is obviously a desire to learn more about the 'science' of GMOs, especially among small-scale farmers in the rural areas, the debate has been hijacked by groups who have politicised arguments against the entry of GM food and emphasised the unequal power relations between rich and poor nations as well as the role of multinational corporations in pursuit of 'scientific' evidence to justify GMOs. The government, supported by the media, has marginalised the voices of those who would argue in their favour. ❏

Fackson Banda *is the director of Panos Southern Africa*

AID AS A POLICY TOOL –
THE CASE OF SERBIA

SONJA LICHT

POST-CONFLICT AID IS BEST DEPLOYED
IN SUPPORTING EXISTING CIVIC AND
DEMOCRATIC INITIATIVES

After 5 October 2000, when the Serbian 'democratic revolution' became the topic of the day, many foreign journalists were keen to find out whether international aid had been a decisive factor in ousting the Milošević regime. Some of them were upset when the answer they were given was not a simple 'yes'. My main example that contradicted the stereotype was the simple fact that the Kolubara miners never received a penny of international aid yet had been the engine of the general strike that made 5 October possible.

However, if we reflect on the nature of the general strike/uprising that led to the political change in Serbia, it is obvious that the aid given to independent media, numerous civic initiatives including the Otpor (Resistance) movement and to the free cities where the political opposition had won the local elections in November 1996 played an important role in preparing the atmosphere for change.

Most of these various organisations and institutions were receiving bilateral and/or multilateral aid from public and private donors from Western Europe and, especially, the USA after the NATO intervention ended in summer 1999. The European Commission assistance to the 'free cities', where local governments were in open conflict with the national one, is probably unique. This was provided through two outstanding programmes, 'Energy for Democracy' and 'Schools for Democracy', and I'm not aware that the EU has intervened in such an overtly political way before.

So is Serbia the success story of international aid to the forces of change? The answer is yes and no. Yes in the last days of the Milošević regime after the NATO intervention; and no in those long years of the 1990s.

The Soros Foundation Yugoslavia was established in Belgrade back in 1991; in 1993, it opened branches in Vojvodina, Kosovo and Montenegro. It was the first donor to provide funding to various emerging civic groupings, educational and cultural initiatives, independent media and independent publishers. With the exception of a handful of NGOs mainly supportive of independent media such as the Swedish Helsinki Committee and the Dutch Press Now, Soros was virtually alone in its efforts until 1997. A few governments made a number of financially modest but morally important grants: the UK, USA, Germany and Sweden.

When the Soros Yugoslavia Foundation was closed in February 1996 – it was reopened in June under its present name – there was a real danger that most of the independent anti-war, human rights, women's, educational, cultural and humanitarian civic organisations, independent media, including the by then famous Radio B92, and independent publishers would disappear. Even this was not enough to shake up the international community which, some months later, was shocked by the realisation that the democratic movement was without political and financial support.

Most analysts believed this lack of interest was generated by the post-Dayton spirit, which saw Slobodan Milošević as a source of 'peace and stability'. Others attributed it to apathy on the part of the US and EU over future democratic development in Serbia and the

COULD THE KOSOVO CRISIS AND THE NATO INTERVENTION HAVE BEEN AVOIDED HAD THE INTERNATIONAL COMMUNITY SUPPORTED THE ANTI-WAR, ANTI-NATIONALIST, DEMOCRATIC FORCES IN SERBIA EARLIER?

rest of the Balkans. Whatever the case, the first serious donor support to Serbia's democratic forces did not reach the country until late 1997. Nor did it include Kosovo, where civic initiatives and independent media were left without significant financial assistance other than from Soros as late as the summer of 1999.

Could the Kosovo crisis and the NATO intervention have been avoided had the international community supported the anti-war, anti-nationalist, democratic forces in Serbia earlier?

The Milošević regime was ousted by the Serbian people acting as a united democratic front. Throughout 2000, the independent media played a crucial role as one of the most trusted sources of information but also a political alternative to authoritarianism. NGOs mobilised themselves to 'get out the vote', often literally going from door to door encouraging people to take their destiny in their own hands – and go to the ballot boxes. Otpor finally became a genuine people's movement and proved that every single repressive act, police harassment and brutality only increased the number of those who were ready for active resistance. And, finally, the leadership of 'free cities' demonstrated that representatives of the political opposition were ready to accept responsibility for their constituencies, including the establishment of an intensive communication with the international community. These initiatives represented various types of international assistance, both political and financial – together they proved an unbeatable force.

IT SEEMS OBVIOUS THAT IF ANY DEMOCRATIC STRUGGLE IS TO SUCCEED, SUPPORT FOR INDEPENDENT MEDIA, CIVIL SOCIETY AND POLITICAL OPPOSITION IS CRUCIAL

It seems obvious that if any democratic struggle is to succeed, support for independent media, civil society and political opposition is crucial. Although democratic power must be generated by the people themselves, flexible, well-targeted international aid can play a decisive role in accelerating the process – and is always more cost-effective than military intervention and the reconstruction that inevitably follows. ❏

Sonja Licht is the president of the Fund for an Open Society in Belgrade

INTERVENTION GOES GLOBAL

JOHN LLOYD

INTERVENTION BY THE WEST
ON HUMANITARIAN GROUNDS
SEEKS TO REFASHIONTHE
WORLD IN ITS OWN IMAGE

Earlier this year, I went with the UN High Commissioner for Refugees and former Dutch Prime Minister Ruud Lubbers to see refugee camps in the southern part of Afghanistan, between the Pakistani border and the city of Kandahar. As we got near the main camp of Spin Boldak, we saw long trucks lining the deeply rutted road, each with bags of flour and the donor country stamped on its side, each one an advertisement for Western generosity. Inside the camps were a mixture of thousands of desperate people, some displaced by the Taliban, some by those who had fought the Taliban, others by drought and famine.

Later, in the evening, we went back to Kandahar and met the governor-cum-warlord of the region, Gul Agha Sherzai. It was quickly evident that he had a different vision of the refugees from Lubbers. Where the Dutchman saw a humanitarian crisis, the Afghan saw a breeding ground for his enemies in camps a few kilometres from the Pakistani border, with former Taliban members among the refugees.

Both were right. The Afghans have returned in much greater numbers than expected: Lubbers was making emergency plans for feeding and heating these thousands through the winter, knowing he did not then have the resources to cope. But Gul Agha was right, too: the week after the two met, an assassin tried to murder President Karzai while he sat beside Gul Agha on the way to the wedding of the president's brother, who lives in Kandahar. The president narrowly escaped; Gul Agha was wounded; the assassin, with two others, was killed by the US Special Forces bodyguard that surrounds Karzai at all times.

It was a case study in globalisation. Of the two main actors in the case, one was a northern European brought there by his UN mission, the other an Afghan who had spent much of his life in exile because of his country's invasion by the Soviet Union and then its seizure by the Taliban, themselves trained in Pakistan, funded from Saudi Arabia and supported by militants from all over the Muslim world. The refugees were kept alive by food from all over the Western world; at least some had grown poppies and marijuana, which were supplied mainly to that same world.

At Kandahar airport, the US 6th Airborne – 'the world's finest fighting men' – had established a base. In the main street of the town, a score of NGOs had set up shop; back in the capital, Kabul, there were nearly 200. Afghanistan, for decades the most remote of the world's states, is now among its most 'globalised'. It would be better, if even less elegant, to say it is its most 'intervened-in', for it is now the subject of more interventions than anywhere else in the globe. A military intervention, largely conducted by the US, still goes on; the humanitarian intervention which brought Ruud Lubbers to Kandahar is among the largest the UN is mounting; a state-building intervention consumes the energy and resources of the hundreds of NGOs and UN agencies now based in the country; an economic intervention is seeking to re-establish an economy independent of drugs and foreign aid, for ever.

Afghanistan is the beneficiary – the radical no-global movements would say the victim – of the extraordinary change, and surge, in intervention in the past decade. Globalisation, defined by David Held and Anthony McGrew in their *Globalisation/Anti-Globalisation* as 'the expanding scale, growing magnitude, speeding up and deepening impact of transcontinental flows and patterns of human interaction', is bit by bit bringing with it the more generally diffused habit of seeing the globe as a whole. That which was once the preserve of the greatest empires – and even they had blind spots – is now available to all. The world is seen as a market; it is also seen, if imperfectly, as a society.

The world as a market has been the main focus of the hostility of the no-global movements. This is in part because of the changed nature of intervention: the main institutions of global economic management – the International Monetary Fund and the World Bank, together with the trade regulation agency the World Trade Organisation, the rich nations' club the Group of 7/8 (Russia is a part-member) and others – became much more demanding of the states they aided, or which became their members, than they had been in the past. The 'Washington consensus' – adumbrated in the 1970s by the British economist John Williamson, which included a commitment to low inflation, low-budget deficits, free trade and expansion of the private sector – became and remains the basic model for all economies. In pursuit of these commitments, the international institutions

Peshawar, Pakistan 2001: aid for the Afghans, victims and beneficiaries of a global world.
Credit: Camera Press / Dag Grundseth / Scanpix

seek to guide and push their clients towards conformity with their demands, rewarding compliance (at least in theory) by more aid and punishing deviation with the withholding of aid.

The reconstruction of the post-communist states of the Soviet Union and the Soviet bloc has been the largest and most controversial of the economic interventions undertaken in the past decade. It was the more complex and contested because Russia, in common with most of the republics that had made up the Soviet Union, had very little experience of capitalism. The project to make it capitalist thus stirred the most profound levels of its social and cultural fabric in ways that were not foreseen either by the foreign experts or by the post-Soviet politicians, business people and officials who drove the thing through.

It is also true that the West's intervention in post-Soviet Russia was largely driven by the US. Though it took a largely economic form and its main agents were the International Monetary Fund and the World Bank, Russian reform has been and remains heavily influenced, though not determined, by a US geo-strategic-cum-political calculation. The question 'Who Lost Russia?' was dismissed by Condoleeza Rice, secretary of the National Security Council, when I interviewed her in the summer of 1999 as she was preparing to join the advisory team for the Bush presidential bid. 'Russia is not ours to lose,' she said. 'The US should not be so involved that it is compromised by association with corruption around the Yeltsin presidency, and by praising reform which was not reform.' However, as she has since discovered in office, geo-strategic considerations mean all bets are off. Russia is again seen, for different reasons, as a state to be nice to; included in that calculation is a downplaying to the point of invisibility of any complaints that human rights are being violated in the continuing campaign in Chechnya.

The performance of the IMF and the World Bank in the Soviet bloc, in Latin American countries and in Africa has made them the subject of ferocious criticism. Most of this has been beside the point, which is that the main elements of the Washington consensus are those by which all healthy economies live. There is room for endless argument about the details, the timing and the strength of the stages of reform, but no alternative system, after the collapse of the state socialist model, has been proposed. Economic intervention will continue because states need it; its terms are and should be under constant debate.

The end of communism had another, wider effect. It meant the end of a certain sort of clientelism – one that saw the two opposing ideological blocs adopt large tracts of the developing world on the basis of their affiliation to one system or the other. The sponsoring of tyrants who mouthed pro-capitalist or pro-communist rhetoric is not something that will be missed, but the downside has been that the money shovelled into these states to keep them onside has, in the past decade, been cut dramatically. Aid to Africa shrank, in the 1990s, from US$32 to US$19 per capita as politicians and officials discovered, with a horror that must have been at least partly feigned, that a great deal of it had stuck in the hands of corrupt rulers and senior officials.

There is now a different spirit abroad, though it is too early to say if it will bring in deep change. Britain's Department of International Development has led on this – among Western politicians, its secretary of state, Claire Short, has become one of the most effective and tough-minded advocates for the poor. In a paper put out by her department in spring this year, she argued in unusually unambiguous terms that to address the causes of poverty was 'not just central to peace and security, but because to do so is right. This is a moral imperative, an economic necessity and a social duty.'

In an interview, she stressed that the approach to aid had changed and was changing still, with what she saw as the more progressive states – such as the UK, Scandinavia and The Netherlands – pressing for longer-term aid. 'People need to change their mindset on aid,' she said. 'You need to see things over long periods. You need, for example, an investment fund which would pay for kids to go to school. The poorest countries need all kinds of help – with policy, with delivery, with services, with everything.'

The new forms of aid – essentially contracts with governments under which money is disbursed against a checklist of reforms – lie behind the new approach to aid to Africa, advertised at the last G7 summit in Canada and now launched on its way. It has less money than its main sponsors hoped; Africa remains a continent in which the problems of endemic and deep poverty are made the more hellish by the still ravaging spread of Aids (De Waal, p176). The moral force that leaders like Tony Blair and Gerhard Schroeder could muster are, by the nature of the political process, fitful, and are now drowned by the war on terror.

The post-11 September interventions have tended to drown out everything else. Terror and its pursuit are rewriting the rules on intervention in ways that are paradoxical and still illegible. The consensus before the attack on the World Trade Center was that the US administration was unilateralist in its approach to the world; determined to do the opposite of Bill Clinton in foreign policy, it withdrew from or refused to accede to international treaties and refused to take an active role in such crucial theatres as the Middle East.

Since that date, it has become the supreme interventionist. It has deposed the government of Afghanistan and is now proposing to depose that of Iraq. It has roused governments around the world to follow its lead in making war on terrorist groups: it has won over doubtful or hostile governments to its side; it has put US soldiers in bases across Central Asia; has hugely increased its defence budget. It now sees the world as if from the hub of a wheel, with spokes leading down to regions that are more or less troublesome to it. Its huge power lends credence to those who see it as a new kind of imperial force, yet if this is so, it is reluctant to acknowledge its destiny.

Post-9/11 interventionism is unclear because the temper of the world is unclear. If terrorist acts on a large scale continue – and the murderous bomb on the Indonesian island of Bali in mid-October may show that the al-Qaida network, or an organisation sympathetic to it, is still capable of outrages – then the world will tend to take on some of the appearances and practices of a police state. At the same time, though, the developed world continues to move towards the practice of 'soft power' – that is, a politics and diplomacy in which borders, as in Europe or North America, become less important, and the proportion of trade, cultural exchange and the merging of policy is more and more the norm.

We who are citizens of the rich states live presently in the paradoxical situation of being unprecedentedly secure from attacks by neighbouring or powerful states, and unprecedentedly insecure about our economies, our travel and our futures. This insecurity will lead us to intervene more and more in the troubled areas and failed states of the world, to seek to refashion them if not in our image then at least in a simulacrum of market-based democracies. It is in this arena that the arguments on intervention will rage: how much of it should be military, how much aid, how much state-building? The questions that have been growing over the last half-century, which have become urgent in the past decade, are now at the top of the international agenda. These revolve round the nature of security and the lengths to which it is permissible to go to get it. We were already in a new era of intervention, and now yet another new era dawns. ❑

John Lloyd is a freelance journalist

INTERNATIONAL JUSTICE, WAR CRIMES AND TERRORISM: THE U.S. RECORD

Vol 69:4 (Winter 2002)   Arien Mack, Editor

* **JUST AND UNJUST WARS**

* **THE TRAINING OF THE MILITARY: NATIONAL LAW AND TEACHING THE GENEVA CONVENTION**

* **KEYNOTE ADDRESS: TERRORISM**

* **INTERNATIONAL LAW AND JUSTICE**

* **PUNISHMENT OF WAR CRIMES AND ATROCITIES: INTERNATIONAL AND NATIONAL TRIBUNALS**

* **DEFINING AND RESPONDING TO TERRORISM**

* **WHERE DO WE GO FROM HERE? NEW AND EMERGING ISSUES IN THE PROSECUTION OF WAR CRIMES AND ACTS OF TERRORISM**

An International Quarterly of the Social Sciences

ISSN 0037-783X. Available in Borders and independent bookstores throughout the U.S. or by order for $12.00/copy. Subscriptions $30/year. Foreign postage: $5.00/year or $2.50 for first back issue plus $1.00 each additional issue. Payment by check (in U.S. currency, payable to Social Research), Visa or MasterCard. Contact us at 65 Fifth Avenue, Room 344, New York, NY 10003. Phone: (212) 229-5776; Fax: (212) 229-5476; socres@newschool.edu. Visit us at www.socres.org

Contributors: Michael Walzer, Professor, School of Social Sciences, Institute of Advanced Studies; **Richard Holbrooke**, Former Permanent U.S. Representative to the U.N.; **Martin Peretz**, Editor in Chief, the New Republic; **Col. Charles Garraway**, Directorate of Army Legal Service, Ministry of Defence, Great Britain; **Col. Anthony Hartle**, Professor of Philosophy and English, United States Military Academy; **Col. Hays Parks**, Special Assistant to the Judge Advocate General of the Army, the Pentagon; **Arthur C. Helton**, Director, Peace and Conflict Studies, Council on Foreign Relations; **Bob Kerrey**, President, New School University and Former U.S Senator from Nebraska; **Richard J. Goldstone**, Judge, South African Constitutional Court and former chief prosecutor, International War Crimes Tribunals for the Former Yugoslavia and Rwanda; **Stephen Holmes**, Professor of Law, New York University; **Samantha Power**, Executive Director, Carr Center for Human Right Policy, Harvard University; **Michael Ignatieff**, Director, Carr Center for Human Rights Policy, Harvard University; **Gary Bass**, Assistant Professor of Politics, Princeton University; **Andrew Arato**, Hirshon Professor of Sociology, Graduate Faculty, New School University; **Aryeh Neier**, President, Open Society Institute; **Patricia Wald**, Former Judge, International Criminal Court, The Hague; **David Scheffer**, Former Ambassador at Large for War Crimes Issues; **Kenneth Roth**, Executive Director, Human Rights Watch; **David Rieff**, Fellow, World Policy Institute, New School University; **Kenneth Anderson**, Professor of Law, Washington College of Law, American University; **Theodor Meron**, Denison Professor, New York University and American Judge, United Nations War Crimes Tribunal, The Hague

BEYOND CHARITY

DAVID RIEFF

BY OPTING FOR A RIGHTS-BASED
SOLUTION TO THE DELIVERY OF
HUMANITARIAN AID, RELIEF WORKERS
HAVE COMPOUNDED THEIR DILEMMA

The malaise among emergency relief workers about humanitarian action dates back at least to Bosnia and Rwanda. Although previous man-made disasters – such as the refugee emergency along the Thai–Cambodia border in the aftermath of the fall of the Khmer Rouge, and the Ethiopian famine of the mid-1980s – had already made clear the unintended malign consequences of aid, the fact that humanitarianism was so clearly misused in the Balkans and in the Great Lakes region of Africa made the lesson an inescapable one.

Humanitarian relief had provided the Western powers with a moral warrant for non-intervention in the Balkans; to have acted politically, it was said, would 'get in the way' of the aid effort. In the Rwandan case, the desperately needed relief that aid workers brought to the refugee camps of eastern Democratic Republic of Congo in 1994 in the aftermath of the genocide actually helped revive the fortunes of the architects of the slaughter who had fled there. As a result, the idea that aid was not a morally unambiguous activity – something that had been controversial among aid workers before the mid-1990s – became commonplace, and took the form, in its encapsulated version, of the conviction that there were no humanitarian solutions to humanitarian problems.

But although this truism was certainly a welcome reality check for a world of organisations that had too often tended to take their own millenarian slogans at face value – think of Oxfam's boast that it is 'working for a fairer world' or Médecins sans Frontières' 1980s boast that it had 'two billion people in our waiting room' – it did nothing to answer the question of how aid workers should cope with the dilemmas they faced. Aid, it was clear, might easily extend wars and inadvertently exacerbate the most grievous human suffering and debasement even as it saved lives. And aid was also recognised as serving as a moral flag of convenience for the political agendas of the great powers who provided relief agencies with both the bulk of their funds and with the institutional support they needed to operate effectively.

But if, by the end of the 1990s, the dilemmas were clear enough, how to respond was not. If anything, the dependency of aid workers on governmental and intergovernmental grants (to some extent a distinction without a difference, as the UN funds NGOs received were largely recycled monies from the major donors, the European Union and the USA) continued to increase steadily. Programmes had been vastly expanded as the money flowed in, as had, not coincidentally, staffs at headquarters. To say this is not to try to score any cheap points about why aid workers found (and still find) themselves in the predicament they did. Venality exists in every profession, but it was not the underlying motivation for the challenge that confronted the humanitarian world. On the contrary, increased funds and the support of national militaries with their vast airlift capacities and budgets, seemed to promise that aid workers could act to save lives in places to which they would otherwise never have been able to gain access. If there had been expansion – with or without humanitarian hubris – it had been for the most decent of motives.

But it is not just a biblical bromide that the road to Hell is paved with good intentions. Aid workers might have the best of moral and operational ambitions, but their success in the field, their unparalleled influence in the media, and their previously undreamed-of access to power was as much due to how the prestige of the humanitarian enterprise benefited the policy goals of great powers as it was to any new altruism in Washington, London, Paris or Brussels. Like human rights, aid in the post-communist era was clearly one of the few saving moral ideas. It had become, in other words, not just a practice but an ideology. The difference was that, unlike explicitly political ideologies, and in a similar way to the human rights idea (another saving secular notion whose ascent can be tied historically to the end of the communist 'faith'), humanitarianism claimed to be not just apolitical but anti-political.

UNLIKE EXPLICITLY POLITICAL IDEOLOGIES, HUMANITARIANISM CLAIMED TO BE NOT JUST APOLITICAL BUT ANTI-POLITICAL

It is difficult to imagine a world view more likely to recommend itself to a neo-liberal order that also proclaimed that politics in the high, ideological sense was at an end. At the same time, again like human rights, humanitarianism was attractive to policymakers in the West – at least judging from the extent to which so many of them have cited it not just as a flag of convenience for their policies but as the expression of the 'moral' essence of those policies (think of Tony Blair) – because it gave a necessary content to policies that otherwise might have seemed simply a pursuit of trade advantage. After all, globalisation could not just be about free markets: to make sense to its advocates, it had to offer the promise of a better world as well. But at the same time, humanitarianism threatened no serious vested interest in the West. It posed no challenge to the liberal order. On the contrary, its practitioners tended to view the liberal order as the one thing that would make the need for their interventions unnecessary.

Again, the parallel with human rights is instructive, and it is hard not to see both movements' adoption by Western governments as injecting the necessary ideological content into globalisation. In an age when globalised media and abiding fictions about progress made it difficult for policymakers to admit that they did not particularly care about the tragedies of faraway peoples (no Western politician today could say of the Rwandans what Neville Chamberlain had said of the Czechs in 1938, that they were a faraway people of whom the British knew little), humanitarianism also served as the proof that the West really did 'care'. In this sense, although the power realities of the world had not in fact altered all that much (had they really done so, the ruin of Africa would be a central concern of powerful states, not a tangential one), humanitarian action made it seem as if they had.

NO GREAT IDEA THAT HAD SERIOUS POLITICAL FUNCTIONS THAT WERE OF VALUE TO THE ESTABLISHED ORDER HAS EVER REMAINED THE EXCLUSIVE PROPERTY OF THOSE WHO ORIGINATED IT

To say this is not to blame the humanitarians themselves. If any group of people in the past few decades has distinguished itself by the quality and seriousness of its commitment and the sincerity of its mission, it has been the relief world. But no great idea that had serious political functions that were of value to the established order – whether that idea is Christianity, or human rights, or humanitarianism – has ever remained the exclusive property of those who originated it. Aid workers might go along on their millennial way, believing that somehow they could bring a world of genuine human solidarity closer, but by the end of the 1990s the aid idea was rapidly being taken away from them. Again, the main reason was their ever increasing dependence on the major donors for funds.

It was a cruel choice that confronted the humanitarians. Allow yourself to be treated as a subcontractor, at least in crises that were of interest to major Western governments – a process that began in the Balkans but has grown more comprehensive in Afghanistan and, lately, in US preparations for a possible conflict in Iraq – or see yourself marginalised or even replaced by business contractors without the slightest commitment to humanitarian principles. For many aid workers, particularly in the US, the imperial train has already left the station and there is really nothing to be done but try to mitigate the worst human effects of the crises that wars like the impending one in Iraq will almost certainly produce. But even for European aid workers, the desire to help has usually been more powerful than any reluctance to be implicated, at least tacitly, in the policy goals of the NATO countries.

For their part, Western governments increasingly tend to see aid workers as subcontractors and to expect the compliance from them that any boss expects from any employee. It is because aid workers have realised this that many of the best of them have been drawn to the idea of human rights. For the human rights paradigm, which insists that people in need are not only beneficiaries of others' largesse but have rights, and that the function of relief work is to provide people with services and help to which they are legally entitled under international law, seems to offer a way out of the subaltern status in which the mainline NGOs now find themselves. At the very least, they have a stronger case for arguing for their presence if what they are doing fulfils internationally recognised legal dictates and norms than they do if they are simply providing charity, with all the elective quality that philanthropy of this sort implies.

> WESTERN GOVERNMENTS INCREASINGLY TEND TO SEE AID WORKERS AS SUBCONTRACTORS AND TO EXPECT THE COMPLIANCE FROM THEM THAT ANY BOSS EXPECTS FROM ANY EMPLOYEE

The difficulty is that the actual practice of humanitarian relief could not be more different from that of human rights work. By definition, human rights is absolutist, fundamentalist. The moment a human rights worker justifies an abuse or a war crime on the grounds that the person who has committed it was oppressed or on the correct side morally or politically, that human rights activist loses all credibility. In contrast, relief work on the ground is, equally by definition, about compromise. The paradigmatic aid action is not the report or the advocacy campaign, but the attempt to move a needed commodity (or aid worker with some technical expertise such as sanitation or medicine) through a checkpoint manned by a monster with a Kalashnikov and, subsequently, to operate in that monster's fiefdom. Thus the aid worker's stock-in-trade is compromise – he has to make an ally of the monster. And unless one is naive enough to believe that those who commit atrocities in our world mainly do so out of ignorance of the law, it is hard to see how the legalism or the absolutism of the human rights approach can be of much value to relief workers.

Of course, this would not be the case if aid workers really wanted to gravitate (as a worrying number of mainline human rights groups seem to be doing) towards the view that if abusers continue to defy international law there must be military interventions on humanitarian and human rights grounds. That, at least, would make sense logically. But the spectre of these endless wars of altruism, not to mention that of the human rights and humanitarian movement providing the ideological shock troops for a movement to recolonise so-called failed states, should give pause to those with enough historical consciousness to remember that humanitarian and human rights justifications also provided the basis for much of nineteenth-century European colonialism. And, to be fair, that enterprise, too, often saved lives as well as taking them, and certainly improved health outcomes in many parts of the world.

Where humanitarians go wrong is in imagining that human rights norms and, more generally, the edifice of international law, can exist independently of power. In this sense, conservative interventionists in the US have a firmer grasp of the realities of the world. For if relief workers are really demanding consistent access to beneficiaries on the basis of law, they will, more often than they would be comfortable admitting, actually be demanding occupation by soldiers strong enough to guarantee such access. And that means NATO and, finally, the US. Perhaps the choice is between liberal imperialism and barbarism. But even if it is, the idea that the choice can be sanitised by appealing to law or human rights norms has made the relief workers' rights-based 'solution' to the dilemma that confronts them as bad as, perhaps even worse than, the original problem. ❏

David Rieff is a writer and journalist. His latest book is A Bed for the Night *(Vintage 2002)*

CULTURE

Buenos Aires, 26 November 2002: mother of the Plaza de Mayo protests against a police blockade at a hunger march. Credit: AFP Photo / Daniel Garcia

IN LABOUR

MARTA BETOLDI

Who are we when we say who we are? And what do we remember about being?
These are two items (among many more) that the twentieth century bequeathed
without explanation. Globalisation, with all its faults and triumphs, has failed
to tell us where we belong, and why. Hence the worldwide struggle for an identity.

For convenience we have placed this search in Argentina: evil dictatorship, brutal
repression, beautiful people murdered, many questions, few answers. But the problem
we project from Argentina belongs to twentieth-century Europe and much of the
world beyond. This is just a small sample. Irrelevant to most of the world, but
ignore it we cannot.

Between March 1976 and December 1983, one of the bloodiest military
regimes in modern Latin American history ruled Argentina. 'State terror' was
reflected principally in the policy of making opponents 'disappear'. The military of
Argentina contributed that word to the language; people did not die or go away, they
'disappeared', there was nothing known of them or even traceable. People vanished
(the figures range from an official inquiry into 10,000 victims, and 30,000 claimed
by the relatives of the 'disappeared'). The Mothers of Plaza de Mayo (the main
square in front of Government House, where relatives of the 'disappeared' marched
in protest) still search every Thursday at 3pm for information on their children.

The Grandmothers of Plaza de Mayo were formed more recently, to search for
the children known to have been born in captivity. The pregnant women who were
captured were allowed to give birth, their babies were taken from them and given up
for adoption among 'friends' of the regime. The mothers were murdered.

In June 2000, the Grandmothers launched a theatrical season entitled 'Theatre
for Identity', in the belief that many unanswered questions could prompt a response
if asked from the stage. The first of the series, 'A propos of doubt' by Patricia
Zangaro, was published in English (Index 1/01). The plays ask two eerie
questions: 'Do you know who you are? Do you have any doubt about your
identity?' The series eventually generated 41 plays that have been collected in
Teatro por la identidad *(Eudeba, Buenos Aires, 2001).*

Argentine actress and playwright Marta Betoldi's 'In Labour' is the second
to be published in English. It topped the list of seven selected by Estela Barnes
de Carlotto, president of the Grandmothers of Plaza de Mayo.

Andrew Graham-Yooll

IN LABOUR ('CONTRACCIONES')

(Stage is in darkness. Stage left a light shines on ANDREA, a woman aged 42. She looks younger. Her clothes are brightly coloured. She sits at a desk writing a letter which she reads aloud.)

ANDREA Hello son, or daughter. I've just had the tests, which explain my morning sickness. It's my birthday today and I want to thank you for this present. I'm a little shocked, but happy. Dad knows nothing yet. I thought you should be the first to learn of your existence. I'll put the tests here.

The written word, I think, suits me better to speak my feelings. I am usually quiet and shy, you will soon see, but this moment is so big I think I must be as talkative as possible. Oh, we've had your name for ages. Juan if you're a boy, Laura if you are lucky to be the stronger sex. And as I know about these things . . . I am sure you are Laura.

A light goes up stage right to show LAURA, a woman aged 23, seated at a desk writing a letter. When action moves to LAURA, ANDREA continues to write in silence.

LAURA Today I was told what a mother's intuition had heard from the heart. The tests showed you're a real . . . girl. Dad was a little crestfallen. He's quite macho, even if he denies it. I am delighted.

I didn't start writing earlier without knowing all was well, and you are! I am a manic letter writer, to my mother's regret. She even threw out the letters I wrote as a teenager to an imaginary boyfriend. This is a secret diary that belongs to you and me. The others will only see the scans and the photos.

ANDREA Mum says that letter writing is a family habit I've got from Granny Antonia. The story goes that when she stopped being illiterate she wrote letters to the whole village. I hope I pass down the best of us. Dad is besotted: he has already bought six pairs of booties.

I think you are going to be a Taurus, according to my astrologer aunt. The sun will give you beauty, the arts and a strong character, pigheaded even. To me, you will be perfect whatever your date of birth.

LAURA You will be born in October, like me, unless you decide otherwise. I saw you on the screen today, so clearly! You were sucking a finger on your right hand and looked happy, and you moved all the time like an astronaut as if you knew you were on film. I think you look like me. I think, because Mum doesn't have any pictures of me as a baby. The family photo albums were lost in one of our many moves. In my first ten years, Dad's work had us moving all over the country. I would have liked to have at least one photo to compare us. I'll make copies of everything, including the scans, and keep them in a safe place.

ANDREA I will stick this first photo of you inside me and I hope you like it. I feel a bit fat, but I've never felt so lovely and radiant.

LAURA It's time we decided a name. I don't want to go on calling you Daughter. Even if it sounds big it is not enough. It's a difficult choice, difficult for me. A name is like a face. A person in itself, a name speaks of who you are.
   I've almost decided on María, which your dad likes and . . .

ANDREA Laura. Don't let anybody call you Laurita, Lala, Luli, or anything like that. I've always disliked nicknames. You are Laura.

LAURA Laura? Not Martina. Why did I write Laura? Laura? It doesn't sound right. It sounds better with my surname, Laura González.

ANDREA Laura Olivares. It's strong, has personality. 'Hello, Miss Laura Olivares. How are you today?'

LAURA I am feeling fine, though I still vomit. They say that stops after three months.

ANDREA I am in the fourth month and I still have to open the window in the bus, and hang on to trees. The vomiting doesn't stop. The doctor says that's normal, just nerves. I have trouble studying, I feel sleepy all the time. But I must get into philosophy. Your dad is in his psychology finals. I don't see him much now he works at the Student Union. He left me his photo. Nice Freud we have, eh? He has style. I love him so much, and he loves me. I feel so full today. I am happy.

LAURA Sometimes I feel strange. I can't stop crying. There is a pressure in the middle of my chest, concentrated anxiety. My doctor says pregnant women have this, but it happens more to me. Mum says don't be silly, forget it, so I don't talk about it much.

ANDREA I think of you all the time, I cuddle you. I imagine your feet, fingers and hands. It is so moving to feel you in me. I'm sure you will have dark hair like all my family and your father's.

Contracciones, 2002: (l–r) Laura Azcurra (actress), Leonor Manso (director), Marta Betoldi (actress and playwright). Credit: Andrew Graham-Yooll

LAURA I think you will be blonde. Your father is. And my parents are fair. I am the only dark one. There's a lost great-grandfather somewhere who left me his genes. My mother insists that my hair darkened over the years.

ANDREA I have three pieces of good news. First: no sickness for a week. Second: Granny Clara's sister came yesterday from Mercedes and said you are a girl, and she is never wrong. Third: people already give me their seat on the train. Thanks, Laura! Such privilege makes me feel like a queen.

(PS: I found a part-time job.)

LAURA Your father and my mother are getting on my nerves telling me to stop working, but I can't think of myself at home all day. I'd die. You've got a hyperactive mother. I must have got it from all the moving.

ANDREA It is so hot. I've got a week off in March and Dad wants us to go to Córdoba. I hope the doctor approves because I'll be in my seventh month. Dad is painting our portraits on the quiet. I saw him by chance this morning and he will be flattering. I won't say I saw it so it stays a surprise.

LAURA Ximena, my best friend, gave me a book of proverbs. The first I read was by a native Indian group. It touched me so I could not stop crying until I had written it for you: 'When a child is born the father shows him the world and the mother embraces him to show that he is the world.'

ANDREA I was looking at carrycots, and though I am betting on pink, I'll buy white.
     PS: Can you believe it: Father bought you a Boca squad shirt!

LAURA Boca won and it makes me happy. I didn't tell you, and even if my parents don't like it, I'm a real Boca fan.

ANDREA Dad is very nervous and won't tell me why. Today he suggested we bring forward the holiday. I suppose he is like that because he is going to be a father. Men get more scared than we do as the time gets closer. That's what my mother says, and she had five children.

LAURA Two victories. One: Dad agrees to be with us when you are born. I am relieved not to be alone. Second: he agrees to your name. It slipped out when we were looking at the screen, I looked at him and we giggled. Anyway, I wasn't going to give up that easily. Laura, the five letters are all yours, with all the strength of its brilliance. Laura, I love you. I am happy.

ANDREA Sorry I haven't written for a week. We've had a military coup. There's a lot of trouble. Your granny is worried about me going to university. Your dad had to leave suddenly for Salta because of problems in the Student Union. He asked me to go alone to Córdoba and we'll meet at the bus terminal. He doesn't sleep much these days, and his asthma's back. He was sweating too much. He left at five in the morning, there was not much light and I pretended to be asleep, I've always hated partings. He kissed my belly, my eyes, kissed me all over and stood in the room for some time.

He left us the portrait on the bed, signed 'I love you'. That filled me with sadness. How strange. I rubbed my face in his pillow to smell his scent.

LAURA After you're born, I am going to write down every detail, so that when you are grown up I can help you. Can you believe my mother doesn't remember anything and can't explain it?

ANDREA I have milk in my nipples, it's called colostrum. It's good to know we are stocking the pantry. Buenos Aires is so strange it frightens me. All I want now is to get to Córdoba. Dad called today in a great hurry and sent us kisses.

LAURA When I eat chocolate you jump like a little rabbit. It makes you happy. Like it does me eating it. Our hearts beat together and in harmony.

ANDREA I get nervous when you stop moving and worry that something's wrong, but if I eat a chocolate you immediately get going. You're a fatty at heart, like your mother!

LAURA I love you.

ANDREA I love you more than myself, I love you madly.

LAURA I feel you.

ANDREA I can see you barefoot, running naked.

LAURA Dawn embraces us; the fading moon touches me.

ANDREA I am in love with you and you make me fall in love with you.

LAURA And I am happy.

ANDREA Happy.

LAURA The doctor says you are well formed. You just have to grow and so must I. Dad is in doubt again about being with me. I'll panic. If he doesn't come, I'll ask Ximena.

ANDREA Everything was on time. Green wallpaper in your room and I bought your cot. Your grannies are in a frenzy of knitting, they are embroidering your sheets. And I have your bag ready just in case you decide to give us a surprise. Two months and you'll be here.

LAURA I'm betting on life. A child is a bet on life. That's what matters now.

ANDREA Dad was very strange. He called early and suggested we don't go to Córdoba, but I won't have that. We are going there tonight . . . and we'll be having breakfast together at the station. Just a few hours feel like years. I'll write to you there.

The light goes out over ANDREA. She exits.

LAURA I had a check yesterday, and I heard your heartbeat; it was regular, rhythmic, with mine. I cried a little.

A person at the clinic mistook me for somebody else. She called me Andrea . . . and was very overcome . . . her eyes filled with tears. I didn't understand what was going on. My husband was in a hurry and took me to the car, but I felt she had more to tell me.

Anyway, all that matters now is you.

Short silence on stage. LAURA looks to where ANDREA was sitting.

LAURA I couldn't sleep last night, even though I practised all the relaxation I was taught on the course.

I couldn't stop thinking of the face of that nurse . . . or maybe doctor. I feel my chest closing and I am filled with anxiety.

Short silence.

Two days now and I can't stop thinking of that woman. I think I'll go to see her.

Silence.

I worked up courage and went to the clinic to find that woman. She is a doctor, a specialist in contagious diseases. Patricia. When she saw me she shook all over again. When she calmed down she offered me coffee and the conversation was a monologue, full of words that hit me strangely. I was a bit shaken, because her words sounded familiar, even the way she moved her hands . . . She kept walking around my chair. She talked of somebody she had met a long time ago and thought that I might be her daughter Laura. That's the name she gave and said she had been at the birth, to help, when she was a medical student. Then she stopped, stared at me, and burst into tears. She hugged me, kissed me . . . apologised, and suddenly I felt very small again.

Silence.

Laura . . . like my Laura . . . I feel faint, short of air.

The lights go out. In the darkness a spot shines centre stage on a space like a basement. ANDREA, looking dishevelled, sits on the floor.

ANDREA It's so hot here, I can hardly breathe. The good news vanished with the pens, but I am not going to stop our chats and I am going to memorise every word until I can write them down when they let me out. They say that us pregnant women will be taken to have our babies outside of here, then they release the babies. I know nothing of your father. They don't talk nicely about him, nor about me, but don't listen to them. I sing to you as much as possible, though my voice is croaking. The pain doesn't let me sleep.

Lights up, showing LAURA.

LAURA Patricia is a ghost, I can't get her out of my thoughts. Her face, her scent. It's as if I knew her. I couldn't tell anybody about her.

ANDREA Felt better today, they are not questioning me so much. There are other pregnant women here and we all try to talk just about you little people. One of them is lovely, Patricia. She's a medical student who helps us with our exercises.

LAURA Patricia calls me all the time and I can't answer. I'm in a bad mood, don't sleep much, and the pain in the chest won't go away. I mentioned a bit to Mum and she went pale and came at me with all that about not talking to strangers . . . and blah blah. I can't stop thinking about the coincidences.

ANDREA I'm terrified. Claudia, one of the girls who was pregnant, had her baby yesterday. A boy. Pablo. She did not go to any hospital and delivered him here, and then he was taken away from her. They said they were giving him to her mother. My God! I worry that my mum is never at home and she might not know that she has to go and fetch you, and she'll be desperate. She won't know the address . . . Laura, I don't want you to leave.

LAURA I feel better. It helped to unplug the phone. I feel less pain in my chest. Your room is a delight. Your cot is fit for a queen.

ANDREA Today I was told that your father was arrested at a friend's house in Salta just as he was leaving for Córdoba. He's alive. He's alive and I miss him very much.

LAURA The old man knows everything. Mum told him. He came to question me. I was angry, he very angry, I ignored him. He wouldn't let go. Quite apart from the silence and the squabble, I know there is something I don't know.

ANDREA I have lost my sense of time and space. I can't remember how many days I've been here. I tried to sing to you but can't. I am very angry. I don't know why this is happening to me. I don't understand, I don't know what they are talking about. I don't understand their language.

I'm afraid. You cheer me with your little kicks. Kick, Laura, please kick! The girls look after me. Claudia can't stop crying and touches our stomachs. I've begun to pray. You are my favourite star, my north, my sun, my everything. I know God will have pity on us and a miracle will happen.

LAURA Patricia brought me this box. (*She puts it on the writing table.*) She told me to look at the photos, baby clothes and a book written for me. And I don't know why I don't tell her to piss off. (*She opens the box slowly.*) My chest hurts. (*She takes out the exercise book and opens it.*)

'Hello son, or daughter: The written word, I think, suits me better to speak my feelings. I am usually quiet and shy, you will soon see, but this moment is so big I think I must be as talkative as possible. Oh, we've had your name for ages, Juan if you're a boy, Laura if you are lucky to be the stronger sex. And as I know about these things . . . I am sure you are Laura.'

ANDREA Laura, I speak to you, I remember you to write to you, and I write to remember myself. If God Almighty will allow it, my darling little one, light of my eyes that are now blind from so much darkness, I know you will not have your first night in your green room or your white clothes, but you will have my nipples to heal you. You will go from me, through me, to an eternity of two, mother and daughter. I will have your taste of milk, of salt and sea in the mornings.

The pains are coming more quickly now . . . I feel so bad about partings . . . You will give me the joy of being a mother and nobody can take that from me and you will be my light now and for ever. One more heave and you will be mine. I love you more than myself, I love you madly.

(*She calls.*) Patricia . . . !

Help me, Patricia.

You come into my heart. I bless you, smell you, lick you and hold you. Eternity in an instant, my sun in this hole. (*Pushing.*) Nobody will erase your name, Laura, daughter of Andrea and Marcos, not guilty, in love, human. Lauraaa! (*Baby cries.*)

LAURA (*Her call mixes with the shout of her mother and the baby's crying.*) Mother!

(*Light out over ANDREA.*) I am me. One can't be so blind nor so deaf not to see or hear, nor so dumb not to speak truths, one can't be so alone from loneness.

ANDREA (*Speaking softly. Alone. She walks and the light comes up.*) You were born to look like me, like my first photographs. With black, very black hair, and dark eyes like your father's. You stuck to my breast and were silent. Not a peep, sure of yourself you felt your way. You were born Taurus, on 10 May 1976. (*She sings the first lines of 'Necesito', a popular song, as a lullaby.*) I love you from deep inside, with my heart I open your wings. I embrace you and surround you in your world as we create a new one. I feel you large, open. I touch your skin, your salt, your eyes, your light, your smell, and our senses dance for joy that the miracle is possible even in the shadows, where you are the Light.

LAURA I wonder how many times I will have your little hand in mine.

ANDREA I hold your hand five hundred times in mine. I kiss you all over, I include you in my heart and like magic I find a mole in the middle of your chest, and that is my signature for ever.

LAURA (*Starts panting.*) You are coming, little one. You are coming, Laura, my Laura.

The light goes down slowly. A baby cries. ❏

First staged in 2001 at the Sala Del Nudo theatre in Buenos Aires. A shorter version, directed by Leonor Manso, was staged in Buenos Aires on 8 October 2002

First English-language publication in Index. *Translated by Andrew Graham-Yooll*

BOMBAY CUSTOMS

KAVITA BHANOT

As Asha neared the finishing line she suddenly thought of giving up and returning to Start, where the territory was familiar. Yet her feet ignored her head and drove her trolley forward. And Asha followed them round the last corner, where, from an emailed photograph she had memorised, she recognised an unfamiliar ocean of faces before her.

Among them stood her five-foot-five moustachioed prize, his eyes as downcast as Sita's had been during the archery competition in *Ramayan*. Sita, the trophy for whoever lifted the divine bow and arrow, had shyly approached the victorious Ram to garland him as her husband. And as Ram surely then did, Asha looked ambitiously beyond the trophy to survey the reward she had mainly been competing for: her newly inherited kingdom.

She had fought a long and lone battle for this land. Her parents had been disappointed when she first expressed a desire to marry in the land of her forefathers.

'Why can't you find yourself a nice boyfriend in Bexleyheath?' her mother had said. In the hope that Asha would give up the impossible scheme, they had refused to loan her their contacts from back home and Asha had been forced to find her own way. Typing 'Indian husband' into the search engine, she had been surprised to see so many matrimonial sites displaying potential husbands.

Asha took a satisfied sniff. She deserved this scent of rosewood mixed into vomit that hovered beneath her nose. The smell of India. She spied a begging bundle making its way towards her; one hoping eye adjoined to three-quarters of a pair of legs.

'Asha . . . welcome!' hollered Ashok Mama striding forward. As he did so, he overtook and almost knocked over the man with the hopping leg and hoping eye. Ashok Mama, her widowed mother-to-be's big bubble-wrapped brother, enveloped Asha in a hug before she had a chance to kiss his feet.

She unpeeled herself from his soggy shirt. All her life she had been fed with horror stories of the unbearable heat of this country, which she had greedily devoured as sprinklings of pistachio on white *barfi*. She could not survive in the climate, she had been warned by her sceptical family and, in defiance, she began to practise. Beginning humbly with extra clothing, she had worked her way up: permanently leaving the central heating on full, meditating for hours before the gas fire and eventually, working night shifts at Tesco so she could sleep the days in the sauna at Bexleyheath Leisure Centre. That morning, about to get off the plane, she had taken a deep breath, preparing herself for the gust of heat about to assail her. And felt nothing. Indeed, a few goose pimples had rippled the surface of her bare arms and she wished she had brought a shawl with her.

'How are you, *beti*!' said Ashok Mama. He clicked his fingers at the one-legged coolie who was still trying to regain his balance, indicating that he should push her trolley.

'Why have you brought so much luggage with you, we have everything here you know, how was your flight.' He stepped back to survey her, 'You look naked.' Asha froze. Straining her eyes, she checked her strained blouse for burst hooks or gaping holes. Her sari was precarious but it hadn't yet given way. She sighed with relief when she realised he was referring to her tired eyes and slumped figure.

She joined her hands in *namaste*. 'It was fine. I was . . .'

'You know, my first time on a plane,' he interrupted, leading her closer to where the ocean was lapping its waves impatiently, 'I was so scared, I thought . . .'

One of the waves engulfed him. 'Yes, yes, there'll be plenty of time to tell her your sob story later,' said mother-to-be. 'Let *me* see my new daughter.' And a pair of pointy eyes started their journey at two tired feet and travelled north via a precarious creased blue silk sari. After a diversion that took them past twelve gold bangles, they took a short cut to her neck where they snatched a rest depot at a gold necklace, before terminating at a three-inch nose.

Determined-to-be-dutiful, the nose suddenly went out of their view as it inclined towards a pair of red Prada shoes. 'What you doing?' the shoes remonstrated, stepping back, refusing to be kissed. 'We don't do that old thing any more, come.' And Asha, for the second time, was stuffed into an envelope; this one smaller and minus the bubble wrap. She was then posted to, opened and skimmed by every member of the huge family until she reached the intended destination: her princess prize.

As Anil stood before her, she peered down into greasy hair sliced precisely in the middle, its perfect parting adorned with white snowflakes instead of Sita's red *sindoor*. At last he looked up. Focusing on something just past her left shoulder, he mumbled a greeting and Asha, looking beyond his right ear, muttered an equally incomprehensible reply that concealed her delight with him. She had known he was the one, as soon as she had read the advert his mother had written for him. A man who let his mother find him a wife, Asha had figured, was bound to be compliant. And now she congratulated herself on inheriting this grateful lump of pliable putty that she would mould according to her fancy, that would not interfere with the plans she had neatly packed in her suitcase.

The tide carried Asha forward and she bobbed along like a boat in a storm, each wave jealously pulling her in its own direction. Only Anil trailed in the distance, his head down, his feet dragging. Waiting outside were two Mercedes fitted with stereos, leather seats and drivers. Looking round, Asha saw that all her suitcases, except one, had found a place in the boot of the car. The one-eyed coolie seemed to be having difficulty lifting the last case off the trolley. Gritting his teeth and straining every muscle in his two arms and one and a half legs, he failed to budge it. One by one every member of the clan tried to lift the divine weapon; nine-year-old Motu puffing out an already protruding chest, a reluctant Anil urged on by the others.

Ashok Mama impatiently huffawed his way over to the stubborn suitcase and bent to lift it. He breathed and tried again. 'What you got in there, Asha, bricks?' he joked, weakly. Eventually, with resignation and ignoring the quips and laughter, Asha trailed towards the suitcase. She closed her eyes and joined her palms in prayer to her swami, HH Hansamarana Swami Maharaj, before bending to lift the bricks he had blessed. Fitting the suitcase in the boot, she made her way into the car, ignoring the astonishment that followed her.

'Your wife does body-building.'

'You're marrying a *phelwaan*,' voices called out, teasing Anil.

Asha, along with the other women and children, squeezed into the back seat, strategically organised and positioned in neat rows on the basis of body mass, bone density and muscle strength. Asha, with her newly acquired status as a *phelwaan*, Motu and Shanti Aunty sat first, like potatoes at the bottom of a shopping bag. Topmost perched purple grapes that shared an uncanny resemblance with Sonu, Monu, Tilu and mother-to-be. Next to Jimmy the driver, staring straight ahead in silence, sat Anil.

Asha soon grew tired of trying to catch and return the questions that
the children threw at her from all directions. Wishing she were sleeping,
she turned her head towards her window and pretended she was. Instead,
her eyes searched the landscape for suitable patches of earth. Closing
her eyes, she saw herself taking the bricks blessed by Swami ji out of
the suitcase, and laying the foundation of the temple. She imagined the
opening ceremony once it was built. Flocks of followers, as far into the
distance as the eye could see, chanting her Swami ji's name. Wearing
a smiling beard and holding a pair of scissors, HH Hansamarana Swami
Maharaj from England stood before his devotees, hand raised in blessing.
He turned to cut the ribbon across the entrance to the red-brick building.
And next to him, President of the Hansamarana Spiritual Mission, Indian
branch, stood Asha.

Soon, deception became reality as Asha drifted into sleep. Both temple
and followers faded into the distance, until all she could see was her Swami
ji. He turned to her, lifting a grateful hand to bless her. He stroked her
head, then her hair, her neck, the small of her back, the big of her front.
Except it was poking rather than stroking, and 'it', she painfully realised,
was an elbow not a hand. Without opening her eyes, she pushed the elbow
away and tried to resummon the dream that had been filling her body
with a pleasant warmth. As her conscious mind remembered the scene,
a mixture of shock and disgust forced her eyes open in an instant.

She found the neat order at the back of the car in disarray. Mother-to-
be was now sitting on her lap, her pointy eyes giving Asha's gold-plated
neck a loveless bite. It was minutes before they travelled north to catch
up with Asha's waiting eyes.

'Where did you get your gold from, *beti*?' she asked. As Asha tried to
explain what Argos was . . . that she hadn't been able to afford Indian gold
. . . a superstore, mother-to-be's face contorted with disgust.

Later that evening, Asha rested on a king-size satin-soaked bed, looking
round her large room, further magnified by the surround-system mirrors
that had turned out to be wardrobe doors. Next to her, on the bedside
table, she had placed a framed photograph of Swami ji. Asha closed her
eyes, willing them to sleep, but the more tightly she squeezed them shut,
the more conscious she was of being awake. Every noise was magnified:
the buzzing of a fly, the trickle of water from the fountain in the hallway,
a voice that seemed to come from next door.

'. . . so ugly . . . big and chunky . . . hollow as a dry coconut,' she heard, '. . . cheap! We've got standards . . . but what do you expect . . . a *supermarket* . . .'

Asha sat up, her ears burning with indignation. It was mother-to-be's voice. Maybe Asha hadn't been exactly honest when she had clicked the 'attractive' option under 'physical description' and it was true that she had worked in Tesco. But Asha knew she was a catch. The elders in the mission had always said so: girl from England, who could cook and clean, who spoke, read and wrote Hindi fluently, who knew about her religion and practised it too. Such girls were rare, even in India, they had said. And now here she was, being rejected by her mother-to-be, before she had had a chance to display her assets.

When mother-to-be walked into the room, she was holding a miniature suitcase covered in red velvet, with 'Joshi Jewellers' printed goldly in the corner. She set the digits of the combination lock to '420' and opened the case. Asha blinked, shielding her eyes from the bright glare that emerged. As they became accustomed to the light, Asha was able to identify the form of an intricate solid gold snake that wound its way around a plastic, velvet-covered neck. Mother-to-be gently took the coil from the plastic neck and entwined it around Asha's own.

'I designed it myself . . . especially for my *bahu!*' she whispered. 'Nobody in my family wears cheap metal from an English supermarket.' Asha's neck felt constricted by the weight of the gold.

'Isn't it beautiful? When we go to England, everyone will want real gold like this, won't they?' The serpent seemed to be winding tighter and tighter round Asha's neck.

'Joshi Jewellers will be "Joshi Jewellers International". I'm so happy.' She hugged Asha. 'Now sleep, and tomorrow, it would be good if you spend time with Anil. Silly boy is sulking, says he wanted a girl from America. I know he will change his mind when he sees that you are a nice girl. And you can tell him that England is as good as America.' Asha did not hear her. She was trying to breathe. ❏

Kavita Bhanot is studying for an MA in creative writing at Warwick University

IN SEARCH OF UTOPIA
PATRICK WILCKEN

As Luiz Ignacio Lula da Silva – universally known as 'Lula' – arrives in
Brasília to assume the presidency, Brazil moves on. After three unsuccessful
attempts, the former lathe operator and radical union leader is in office.
He heads the Partido dos Trabalhadores (PT), a mass-based, activist
organisation whose Marxist leanings have up until now prevented it
from gaining power at the federal level.

Needless to say, it is a very different Lula who is now settling in to his
new quarters in the capital. Long gone are the jeans and T-shirts of archive
footage – Lula manning the barricades in the strike actions that made
him famous in the 1970s. Besuited, almost avuncular with his beard and
the beginnings of middle-age spread, Lula now speaks in softer, more
conciliatory tones. His rhetoric has eased into the fuzzy language of
electability – peace and social justice were campaign themes, his goal
the creation of a 'decent Brazil'.

But this is not to say that it will be business as usual in Brasília after
Lula takes office. The very fact that Lula is president at all says something
profound about Brazil and its democratic deliverance. Past campaigns have
seen Lula pilloried in the press, television debates manipulated in favour
of the establishment candidate – a general closing of ranks against the left.
Lula's humble background as an economic migrant from the impoverished
north-east, a shoeshine boy made good who rose through the union
ranks to become party leader, were used against him. His lack of formal
education, his lisp, his uncertain grasp of Portuguese grammar and the fact
that he could not speak English, marked him out as somehow unsuitable –
too common to hold high office.

This time around it was different. It was the establishment's preferred
candidate, José Serra – an anonymous-looking technocrat, the former
health minister in Fernando Henrique Cardoso's outgoing administration –
who looked somehow awkward and out of touch. Lula's against-the-odds
life story was a vote-winner, striking a chord with the millions who
struggle daily to make ends meet. Pointed comments from Wall Street
analysts about the dire economic effects that a PT victory would bring,
speculation against the Brazilian currency – the *real* – and IMF interference

were not enough to tip the balance. Serra battled on, but never looked like overhauling Lula's comfortable lead.

Brazilians had wearied of their political elite; they were looking for something new, someone who stood for a more humane, social agenda. Responding to this yearning, at times the Lula campaign took on a surreal, utopian air. In one PT campaign broadcast, hundreds of pregnant women dressed in flowing white robes strolled, smiling, hands on bellies, down a grassy knoll. When it was all over, celebrations broke out across the country. 'Brazil voted for change,' said Lula in his carefully scripted acceptance speech. 'Hope overcame fear.'

My apartment window in an inner-city suburb in Rio looks over on to a small *favela*, perched on a hillside opposite. As I sit watching the candidates slug it out in an epic television debate, small-arms fire echoes across the way. There is a dull, irregular response from some far-off position. The to-and-fro goes on through the night. At one point, tracer-fire arcs across the night sky, a luminous streak trailing over the city. While the political battle continues, another conflict is coming to a head in the narrow alleyways that criss-cross Rio's shanty towns.

A week before the first round of voting, Rio came to a halt. On a Monday morning, the city gradually emptied out. Small traders shut down, then large stores, banks, schools and universities. Threats circulated, gunmen toured the streets and deserted government buildings were defaced with graffiti. 'PARALLEL POWER' and 'WAR WITHOUT END' read the slogans, daubed in red paint. There were isolated incidents of violence; several buses were burnt out. Initially, there was confusion about what exactly was happening. Was this a case of rumour-driven mass hysteria? Was it a show of strength from the Comando Vermelho (the Red Command), a criminal organisation, the hub of Rio's drug-trafficking underworld? Or was this a more sinister political protest against the PT's incumbent state governor, Benedita da Silva?

The background to these extraordinary events lies in a prison complex called Bangu in Rio's West Zone. There, 9,000 prisoners are incarcerated in what amounts to a small city. Businesses operate within its walls, using prison labour. A dedicated bus route, advertised as the 'Bangu day trip', serves the prison, bringing in family members from the surrounding districts. On a typical weekend the facility receives 30,000 visitors. Inside, conditions are appalling, with up to 50 per cell. 'Prison' is perhaps an exaggeration: around 70 inmates escape each month, the number rising

Rio, September 2002: Lula da Silva on the hustings.
Credit: Rex Features

as Christmas and New Year festivities approach. Mobile phones circulate freely; heavy arms, drugs, large amounts of cash (in one recent instance in Iraqi currency), even a laptop have been seized in raids.

The notorious Red Command leader Luiz Fernando da Costa, more commonly known as 'Fernandinho Beira-Mar' ('Freddy Seaside' in the *Miami Herald*'s comical transliteration), was held at the 'maximum security' end of the operation (Bangu 1), running his empire from the inside. Several rival gang members were also imprisoned there, before, in the course of a riot that left Bangu 1 out of control for 24 hours, they were killed. 'I will only let the police into the prison when the job is done,' Beira-Mar is reported to have said during the siege. After a tense stand-off, Beira-Mar and his men surrendered.

The following day, Beira-Mar appeared on all the front pages, handcuffed but smirking for the cameras. His arrogance, his flaunting of state authority caused severe embarrassment for the governor, Benedita da Silva. It also created a problem: where was Beira-Mar to be held in the wake of the Bangu fiasco? One suggestion was that he be imprisoned on an island in Rio's Guanabara Bay; another that he be transferred to a facility in another state; even that he be handed over to the USA on the pretext of his links with the Colombian rebels, the FARC. In the end, he was moved to a military police compound, stripped of his visiting rights, his legal consultations restricted to half an hour a week. It was at this point that the order went out to shut down Rio. Whether or not the goal was political, it made a mockery of Benedita da Silva's administration. So serious was the situation deemed as Rio went to the polls that the army was brought in to secure the streets. While Lula cruised to easy victory, Benedita da Silva was crushed in the first round.

The shocking death of well-known investigative journalist Tim Lopes while gathering information for a report about the use of child prostitutes by drug traffickers has also focused attention on the growing lawlessness in the city's slums. Tim Lopes was tortured, murdered, then burnt. His alleged killer, Elias Pereira da Silva, also known as Elias Malucoí (Crazy Elias), was captured after a highly publicised police hunt just after the Bangu debacle, filling the papers with yet more sinister images of handcuffed drug lords. After a brief hearing, he joined Beira-Mar at the military police compound.

The current law and order crisis has crept up on Rio. The drug trade has always operated out of the *favelas*, but over the last ten years it has grown exponentially. Sophisticated weaponry – grenade launchers, night-vision equipment and Israeli Uzi machine guns – are often captured in police raids. Many parts of the city are no-go areas. Two of the city's main highways, which run through some of Rio's worst slums, are no longer secure by night. In a series of recent incidents they have been blockaded by bandits dressed up as policemen, robbing motorists they stop. Many in Rio are now sensing that control of their own city is slipping away.

The unease has been heightened by the timely release of *Cidade de Deus* (*City of God*), a film by Fernando Meirelles, co-directed by Katia Lund. The title refers to one of Rio's most dangerous *favelas* and the film traces a generation of turbulent change within the shanty town, from its semi-rural innocence of poverty and petty theft through to today's ultra-violent world of competing drug barons. It centres on a group of boys, following their lives as they gradually become enmeshed in the drugs and violence that surround them. The film's appeal is as much in its form as in its content. This is no worthy, neo-realist essay with slow pans and long silences. Sharp, witty and superbly edited, *Cidade de Deus* is a headlong rush through the 1970s and 80s, a kind of *Goodfellas* set in the tropics. But unlike Scorsese's nostalgic recall of a world that no longer exists, Meirelles's 1970s dystopia rings truer than ever in today's Rio.

The film divided the critics, but on its release proceeded to break all national box-office records. Clearly a chord had been struck, an authenticity achieved. The project did, indeed, have deep roots in the world it was setting out to depict. It was based on a book by Paulo Lins who grew up in the Cidade de Deus *favela*; the actors were almost all non-professionals, recruited from the shanty towns.

Its making involved many ironies. 'The main character of the film is not a person,' runs the press release, 'it is a place.' But not, unfortunately, the Cidade de Deus *favela*. The notorious shanty town of Rio's North Zone was deemed too dangerous to shoot in. The eventual location, Cidade Alta, was no less problematic. Access was only granted through negotiations with 'community leaders' (read drug barons) and an unorthodox form of script approval involved input from the dealers themselves.

The story became even more involved on the film's release. The premiere was attended by drug boss Paulo Sergio Savino Magno, but he would never get to see the film portrayal of his own community. He was arrested as he arrived at the cinema. Police are also trying to force Meirelles and Lund into attending an inquiry on their relationship with the traffickers during filming.

This is, though, an epoch-making film for Brazilian cinema. Endlessly discussed in the media, it has become a reference point for the country's current travails. *Cidade de Deus* has shown Brazilians what they already knew, but were too caught up in to articulate: how bucolic housing projects turned into nightmare slums; how the Beira-Mars of this world grew up in poverty, entered the drug trade and built their empires; how large swathes of the city were abandoned by the authorities, in effect turned over to the traffickers who took on the paternal role of the state, albeit in a violent, uncompromising way.

Voters' reactions to these issues resonated at the polls, with varying outcomes for the PT. During the campaign, even the middle classes were realising that root causes needed to be addressed, social programmes implemented to stem the tide. This was no time to follow the economic orthodoxy of the rich countries, slimming down the state, cutting the scant provision that exists for the huge numbers of needy in Brazilian society. This was time for a radical rethink.

The *favela* across from my apartment seems quiet the day after the shoot-out. Small boys fly kites from rooftops; dogs bark; a cock crows. Rural aspects still survive in this most urban of settings. Then there is another noise, a low pulse that grows louder and louder. Soon it is a deafening clatter, as a military helicopter hovers not 50 metres overhead. A soldier hangs out of the cabin, a machine gun held loosely in his one free hand. The whole scene lasts no more than a few minutes, before the helicopter gently tips forward and powers off across Rio's Guanabara Bay. It leaves behind a trail of vapour and lingering images – Vietnam newsreels, footage from futile wars fought out in the African tropics.

Rio, like Brazil as a whole, is at the crossroads. But there is now a willingness on the part of the voters to face down their country's enormous problems. Lula may well be forced by economic circumstances to spend his first months in office dampening down the expectations that the PT's victory has unleashed. As a conviction politician from the left, though, he at least represents something other than capitulation to the markets. With the horse-trading under way in Brasília, it remains to be seen if the politicians can capitalise on this mood change and steer Brazil away from the dangers that lie ahead. ❏

Patrick Wilcken is about to publish his first book, In the Wake of Empire *(Bloomsbury, July 2003)*

Support for

It is the generosity of our friends and supporters which makes *Index on Censorship*'s work possible. *Index* remains the only international publication devoted to the promotion and protection of that basic, yet still abused, human right – freedom of expression.

Your support is needed more than ever now as *Index* and the Writers and Scholars Educational Trust continue to grow and develop new projects. Donations will enable us to expand our website, which will make access to *Index*'s stories and communication between free-speech activists and supporters even easier, and will help directly with our Sponsored Subscriptions Programme which provides free copies of the magazine to activists in the developing world and the former Soviet states.

Please help *Index* speak out.

The Trustees and Directors would like to thank the many individuals and organisations who support *Index on Censorship* and the Writers and Scholars Educational Trust, including:

IF YOU WOULD LIKE MORE INFORMATION ABOUT INDEX ON CENSORSHIP OR WOULD LIKE TO SUPPORT OUR WORK, PLEASE **CONTACT HUGO GRIEVE, DEVELOPMENT MANAGER, ON 020 7278 2313 OR EMAIL HUGO@INDEXONCENSORSHIP.ORG**

WWW.INDEXONCENSORSHIP.ORG
CONTACT@INDEXONCENSORSHIP.ORG
TEL: 020 7278 2313 • FAX: 020 7278 1878

SUBSCRIPTIONS (4 ISSUES PER ANNUM)
INDIVIDUALS: BRITAIN £32, US $48, REST OF WORLD £42
INSTITUTIONS: BRITAIN £48, US $80, REST OF WORLD £52
**SPEAK TO TONY CALLAGHAN ON 020 7278 2313
OR EMAIL TONY@INDEXONCENSORSHIP.ORG**

Index on Censorship (ISSN 0306-4220) is published four times a year by a non-profit-making company:
Writers & Scholars International Ltd, Lancaster House, 33 Islington High Street, London N1 9LH. *Index on
Censorship* is associated with Writers & Scholars Educational Trust, registered charity number 325003
Periodicals postage: (US subscribers only) paid at Newark, New Jersey. Postmaster: send US address changes
to *Index on Censorship* c/o Mercury Airfreight International Ltd Inc., 365 Blair Road, Avenel,
NJ 07001, USA